Praise for THE NEXT REVOLUTION

"As a Boomer executive working with Gen Xers, I had an 'Aha!' experience when I read this book. The NeXt Revolution *offers understanding, practical solutions, and an excellent road map for dealing with these issues now and in the future."*

—BEVERLY JOHNSTON, Vice President, Human Resources,
North Kansas City Hospital

"What a team to discuss the next revolution and the generational challenges ahead for all! Charlotte and Laura share inspirational moments and strategies for moving forward with the next generation of leaders poised to undertake both life and career opportunities."

—JILL KICKUL, PH.D., Professor of Entrepreneurship,
Simmons School of Management

"Today's Employers of Choice are Boomer-focused and need to change gears quickly if they are to attract, motivate, and retain Gen X top talent. The NeXt Revolution *takes the reader into the work world of what* must *be if organizations are to succeed beyond 2010."*

—NANCY AHLRICHS RAICHART, author,
Manager of Choice and *Competing for Talent*

"As a Boomer with a Gen X daughter, I can directly relate to The NeXt Revolution. *This is a good read for employers and managers who need to plan for the exodus of the Boomers by aligning their employment strategies to retain the talents of the Xers!"*

—MARGE CONNELL, Order Fulfillment Manager, Hallmark Cards, Inc.

"Bravo to the Sheltons for their provocative insights into the unique motivators of Xers and Boomers. The NeXt Revolution *provides a greater understanding of and appreciation for how each generation derives meaning and possibility. Be ready to transform your perceptions."*

—MARTHA LYNN, PH.D., Chief Learning Officer, The HNTB Companies

"The NeXt Revolution *hits the proverbial nail on the head. It explores the relationship between work, parenthood, and members of Generation X like no other book, exposing fallacies and hidden truths alike. As a Gen X mother, I recommend that every new Gen X mother and working professional read this book."*

—STACI MONK NELSON, Technology Delivery Specialist,
Metropolitan Community College

"The definitive reference for where we came from, where we are, and where we are going. You don't have to be a woman to feel refreshed by the introspections and reflections presented in this book."

—STEVE WOLFRAM, Founder, WolfJam Productions

"I wish I had had the ideas in this book when I naively entered the workforce. It contains many of the tools I was left looking for after the initial awe of a first job had come and gone."

—MELISSA WOOD, CFS, Investment Research Associate,
Center for Financial Planning, Inc.

"Charlotte and Laura have eloquently added their voices to an issue that until recently was treated as the 'elephant in the living room'— career confusion. They have managed to deftly guide us on a tour of career introspection."

—KATHERINE MICHELLE MARTIN, Health Policy Advisor

THE NeXt revolution

THE NeXt
revolution

WHAT GEN X WOMEN
WANT AT WORK AND HOW
THEIR BOOMER BOSSES
CAN HELP THEM GET IT

Charlotte Shelton

Laura Shelton

Davies-Black Publishing
Mountain View, California

Published by Davies-Black Publishing, a division of CPP, Inc., 1055 Joaquin Road, Suite 200, Mountain View, CA 94043; 800-624-1765.

Special discounts on bulk quantities of Davies-Black books are available to corporations, professional associations, and other organizations. For details, contact the Director of Marketing and Sales at Davies-Black Publishing; 650-691-9123; fax 650-623-9271.

Visit the Davies-Black Publishing Web site at www.daviesblack.com.

09 08 07 06 05   10 9 8 7 6 5 4 3 2
Printed in the United States of America

Library of Congress Cataloging-in-Publication Data
Shelton, Charlotte
    The neXt revolution: what Gen X women want at work and how their Boomer bosses can help them get it / Charlotte Shelton, Laura Shelton—1st ed.
        p. cm.
Includes index.
ISBN 0-89106-200-9 (hardcover)
1. Women in the professions—United States—Attitudes. 2. Generation X—United States—Attitudes. 3. Job satisfaction—United States—Public opinion. 4. Quality of work life—United States—Public opinion. 5. Baby boom generation—United States. 6. Organizational change—United States. 7. Intergenerational relations—United States. I. Shelton, Laura. II. Title.
HD6054.U6S54 2005
306.3'6'0820973—dc22

2005023355

FIRST EDITION
First printing 2005

To Dr. Myles Gartland, statistician par excellence,
whose assistance with survey design and data analysis
made this book possible

To Dr. Jim Moore and Charles Garfield III (our husbands),
who selflessly supported this project and who themselves are
models of X-friendly management

>> | CONTENTS

My daughter, Laura, was born in 1974. I was just out of graduate school, trying out my wings in my first professional position. Over the ensuing years, Laura grew up and so did I—professionally, at least. I moved from counseling psychologist roles in nonprofit educational and health-care organizations to senior executive positions in banking and energy corporations. It was a heady time. I was determined to break the glass ceiling. I discovered that I could achieve more than I had ever dreamed and make more money than I had ever imagined. Along the way, I kept Laura engaged with my journey. I took her to work, introduced her to my colleagues, and talked about my adventures at the dinner table. All along the way I told her, "Dream big! Reach for the stars! Go for it! You can have it all!"

Now, in my mid-fifties, I look at my frustrated twenty-something daughter and her disillusioned twenty-something female friends and I realize that I (we?) didn't tell them the whole story. Yes, they should dream big! Yes, they can have it all! However, the "all" won't necessarily be easy to attain. And, some of their dreams may be impossible to actualize within the structures of traditional bureaucratic workplaces.

The so-called feminization of the workplace remains an idea whose time has not yet come. The values of twenty-first-century organizations are still primarily white male values—power, control, and status. Our male Boomer leaders have built organizations whose practices and policies reflect these values. Interestingly, these values are not only unattractive to our daughters, they are increasingly frustrating to Gen X males as well.

The NeXt Revolution explores the workplace experiences of Generation X using both quantitative and qualitative data. As a part of our research, we administered a career satisfaction/expectations survey to 1,200 Gen Xers—780 women and 420 men (see Appendix). The survey results are scattered throughout the book, and they are discussed at length in Chapter 5. In addition, Laura, her Gen X friends and co-workers, and hundreds of other survey respondents gave us a peek into their lives. This book is filled with their stories—personal and poignant stories of frustration and success.

This book focuses primarily on Gen X women and the role they can play in leading a workplace revolution. Laura wrote the first four chapters. These chapters focus on describing the legacy of this generation and how their workplace experiences have been shaped by the Boomer generation in general and their mothers in particular. At the end of Chapter 4, Laura passes the pen to me, and in Chapters 5 through 8, I describe our survey results in more depth, identify the characteristics of X-friendly workplaces, discuss four roads to revolution, and present a set of "Quantum Skills" Xers can use to change themselves and their workplaces.

The NeXt Revolution is a look at what is, as well as a vision of what might be. It is, above all else, a call to action. It challenges Gen X women to continue the work of workplace transformation that we, their moms, began almost fifty years ago. This is not easy work. The task is Herculean. The challenge is to transform our workplaces from soulless to satisfying, from fear based to fun, and from competitive to collaborative. Like Moses in the Hebrew scriptures, we Boomer mothers probably won't live to see the "promised land," but our daughters may. They are, after all, daughters of our revolution, and they are well suited to lead the neXt.

—Charlotte Shelton

>> | ACKNOWLEDGMENTS

We'd like to thank all the Gen Xers who so fearlessly let us explore their lives and spill their stories on these pages. They include Alicia Young, Bianca Garchar, Jennifer & Dr. Matt Shelton (and baby Will), Chuck Garfield, Dr. Lisa and Steve Wolfram (and baby Lily), Lisa and Dr. Myles Gartland, Jenny McCarthy, Christy Glaser, Sheila Lucas, Staci Monk Nelson, Melissa Wood, Julie Weber, Stacy Tyler, and Brenna Willingham.

We also appreciate the Rockhurst University MBA and EMBA students who helped launch the survey and whose stories are anonymously sprinkled throughout the book. A special thanks goes to former MBA student Jesyka Simpson, who helped conduct the initial review of the literature, and to graduate assistants Angela Watson and Ellisha Winfield, whose editing and research assistance were invaluable.

To co-workers and friends who helped shape this book, including Jackie Damico, Paul Rodgers, Beverly Johnston, Dr. Mindi McKenna, Doug Beddome, and Twyla Dell, we send much appreciation.

To our Davies-Black "family," who loved the idea from the beginning and supported our vision in every way possible—our amazing editor, Connie Kallback; our marketing guru, Laura Simonds; the creative force behind our cover design, Laura Ackerman-Shaw; our guides through production, Jill Anderson-Wilson and Francie Curtiss—we say a great big "thank you" for the encouragement and support you gave us. Also, kudos to Mark McDonald, the cover photographer, for his perseverance in capturing just the right look.

And to all of the 1,200 Gen X women and men who took the time to respond to our survey, and to their Boomer moms (and dads) who paved the way, we say "good job!" Remember, we're counting on each of you to help us lead the neXt revolution.

>> | ABOUT THE AUTHORS

Gen Xer Laura Shelton is a television news reporter at the Fox affiliate in New Orleans. Her job-hopping, Gen X career has led her through four different stations, including stints at NBC and CBS affiliates. Her work experiences, including eight different bosses in only six years, helped launch this project and are woven throughout the book.

Laura is a contributing author to the book *Crime and Local Television News: Dramatic, Breaking and Live from the Scene.* Her master's thesis, "Black and White TV," explored racial issues in television hiring and was selected for presentation at the Broadcast Educators' national conference. Laura holds a B.A. degree in broadcast journalism from Southern Methodist University and an M.A. degree in communications from the University of Nebraska, Omaha. She lives with her husband, Chuck Garfield, and their bulldog, Bogalusa.

Boomer Charlotte Shelton is an author, management professor, coach, and consultant. Her work focuses on championing and supporting personal and organizational transformation. She is a founding member of WiseWork Consulting and also teaches in Rockhurst University's Helzberg School of Management MBA program, where she challenges business students to think outside the box of traditional management practices.

Charlotte spends her summers as a visiting professor at Peking University in Beijing, China, where she teaches innovation and change to MBA students and key business leaders. She is author of *Quantum Leaps: 7 Skills for Workplace ReCreation* and is a frequent seminar/conference presenter. Charlotte lives in Kansas City with her husband, Dr. Jim Moore.

CHAPTER 1

Daughters of the Revolution

It was 8 a.m. and I was wide awake. Someone my age (and still living the single life, I should note) shouldn't have been getting up at that hour on her day off. Weekends are for sleep, or at least for trying to catch up on the sleep I was robbed of during my hectic week. I padded down the stairs looking for some hot chocolate and Mom. I felt about seven years old, rather than one day shy of twenty-seven. Though there's nothing particularly symbolic about turning twenty-seven, I had come home to spend my birthday with my emotional oracle of a mother, who always wants to hear about what's bothering me and then wants me to figure out what I can do to change it.

I made my hot chocolate, trying to keep quiet—Mom was still asleep. Again, I wondered why I had awakened so early. What was wrong?

Moments later, Mom found me in the kitchen and asked me the same question: What was wrong? I thought it might be work. What else could it be? I didn't have children or a husband or even a boyfriend. My life revolved around work. My greatest successes and failures, my sense of purpose, my reason for being, all lay in the newsroom of a television station. We talked and talked about ways for me to make changes, steps to take, what I might do differently.

Finally, Mom asked me a question I'll never forget: "If you're so unhappy, tell me, which of your friends really loves her job?" Hmmmm. For several minutes I pondered the question while mentally running through a list of all my high school and college girlfriends. One of them works on Capitol Hill for a congresswoman, one is a news reporter in Phoenix, one teaches in a school system in the Bay Area, one works for a consulting company in the Twin Cities, and one is a producer in Chicago for a leading talk show host. Other friends are managing investments in Ann Arbor, writing news in Denver and Orlando, selling pharmaceuticals in Providence, computing in Dallas, working on the set of a late-night show in Hollywood, and doing speech therapy in Houston. One is a pediatric resident in New Orleans, one's an anesthesiologist in Kansas City, and one's a photojournalist in Omaha. As I mentally ticked through this list of highly diverse women, I identified a few who had told me they liked their jobs. Most of them are doing exactly what they had planned to do. But does any of them really love her job? Does any of them have the passion for work that I thought I should have? No!

Mom and I brainstormed theories as to why my girlfriends and I weren't thrilled with our careers. Maybe we were unhappy because the workplace wasn't what we had expected. Perhaps we are finding it to be dominated by white males. Or, perhaps we don't like the rigidity and structure of traditional bureaucratic hierarchies. Then again, maybe it's because we just don't like the politics of organizational life and the boredom of entry-level jobs. Or, maybe it's because we are putting all of our proverbial life-satisfaction eggs into one basket—a career basket (while we wait for our perfect Prince Charming to appear). Or, perhaps it's because of our "big dreams." We were taught that we could do whatever we wanted—the sky's the limit.

On that pre-birthday morning, Mom and I spent several hours discussing these hypotheses. We decided we wanted to know more about the causes of my generation's workplace dissatisfaction and whether it is as pervasive as we believed. That's when we came up with the idea of surveying my peers about their expectations of work, as well as about how their parents had affected those expectations. We questioned young workers, starting with my national network of friends and expanding to my friends' friends, and their friends, and, well, you get the picture. Then we took the survey to Mom's MBA students and cast the net to their friends and business associates, all through the power of e-mail forwarding.

We collected an amazing amount of information from 1,200 respondents. The results shed a lot of light on the questions I had asked as I curled up next to Mom the day before I turned twenty-seven: What did I want from work, and how did I come to want it? It turns out that part of the answer was sitting right next to me. We learned from our mothers, participants in the women's liberation movement who changed the face of the American workplace. We are the products of all they fought for, and the benefactors, too. We are the daughters of their revolution. Some of our mothers are, or were, feminists. We are, therefore, daughters of the feminist revolution that rocked (no pun intended) this country in the 1960s. But, before we explore our heritage as daughters of this revolution, we need to examine the broader generational heritage of both the women and men of my generation—Generation X.

A LABEL, LIKE IT OR NOT

According to generational-identity authors William Strauss and Neil Howe (1997), Generation X is the label given to people who were born between 1961 and 1981. Other authors have used 1964 as the beginning of

Gen X, and the generational cut-off dates range from 1975 to 1980. For this book's purposes, we are using the drop-off in birthrates that began in 1964 as the starting date for Gen X and 1977 as the end date for this generation. We picked 1977 primarily because women born after that year were likely to be just entering the workforce when we started our survey, and we wanted to hear from Xers with a little bit of that all-important real-life experience under their belts. So, in 2004, Xers ranged in age from twenty-seven to forty.

If you're close to one end of the scale or the other, born near 1964 or 1977, you may feel you relate a little more to the Baby Boomers who came before Gen X or to the Gen Y group (sometimes called the Millennials) that came after. There are no magic dates that separate the generations. Still, we are called a generation because we grew up sharing experiences—such as the fall of the Berlin Wall, Reaganomics, families with two working parents, and, often, divorce. Events and trends such as these shaped our family lives and personal values, and they added to our generational personality.

Members of a generation are linked through the shared life experiences of their formative years—pop culture, economic conditions, world events, natural disasters, heroes, villains, politics, and technology—experiences that create bonds that tie the members of a generation together into what social scientists call cohorts (Table 1). Because of these shared experiences, cohorts tend to develop and retain similar values and beliefs. This affects everything from their attitudes about savings and sex to their preferences for music and movies. According to an old proverb, people resemble their times and their peers more than they resemble their parents (Smith and Clurman 1997).

This doesn't mean that all the members of a generational cohort think or act exactly alike. Just think about the diversity of the Boomers. This generation comprises Democrats and Republicans, pro-choicers and pro-lifers, fundamentalists and atheists. Some Boomers are workaholics, whereas others don't work at all. Generational labels don't mean all members are alike. They do, however, reflect the essence of the historical era in which that generation came of age.

TABLE 1	GENERATIONAL DIFFERENCES		
	Traditionalists	**Boomers**	**Xers**
Defining Values	loyalty, sacrifice, conformity, respect for authority	personal gratification, wellness, success	balance, self-reliance, pragmatism
Defining Events	Great Depression, New Deal, WWII, Korean War, silent movies	Vietnam, television, civil rights, cold war, assassinations, feminist movement	working moms, *Challenger,* latchkey kids, computers, divorced parents
Outlook	practical	optimistic	skeptical
Work Ethic	dedicated	driven	balanced
Success is a result of	working hard	political savvy, networking skills	holding two jobs
Money is for	security	enjoyment	survival
Education is	a dream	a birthright	a necessity
News Icons	Edward R. Murrow, Walter Cronkite	Diane Sawyer, Peter Jennings	Kurt Loder (MTV), Jon Stewart *(Daily Show)*
Music Icons	Duke Ellington, Bing Crosby, Ella Fitzgerald, Frank Sinatra	Elvis, the Beatles, the Beach Boys, Janice Joplin, the Rolling Stones, the Supremes	Madonna, Bon Jovi, Bruce Springsteen, U2, Prince

We Gen Xers lived with shag carpet, avocado appliances, wood-paneled station wagons, and *The Brady Bunch.* That's a quick 1970s snapshot that should create an instant picture of the time when Xers were growing up. Shag carpet and the Bradys probably didn't change the direction of our lives, but they do represent changing family values and lifestyles that became part of the fiber of who we Xers are. What is the essence of Generation X? We're fast paced and high tech, we're slower to marry and start families, and we want work to be emotionally fulfilling in addition to providing a means to pay our bills. Our defining values include life/work balance, pragmatism, and self-reliance. These are some of our generational fibers, and when you start weaving the fibers together, the fabric of Generation X starts to take shape. Some refer to us as the "Why me?" generation. As a generation, we are often skeptical and sometimes may appear lost, dissatisfied, and frustrated. Much of that comes with the territory of being in our twenties or thirties, but some of it we inherited from our Boomer parents. Some even argue that the generation gap between Boomers and Xers looms larger than generation gaps in the past: "Due to recent rapid changes in Western civilization related to both social conditions and advancing technology, Generation X is growing up under a set of societal conditions that is significantly different from any known before" (Karp, Fuller, and Sirias 2002, p. 3).

OUR LEGACY

To understand Generation X, we have to go back in time. Without the generations before us, there would be no us. So let's start with the *Traditionalists*, who were born between 1920 and 1946. This generation is composed of our grandparents (and, in some cases, our parents), people who are sometimes referred to as the Matures or the Silent Generation. A good word to describe them is *loyal*. They served their country loyally and expected loyalty from others. These were the workers who stayed with a company for life, just as they stuck with their marriage until death. Other defining values include sacrifice, hard work, conformity, and respect for authority. This generation entered adulthood filled with optimism for the future and pride for their country. "The booming postwar economy gave the United States of the late 1940s, the 1950s, and the 1960s a sense that anything was possible" (Lancaster and Stillman 2002, p. 21).

The booming postwar economy also led to a booming birthrate— the baby boom that peaked in the mid-1950s, when the birthrate reached an all-time high of 25.3 births per every 1,000 people (Losyk 1997). This new generation of *Baby Boomers* (or simply Boomers) was born to parents who read Dr. Spock and watched *Father Knows Best* on their black-

and-white television sets. "The availability of jobs and GI loans to Traditionalist parents, the boom in production of consumer goods, and the promise of a good education for all allowed Boomers to grow up in a relatively affluent, opportunity-rich world" (Lancaster and Stillman 2002, p. 83). Those opportunities included a higher education. Fewer than 20 percent of Traditionalists earned a bachelor's degree, but about 30 percent of Boomers earned a bachelor's or beyond.

The boom in the birthrate lasted about eighteen years, from 1946 until around 1964. Then, just like the law of gravity, what went up also came down. The birthrate plummeted into a baby bust (that's when Xers came along), dropping to 14.5 births per 1,000 by the mid-1960s. The boomer birth years came to a screeching halt, making way for the neXt generation. An influential 77 million people make up the Boomer generation. In contrast, Generation X numbers only around 44 million, a little more than half the size of the Baby Boomer and Gen Y cohorts that precede and follow us. You'll sometimes hear the children of the Boomers referred to as the Thirteenth Generation because we're the thirteenth generation of Americans since the founding of this country. However, during the past decade we have increasingly been referred to as *Generation X, Gen X,* or simply *Xers.*

A lot of us Xers don't like our generation's label. It's so nondescript. Just an X? Generational business consultants Lancaster and Stillman (2002) say the label X brings to mind stereotypes of a grunge slacker covered in tattoos, just as the label Boomer brings to mind a workaholic and the label Traditionalist brings to mind God, country, and apple pie. Now, these are sweeping generalizations, and, depending on your generation, you're probably feeling slightly offended by them, but the images do emphasize that each generation is different from its predecessor. That's the way it always works; as the world changes, so do generations (Table 2).

Obviously our parents' generation was named for the boom in the birthrate that followed World War II, but what are the origins of our generation's name? The term "Generation X" was first used in 1965 as a title for a British self-help manual. Later, musician Billy Idol used the name

TABLE 2	GENERATIONAL REMEMBRANCES	
Traditionalists	**Boomers**	**Xers**
FDR, Eisenhower	Kennedy, Nixon	Reagan, Clinton
crew cuts	ducktails	skinheads
no more butter	no more war	no more ozone layer
Sunday drives	drive-throughs	drive-bys
Dr. Spock	Dr. Strangelove	Dr. Kevorkian
(Adapted from: Smith & Clurman, 1997)		

for his rock band. The name appeared again when Douglas Coupland published *Generation X: Tales for an Accelerated Culture* (1991). The characters in this fictional book are described as underemployed, over-educated, and unpredictable. Somehow America's marketing wizards drew a connection between Coupland's characters and the Thirteenth Generation. Soon the Boomers' children had a new generational name, not just a number, of their own.

Will we be Gen X for life? The Baby Boomer label locked itself on tight, but Generation X is so nondescript! It's hard to imagine one day, at age eighty, still being called an Xer. "X" seems open to the possibility that someday we'll find an identity and establish ourselves as more than X. But, for now, a lot of Xers feel a little lost—especially the women. To figure out how we became lost, we must explore our generation's legacy— the blessings and burdens passed on to us—blessings such as a more level playing field with men in the workplace, the chance to enter any career we want and to climb the ladder to a CEO job, plus the option to marry later, or never, and to have kids later, or never.

Those are the chances and choices my mother wanted to give me. Here, she discusses her experiences and our legacy:

>> *Who are the mothers of Generation X? First and foremost, we are children of the fifties and sixties. We grew up playing with hula hoops and wearing poodle skirts and saddle oxfords. We can remember when our parents purchased their first TV. We grew up without VCRs or microwaves. We listened to Elvis and the Beatles on 45 rpm records and eight-track tapes. We watched* I Love Lucy *and* Ed Sullivan *and sang along with* Hit Parade *on Saturday nights.*

In the 1960s our innocence began to disintegrate. Some of our parents built bomb shelters as U.S.-U.S.S.R. tensions escalated. We listened to somber conversations about the Cuban missile crisis and watched as missile silos began to dot the countryside. We learned to live in a world in which it was commonly acknowledged that cold war would likely turn into real war, and real war triggered images of nuclear destruction.

We were saddened when the Russians beat us into space with Sputnik, but we felt redeemed a few years later when our own Neil Armstrong was the first person to walk on the moon. We were moved by his words, "one small step for man, one giant leap for mankind," and his remarkable photos from outer space reminded us of the interconnectedness of our planet—an awareness that eventually led to our generation's slogan "Make love, not war."

When we learned of Rosa Parks' refusal to give up her seat on that Birmingham bus, we were awakened to the reality of racial discrimination. And, as we listened to Martin Luther King Jr., we were awakened to visions of hope. Some of us heard his "I have a dream" speech and began to march for civil rights. Others of us quietly began to change our own behaviors in order to create a more just world.

Some of us tie-dyed our T-shirts and fringed our jeans. Others of us modeled our hairstyles and our wardrobes after our stylish first lady, Jacqueline Kennedy. All of us watched in horror in 1963 as she cradled her dying husband in her bloodstained hands. Soon thereafter, we sent our boyfriends, husbands, and best friends off to Vietnam. Many of them never returned. Some of us marched for peace. Others continued to march for civil rights. All of us remember the 1970 images of dying students on the Kent State campus and burning babies in the jungles of Vietnam. Some of us smoked pot to escape the pain. Others of us burned our bras. None of our lives were ever quite the same again.

We Boomer women were deeply affected by all of this. We entered adult-hood with a significantly different ethos than had our mothers, who were, for the most part, stay-at-home moms. Few of them had college degrees, and among those who did, most chose to forgo their careers for their families. Many of our childhoods were right out of a Leave It to Beaver *episode.* Sex and the City *was still a good fifty years away.*

GENERATIONAL DIFFERENCES

Reading my mom's vivid description of her coming-of-age era, you can plainly see that she has some very concrete images of her generation's formative years. In fact, researchers say that our parents and grandparents have a stronger sense of connection with their generational peers because they all went through some intense and impressive historical moments. Our grandparents experienced the Great Depression, the New Deal, the World Wars, and the Korean War. These defining events shaped their generation, making our grandparents patriotic, loyal, and hard-working. They were proud that their country dominated the world.

Boomers inherited a different nation. The Cuban missile crisis, the Vietnam War, the Kennedy and King assassinations, and the civil rights movement characterized their formative years. They remember President Nixon and the image of their country's failure as Saigon fell in 1975. The Boomers lived through Watergate and war protests. Their lives were greatly affected by the advent of the pill and the subsequent era of sex, drugs, and rock 'n' roll. Many of them participated in a fight for equal rights that initially caused bloodshed but eventually brought reform. Those turbulent, sometimes hopeful, sometimes cynical times turned the Baby Boomers into a generation with values very different from those of their Traditionalist parents.

For a picture of the quintessential male Boomer, the authors of *Defining Markets, Defining Moments* suggest we look no further than former president Bill Clinton. "He is highly educated; came of age during the '60s; avoided the Vietnam War; smoked marijuana (although he says he didn't inhale); married a working woman; has one child; and has strayed from the bonds of marriage" (Meredith, Schewe, and Karlovich 2002, p. 180). Clinton is a highly motivated and intelligent example of a Boomer who also embodies the generation's trademark arrogance and tendency to be workaholics. Female Boomer icons include Hillary and Oprah. Both are so well known that no last name is needed. They are revolutionaries who marched for civil rights and fought for affirmative action—and they still are attempting to level the playing field for mothers and daughters around the world.

FROM CLINTON TO COBAIN

Compare Boomer icon Bill Clinton to the man said to embody Generation X, Kurt Cobain. Clinton and Cobain are, in fact, as night and day as Boomers and Xers. Cobain, the well-known grunge icon of the late 1980s and early 1990s, sang about anger and disillusionment. His dark, self-deprecating songs about pain and despair didn't paint a hopeful picture for us Xers, and the darkness he sang about eventually swallowed him. High on heroin, in April 1994, Kurt Cobain put a 20-gauge shotgun in his mouth and pulled the trigger. In his suicide note, he wrote that he couldn't stand to think of his daughter becoming "the miserable, self-destructive death rocker that I've become." Most Gen Xers remember his drug-induced suicide. It seemed to send a helpless, hopeless message to us all. In fact, my generation has set suicide records.

Kurt Cobain does not stand alone as the poster child for Generation X. We remember plenty of other names from the headlines. Generational consultants Lancaster and Stillman say the highlight reel includes the actors from the Brat Pack, Bill Gates, Monica Lewinsky, the Ayatollah Khomeini, Quentin Tarantino, Clarence Thomas, Newt Gingrich, Ted Bundy, Al Bundy, Beavis and Butt-Head, Dilbert, the Menendez brothers, O. J. Simpson, Madonna, and Michael Jordan. Now, of course, not all of these people are Gen Xers, and some aren't even real people, but they were all big names in the media at the time Xers came of age. And if you begin to analyze the list, you'll find many of them are infamous, rather than idols. "With the explosion of twenty-four-hour media and tabloid journalism, Xers saw almost every role model of their time indicted or exposed as someone far too human to be a hero" (Lancaster and Stillman 2002, p. 24). Instead of having role models to look up to, Gen Xers grew up seeing the famous with their warts exposed. Our icons were tragically flawed.

DEFINING MOMENTS

Social scientists refer to the events that define a generation as markers. Markers form a set of collective experiences that shape a generation's values, attitudes, and behaviors. Markers are synonymous with that generation's defining moments. If the defining moments of the two previous generations were like a six-hour documentary, the markers of Generation X would be more like a thirty-second commercial. My generation has been frozen in horror by senseless acts of violence, collectively gasping as we watched students running for their lives out the doors of Columbine High, shaking in fear as we watched the smoke billowing from the World Trade Center, and then crying out as the buildings collapsed along with our sense of security. But these atrocities did not happen in our formative years (the tween and teen years when we were figuring out our identities). In theory, those are the years when major national and global events have the most impact on a new generation. But most of us Gen Xers had already graduated from college by the time Columbine erupted, and we were likely working the day the Twin Towers crumbled.

Instead our generational headlines read, "*Challenger* Explosion" . . . "AIDS Epidemic" . . . "Operation Desert Storm." We sat in classrooms eagerly watching the first teacher rocket into space onboard the *Challenger;* then, a minute after takeoff, the ship exploded into a fiery ball. Our unconscious lesson from the tragedy was that anything could go wrong; just look at what happened to Christa McAuliffe. When we got to high school (or college), many of us were handed free condoms and told that the era of free love was a thing of the past. The HIV horror stories made us realize that our sexual experiences might be a little like Russian roulette, just as unpredictable and potentially just as deadly. "My generation inherited not free love but AIDS, not peace but nuclear anxiety, not cheap communal lifestyles but crushing costs of living, not free teach-ins but colleges priced for the aristocracy" (Beaudoin 1998, p. 10).

In high school (or college) we sat through a living lesson on war, watching Operation Desert Storm quickly unfold. We saw the swift and decisive guided missile hits of the Gulf War that looked a little more like a video game attack than the battlefield offensive of previous wars. And for the first time, this country's children had front-row seats from which to watch the action. In World War II the news came in front-page stories or in news reels shown before movies. During the Vietnam War, journalists lugged TV cameras into combat zones, but problems with technology impeded the spread of information. Operation Desert Storm was the first war that could be watched in real time—24/7. What turned out to last not quite two months became a war that barely resembled our parents' long years of involvement in Vietnam.

These dramas shaped our worldview but often didn't directly touch our lives. We wouldn't be onboard a space shuttle, but we would learn not to trust the system. Most of us wouldn't contract HIV, but we would bring fear to bed with us. The majority of us wouldn't fight in Desert Storm; instead we watched the war with a sense of detachment. The only war many of us could relate to was on the streets of our hometowns. It was being fought with knives and semi-automatics. As a consequence of gun violence, we became the first generation to walk through metal detectors to get to our classrooms.

Our parents fought in Vietnam or fought against it at home, but for us, military action was something that made gas prices creep a little higher and consumed the evening news. When you're weaned on TV violence, a war halfway around the world, far from your home turf, just doesn't seem all that real. We've seen so many Freddie, *Terminator,* and

Die Hard (and harder and hardest) movies, that as a generation we have become desensitized to real-life bloodshed. Blame it on television, but violence and sex seldom shock Generation X. Janet Jackson's peep show at the 2004 Super Bowl shocked and appalled the FCC (and conservative Traditionalists and Boomers), but Gen Xers barely batted an eye. We've seen it before, and a whole lot more.

Some would say we're pessimists. I think we're just pragmatic. As a generation we have little interest in politics. After all, we've seen scandals from Watergate and Monica-gate to O. J. and Enron. We are skeptical of government. Not many of us read a daily newspaper, and even fewer bother to vote. We distrust the media because we know how easily reality can be distorted. While our Boomer parents believed that "image is everything," we tend to believe that "everything is image." We grew up with spin doctors who manipulated public opinion and TV news that was driven by Nielson ratings. We are a generation of skeptics.

We were the first generation to use computers to write our high school or college research papers (see Table 3 for a list of inventions that shaped our lives). Xers were some of the first to enjoy the dot-com boom and to become casualties of the massive bust. Many of us knew someone who'd been on top of the Internet mountain and later found herself in a Silicon Valley slump. And we learned from it all that we were free agents and that there's no such thing as job security. It's our generation that spent days on end at Starbucks with our laptops and cell phones, hoping to find our way back into the working world after the massive rightsizings of the past few years. We're a generation of iPods, BlackBerrys, and Napster. We were there for the birth of the information age and became some of the first to talk to our friends by computer, something our parents and even grandparents would eventually emulate.

And speaking of parents, Gen Xers are also the products of more divorces than any generation before us. The U.S. divorce rate more than tripled during the birth years of Generation X, and this affected us deeply. Our grandparents had a 15 percent divorce rate as they raised our parents. Our parents had a 50 percent divorce rate as they raised us. While our optimistic Boomer parents grew up in homes where their par-

TABLE 3	GEN X SNAPSHOTS: INVENTIONS THAT SHAPED OUR LIVES
1974	Self-adhesive postage stamps, online ATMs, video games
1975	Light beer
1977	Sports bras
1978	In vitro fertilization
1980	Post-its, Rollerblades, 24-hour cable news
1981	Laptops, Polar fleece
1983	CDs, Cell phones
1984	Twist-top beer bottles, flip-top toothpaste caps, cupholders in cars
1986	Energy bars
1987	Prozac
1989	Carry-on luggage on wheels
1991	World Wide Web

(Adapted from: "Then and Now," People, *April 12, 2004)*

ents stayed married and *Leave It to Beaver* was the norm, many of us grew up in single-parent homes watching shows like *My Two Dads, Different Strokes,* and *Who's the Boss?* Nontraditional TV families became our role models.

We were also a generation of latchkey kids, growing up in homes where parents' jobs often ate into family time. As young children, we not only made our own beds, but we often made our own breakfast and walked ourselves to school. We learned early to take care of ourselves. Some authors have referred to us as the "Abandoned Generation," but our abandonment made us self-sufficient, individualistic, and highly confident in our own abilities (Willimon and Naylor 1995).

Because of the increased job mobility of our parents, many of us moved a lot. We lived in several geographic areas and were immersed in a variety of multicultural experiences. Consequently, as a generation we are appreciative of diversity and open to change. And, we get bored very easily. My generation invented bungee jumping, free cliff climbing, and Rollerblading. We thrive on risk and speed. So it is no surprise that my generation's drugs of choice are speed and ecstasy. The Boomers smoked pot and some ingested hallucinogens. Their goal was to expand their awareness. The Xer high on speed is searching for something very different.

Our propensity for urgency makes us seem impatient. We ask a lot of questions and are quick to express our demands. Furthermore, we often pursue multiple lines of inquiry. We are mosaic thinkers, masters of multitasking. Our moms, as first-generation female professionals, taught us well. This is what Mom, who eagerly entered the workforce in the 1970s, has to say about being a part of a generation of women who attempted to break the proverbial glass ceiling:

> >> *We Baby Boom women went to college in unprecedented numbers—some to find a husband, but many to prepare for a career. Our parents wanted us to get a good education, but we were expected, for the most part, to follow in our mothers' footsteps by marrying young and devoting our lives to raising our children. A few of us did, but many of us didn't. Helen Reddy's lyrics ("I am woman; hear me roar") sparked our imaginations and fueled our ambitions, while Betty Freidan, Germaine Greer, and Gloria Steinem called us to action. We intended to change the existing world order—at least in the workplace.*
>
> *Equal rights legislation and affirmative action programs gave us great hope. We entered the world of work filled with great expectations. We were committed to the revolution. We believed that due to our individual efforts and the collective efforts of organizations like NOW (National Organization for Women), white, male-dominated hierarchies would crumble. Onward and UPWARD! was our battle cry. Beware to those who stood in our way. We reminded our male co-workers that Ginger Rogers could do everything that Fred Astaire could—while wearing high heels and dancing backward!*

By the 1970s we were raising children as well. Some of us traded in our business suits for jogging suits, but many of us were determined to "have it all." We managed departments while also managing households. We rocked sick children at night and climbed the corporate ladder by day (or at least we tried to). The stress of our schedules coupled with the realities of organizational life eventually began to take their toll. By the 1980s the U.S. divorce rate escalated to 50 percent, and we were major contributors.

FOR BETTER OR FOR WORSE?

I vividly remember being thirteen and finding out my parents were getting a divorce. Though emotionally distraught, I was aware that now my family would be like everyone else's. When they separated, I was in sixth grade, and by that time, most of my friends' and classmates' parents were already divorced. I'll never forget my friend Melissa telling me in high school that she felt strange being part of a family that stayed together. Just recently another friend, Jackie, confessed that she "felt like a freak" because her parents never divorced. While divorce was taboo and the subject of gossip or behind-the-back whispering for previous generations, for Gen Xers it just seemed inevitable that our parents would split. Eventually you were going to have to divide your weeks and holidays between Mom, Dad, relatives, and stepfamilies.

We Xers have experienced a plethora of blended family relationships. We've not only had to adjust to stepparents, stepsiblings, stepgrandparents, stepaunts, and stepuncles, we've had to adjust to life with Mom's boyfriend or Dad's ex-wife. These broken (and sometimes awkward) relationships have left us skeptical of relationships, yet needy of them. Because so many of us have been deprived of a traditional family, as young adults we often try to create surrogate ones. We form "urban tribes," making families out of friends.

An urban tribe is a family you pick for yourself. Urban tribes have become the support network that family used to represent for our parents' and grandparents' generations. They are an offshoot of our generational mobility. We Xers often move to cities where we have no relatives, so our tribes are a product of practicality. It's just much easier to live when there are people who've "got your back." Urban tribes are the people we eat dinner with several times a week. These friends have keys to our houses and come over unannounced, maybe even letting themselves in. We go on vacation with them and we celebrate holidays together. Our tribes are always on our cell phones' automatic dial lists (Quinn 2004, p. D7).

My tribe grew out of my work relationships. When I moved to New Orleans I knew two people and was working with one of them. After a year, I'd developed a network of friends who invited me over on holidays and gave me rides to and from the auto shop, and one co-worker/neighbor/friend comes over for dinner at least three times a week. Now, my mom and dad always had friends, but they seemed to rely on family. My generation doesn't always have family, so we turn to our friends.

SEARCHING FOR A SOUL MATE

Some might say that we Gen X women have learned from our parents' mistakes. We are marrying later, we are having kids later, and spending time with friends and families is taking on renewed importance. The latest census and labor data show that the 36.3 million Americans who are in their twenties are getting married later than previous generations. The average marrying age for men a decade ago was twenty-two. Now the average age for men is twenty-seven. A decade ago, the average age for women was twenty, and today it's closer to twenty-five (Eveld 2001).

Some of us aren't marrying at all. The never-married is the fastest growing demographic group in America. In a 2002 segment called "Never Marrieds," ABC News reported that singles constitute more than 40 percent of the U.S. adult population. In the past thirty years the number of people who have never walked down the aisle has more than doubled. In 1965 three out of four college women said they would marry a man they didn't love if he fit all their other criteria. This is far from true for my generation. A recent Rutgers University survey found that 94 percent of people between the ages of twenty and twenty-nine agree with this statement: "When you marry you want your spouse to be your soul mate, first and foremost." Gen Xers want a soul mate or no one at all!

And, if we're not certain whether our current partner really is our soul mate, we may choose to cohabit (much to some of our parents' dismay), rather than tie the knot. For some Gen X couples, living together is simply a matter of economics. For others, it's a way to give the relationship a test run before committing to a lifetime of matrimony. In fact, these days almost half of people thirty-five and under live with their partners before getting married. My friend Alicia is one of them. Here's her story:

Marriage? Maybe

At age 26 I got lucky in Las Vegas, but probably not in the way you'd expect. I was on vacation with a friend from college and the trip ended up changing my life. My friend and I fell in love! Unfortunately, when the weekend was over, I went back to Fort Worth and he went home to Minneapolis. As our relationship grew, it became obvious that we were going to have to live in the same city. Spending one or two weekends together a month wasn't working. We approached it logically at first, with me looking for a job in Minneapolis, him in Fort Worth. But this was in 2002, around the time the job market tanked, and there weren't many jobs to be had. I was at a crossroads in my life. Should I stick with my established career or follow my heart? The heart was certainly riskier, I knew from experience.

My parents divorced when I was very young. My mother never remarried, while my father did—three times. Watching their marriage end unsuccessfully and quite painfully taught me that marriage doesn't always equal stability and lifelong togetherness. Knowing this made the Minneapolis move a tough decision, but I finally gambled on love. I moved to give us a chance. I still hadn't found a job, so we decided it would make more sense for us to live together. Plus, we planned to eventually get married. We viewed living together as a step in that direction. For me, the key was making the commitment to building a life and future together.

It made sense to me, but not to my parents. I would be the first person in the family to live with a significant other without getting married. When I told them, they spouted off statistics about couples who lived together not lasting. They suggested that we just go ahead and get married. So we decided to make a commitment— no, not getting married. We bought a home together. To me, it was a significant event in our relationship. I imagine closing on a house is sort of like saying "I do." Both give you a feeling of permanence.

We have been together now for three years, and while we occasionally talk about getting married, we aren't in any rush. As a friend of mine said, after living with her boyfriend for a year and then getting married, "The only thing that really changed was my last name." Whether we end up getting married soon or sometime in the future or just living together, only time will tell.

Alicia sums it up well when she says, "We aren't in any rush." That's a common theme among Gen Xers who aren't diving into marriage as early as their parents did. Instead, like Alicia, they take the relationship for a test-drive by living together. The test-drives and marriage delays can be tied right back to our experiences growing up and watching our parents divorce. We simply don't want it to happen to us and we don't want to put our kids through the same pain we went through. We're afraid of repeating our parents' mistakes; so Gen Xers are taking their time to marry, and when we do, most of us, unlike our mothers, change our last names.

SHOW ME THE MONEY

Our Boomer parents came of age during a time of unprecedented national prosperity. They grew up believing there was more than enough for everyone, and as adults they became prolific consumers of goods and services. Many of them placed a high value on personal gratification and material success. Consequently, even if our parents divorced, many of us middle-class Xers continued to live comfortable lifestyles subsidized by two working parents. As we grew from childhood into our teen years, our parents' incomes progressively increased as they climbed the corporate ladder, and our lifestyles changed accordingly. We left the ranch house behind and moved into split-levels in nicer subdivisions. Our parents' closets of leisure suits, wide ties, and wider bell-bottoms were replaced by name-brand clothes like Izod and Polo, and they dressed us in little versions of the same.

Some of our parents gave us things because they had so little time to give. Others gave us things just because they could. We came of age during the most affluent period this country has ever known. We didn't have the X-Box, but we had Atari 2600s. Laptops weren't around, but we used our family's first computer to make birthday cards in Print Shop, printing them out on dot-matrix printers. We grew up fighting with our brothers and sisters over personal space in the backseat of station wagons that kept getting nicer as we got older. And, eventually, maybe our mom or dad handed us a set of keys to a car of our own.

Even though our parents' generation has become known as the "me generation" due to their obsession with the good life, their generation also embraced an inclusive social agenda that resulted in affirmative action and civil rights legislation. Our Boomer parents passed their beliefs in the American dream on to us, their Gen X children. They wanted us to inherit, not only a world of material abundance, but also a workplace of unlimited opportunities. We Gen X women grew up believing, not only that we could achieve our dreams, but that, due to our mothers' hard work, we would enter equal opportunity workplaces where we would find encouragement, support, and enjoyment as we rapidly ascended the career ladder. It's the life Mom tells me she'd worked for, dreamed of, and helped deliver. She explains,

>> *Even though we Boomer women encountered a variety of glass ceilings in our male-dominated workplaces, we were deeply committed to creating a world without gender bias. We taught our sons how to cook their own meals and do their own laundry, and we encouraged our daughters in sports and leadership. We believed that we could rear a new generation of equal opportunity kids. We told them that they could have it all. We challenged them to dream big while showering them with material possessions—whetting their appetite for the good life. We programmed them with GREAT EXPECTATIONS!*

CHAPTER 2

Great Xpectations

Gen X women want it all—and we want it all *right now*. Our lives are filled with cell phones and instant messaging, microwaves and PDAs. These technological devices lead us to expect rapid results and instant fulfillment. Furthermore, many of us have put all of our life-fulfillment needs into our careers (some of our moms were good role models). Our quality education, coupled with our desire to delay marriage until we find the perfect partner, as well as our parents' encouragement and our own achievement needs, lead us ever deeper into striving for career success. But, like the proverbial quest for happiness, the harder we strive, the less we seem to be finding. Consequently my generation is now confronted with a huge gap between career expectations and reality. Here's what a few of our survey respondents had to say about how their careers are proving to be different from their expectations:

I expected that if I worked hard and finished college with a good GPA I would get a wonderful job—that has *not* been the case! I have been blessed with jobs that are enjoyable but not prestigious or high paying. From my experience and from talking with friends, it seems that our generation did not get realistic ideas about the working world during college and high school. We were told "you can be anything you want to be" but not given any guidance to get there.

27-YEAR-OLD EMPLOYMENT ASSISTANT

As a high school student I always heard "you can be anything you want to be." I have found that this is not true, particularly for highly competitive careers. I was always told that if I worked hard and got good grades, I would land a good job. Again, not necessarily true.

33-YEAR-OLD MARKETING COORDINATOR

MIND THE GAP

When you're hopping on or off the tube in London, you hear a canned voice repeatedly cautioning passengers to "mind the gap" between the platform and the train. Too bad there's no such voice reminding us Xers to "mind the gap" between our expectations and reality. If we were reminded, we might stop and realize that there's a reason Gen Xers are feeling dissatisfied and unhappy about work. Consider this: Our mothers entered the workforce with very few role models. They set career goals and then climbed the organizational ladder, slowly shattering the glass ceilings they encountered along the way. They had little expectation of reaching the corner office; hence they were grateful for each new opportunity and frequently were surprised that they made it as high as they did (remember their moms, our grandmothers, typically did not have careers). Many of our moms, thanks to their good education and their willingness to work longer and harder than their male counterparts (and the help of affirmative action), wound up in positions that exceeded their expectations.

Due to the success of these Boomer women, we Xers grew up with a very different set of expectations. We set our career goals high, based not only on our mothers' achievements, but also on the achievements of women as diverse as talk show host Oprah Winfrey, TV newswoman Diane Sawyer, eBay CEO Margaret Whitman, and national poet Maya Angelou. We raised our expectations based on their realities and thus aimed even higher than the success levels many of our mothers achieved. Remember, our moms encouraged us to do anything we wanted. And then, alas, not only did we have to start at the bottom of the ladder, but we soon discovered that our expectations were unrealistic. While our entry-level career opportunities were greater than those of our mothers, little has changed on the corporate culture front. The encouragement, support, and enjoyment we expected are, all too often, missing. Like many before us, we, the beneficiaries of our mothers' attempts at social reform, have taken for granted that which they worked so hard to accomplish. And, we've overestimated their progress; consequently, we're living a reality that doesn't measure up to our great Xpectations.

There's a big difference in the direction of the expectation/reality lines (Figure 1). For Boomers it's an optimistic line climbing from expectations to reality. In contrast, the Xers' line shows a steady decline. We expected a lot and haven't necessarily achieved it yet. Logically, that makes sense, because our mothers have twenty-plus more years of work experience than we have (perhaps when Xers are in their fifties and sixties, we will have advanced beyond our mothers' positions); but emotionally we, as a generation of women, feel quite disillusioned with the world of work. Even though I'm sure the intentions were good, our parents', teachers', and career counselors' great expectations for my generation have, unfortunately, created a sense of entitlement. Our reality doesn't actually bite. We're not that far down the career ladder from our moms, but we had much higher expectations to begin with.

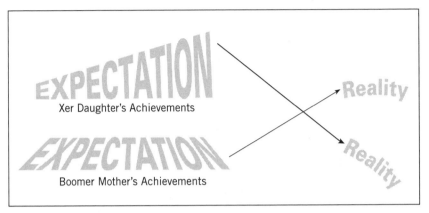

Figure 1 > Boomer-Xer Expectations-Reality Gap

Boomers who don't understand why their younger counterparts in the office have such high expectations of advancement and achievement should ponder Figure 1, which illustrates the Boomer-Xer expectations-reality gap. A good example of those high expectations is given by a thirty-one-year-old finance assistant who believes she should have advanced far faster than she has. She wrote, "I entered banking thirteen years ago and honestly expected to be a lot further than I am currently. I saw myself in a management position within ten years." Many Boomer women had to wait years for management jobs, parking spaces, and corner offices. We Gen Xers walk in the door expecting them. Women like my mother had to fight for good jobs; women like me think we're entitled to them.

We Gen X women entered the workplace with high expectations, and we carried with us our mothers' dreams. As Mom has explained, Boomer women came of age during a time of increased awareness about the importance of social justice and equal rights. The new nation they helped create was waiting there for us Xers to grow into. What Mom didn't realize was that there might be some serious burdens linked to all that opportunity. She probably never imagined that, when I chose to put off getting married and having a family to focus on my career, I'd end up being vastly disappointed that my job wasn't meeting my relationship needs. Or that the workplace she tried so hard to level would still be an uneven playing field for me. I'm certain that when she told me I could be anything I wanted to be, she didn't think I would interpret that as entitlement to huge career successes in record time. And when that dream crashed into the reality that her daughter would end up as another disillusioned Xer, I'm sure Mom wasn't thinking about all that. She was just a Boomer who came of age in the vastly different era of the 1960s, had two kids in the 1970s, and struggled to make the world a better place for all of us. Too bad she didn't tell me to "mind the gap."

PERPETUATING THE MYTH

Not only do we Xers have great Xpectations about finding the perfect job, but we have great ideas about what the ideal workplace should look like and what our place as Gen X women could be in it. However, we can't just point a finger at our parents for our great (and sometimes unrealistic) Xpectations. Our educational systems played a role as well. Remember what your high school guidance counselor told you or the line those university recruiters fed you when you were shopping for a college? They tried their best to make us all believe that if we chose their school, the world would be our oyster. They sent out the videos with kids and teachers in lab coats and goggles, smiling over some important scientific breakthrough and other students sitting in high-tech classrooms preparing for high-paying, high-tech jobs. Those recruiters led us to believe that once we had a diploma from (insert the name of the college of your choice here), we'd be able to achieve high levels of success and satisfaction in the real world of work.

University career centers also played a major role in helping to create our unrealistic expectations. In *Quarterlife Crisis* (Robbins and Wilner 2001), Kristina, a 1995 graduate, says, "When I graduated from college, I thought getting a job would be a snap, because that's the impression we got from the career counselors and everyone around us. Boy, was I wrong" (p. 173). In fact, there's a general feeling among recent college graduates that their schools' career placement programs only helped the I.T. students. "It is interesting that these 'service' centers simply do not prepare students who will have to put in some service time of their own before they will be able to climb into the career of their choice" (p. 174).

Your career counselor may have told you that everything would eventually fall into place. A couple of years out of college, you may have started wondering *when?* Maybe some solid advice would have been more appropriate. It might have been more useful if they had given us the cold hard facts and told us to be prepared to answer phones and do some filing. They could have told us that success rarely comes easily or instantly, so we should be prepared to do some time on the bottom rung of the corporate ladder.

Of course we can't blame our great Xpectations solely on our parents, our high school guidance counselors, or the universities. The new-economy corporations were also pretty busy selling us a glorified image of the working world. In the dot.com boom of the 1990s, many of us were wooed by stories of ideal jobs (and huge salaries) waiting for us right after graduation. But even those jobs often turned out to be disappointing. Just listen to the story of Bianca, a twenty-nine-year-old consultant.

Welcome to Greensboro

Life was good. I was barely twenty-two. I had just graduated with two business degrees from a prestigious university. I had accepted a consulting job offer from one of the Big Five. My life was right on track, just as I had planned.

I didn't want to waste any time—no frivolous trips to Europe to find myself, no lying in the sun reading *Cosmo*. . . . I arrived at my new office for orientation six days after graduation. I wore a tailored navy suit, heels, and hose and carried a new briefcase. . . . I was now the professional I had always pictured.

I remember, one hour into the orientation, looking at my watch and wondering what time I would get to leave. Funny thing is, this thought still crosses my mind every day . . . only now it's six years later.

After suffering through six weeks of so-called training and brown-nosing with executives, I was ready for my first project. I received a phone call letting me know who my new client would be and that it would involve travel. "Travel!" That was the word I had been waiting for! Where would it be—L.A., New York, Paris? Thoughts of jet-setting through airports, holding a cell phone in one hand, palm pilot in the other, winking at the other executives who were hurrying to catch their planes. . . . Then I asked the question, but little did I know the answer would be symbolic of my life as a consultant. "When do I leave?" I asked excitedly. My new manager ordered, "Buy a ticket on American to Greensboro. We will leave from Dallas on Sunday and return on Friday night." Before I had time to digest, I responded, "Yes, sir. I will see you on Sunday," and I hung up the phone.

Questions flooded my mind: "Where the hell is Greensboro?" "Isn't some secretary supposed to buy my ticket for me?" "Sunday through Friday night? What happened to the four-day workweek I kept hearing about?"

After discovering that Greensboro was in North Carolina, employees were responsible for buying their own tickets (to be reimbursed later), and there was only one flight per day to Greensboro, I packed up and arrived at the airport two hours early.

My manager was waiting for me with a stack of material. I couldn't help noticing his close resemblance to Mickey Mouse. He quickly shook my hand and said, "Read this on the plane; it should help you get up to speed." My first thought was, "It's Sunday. The only things I read on Sunday are the wedding pages and my horoscope. Is he kidding?" We boarded the plane several awkward minutes later. I sat between "Mickey" and a two-hundred-pound man in overalls and a straw hat. This was going to be a long flight. I kept my sanity by thinking about the upcoming limo ride to the swanky hotel. I could not wait to crawl into my crisp sheets and curl up with the wedding pages.

Two and a half excruciating hours later, we arrived. It was 12 a.m. Eastern time. The airport was dead. We walked around outside for ten minutes looking for something. I assumed it was the limo. Then it pulled up: the Marriott Courtyard bus. We climbed on and went to the less-than-swanky hotel. After checking in, Mickey told me to meet him at 6:30 a.m. in the lobby.

I woke up at 5:30 so I would have time to curl my hair and press my suit. I did not know about the humidity in North Carolina. I was eyeing the buffet breakfast as Mickey rushed downstairs. He ran past me and said, "Let's go."

My first week was a blur. Each day I sat in meetings pretending to understand what the clients wanted from us. Mickey would later translate the clients' needs into multitabbed spreadsheets and hours at the copy machine. I would spend days in a tiny cubicle squinting at my laptop, trying to make the numbers add up and the column headings straight. I would print each version and lay it on Mickey's desk for approval. Minutes later he would return, red pen in hand, basically telling me to start over.

I learned a lot in my first month in Greensboro. I learned that arriving at the airport twenty minutes early will suffice. I learned that packing hose, heels, and a curling iron is useless. I learned that I could put up with constructive criticism from a mortal cartoon character. Most important, I learned that consulting was not all it was cracked up to be.

Over the past six years, I have also worked on projects in Jacksonville, Seattle, Little Rock, San Francisco, and my home-town of Dallas. Regardless of location, the work is pretty much the same. My role has changed with my experience, however. I am now a manager myself. I am the one giving the stack of material to the new consultants, with a red pen in hand. One thing hasn't changed, though: I still look at my watch every day and wonder what time I will get to leave.

This Xer had a clear image of the perfect job even before she graduated from college. In fact, her education at the right college helped her land her job with the right company. But she quickly realized she'd had the wrong impression. She didn't find the excitement, purpose, or fulfillment she'd expected. Work wasn't what she had hoped for at all, and it was that disillusionment that kept her glancing at her watch every day.

THE IMPOSSIBLE DREAM

Gen Xers long for the perfect job. We yearn for work we can love. It's not that our parents didn't want to be happy at work. But in the past, the career paths were a little more straightforward. "Aspiring doctors went to medical school, lawyers went to law school, and teachers attained degrees in education. Job and life patterns were more clear-cut, and there was less emphasis on 'love what you do' in favor of 'support the family'" (Robbins and Wilner 2001, p. 8). Many Boomers were also more focused on job status than on job satisfaction—on feeding their egos rather than feeding their souls. As you'll see in Chapter 5, status is simply not on most Xers' radar screens.

We want to be affiliated with an organization that feeds our sense of pride (Reich 1998), which could have to do with the place being hip, well-respected, or cutting-edge. Just imagine yourself out at a bar with your friends. You meet a new guy, and one of the first questions after you ask him his name is probably going to be "So, what do you do?" And, let's be honest; we're not asking him to tell us about all the little things that fill the minutes of his daily life. We want to know what his job is because many of us continue to define ourselves by our work. The more we like our job, the more we like ourself. The more dissatisfied we are with our job, the worse we feel about ourself. So, when we are dissatisfied with work, our feelings bleed over into every aspect of our life.

Even though we long for the perfect job, most of us might find it easier to define an imperfect one. In fact, the Gen Xers we surveyed were fluent in the language of frustration. It seems to be all that's spoken in some of their workplaces. One woman, after completing our survey, e-mailed us the following story:

> Some of my Gen X friends were just talking yesterday about the dissatisfaction we're feeling these days. So we found the survey very interesting/timely. One of my friends actually said that of the last five years of her professional life, the best time she had was the forty-five-day recovery period when she didn't have to work after she underwent emergency surgery for a ruptured colon!

This story is quite dramatic and it may be quite disturbing for Boomer mothers who fought for Xers' career opportunities. But it is also typical of the comments we received from many other Gen X women (and men) on survey question number thirty-four: "How has your career, thus far, proved to be similar to or different from what you expected when you entered the workforce?" Here are some of the other responses:

My career is totally different from what I expected it would be back when I first entered the workforce. It is neither glamorous nor exciting and it is certainly not stimulating! I work only to support my life outside of work. If my life outside of work was as dull as my daily working life, I think I would find myself in a severe depression.

29-YEAR-OLD PRODUCT DEVELOPMENT ENGINEER

My work experiences have been similar to living in hell.

29-YEAR-OLD DELIVERY DRIVER

My career, as well as my life, is nothing like I expected when I was young. You have these dreams about all the great things you will do and they all seem to fade away as the years go by.

30-YEAR-OLD OPTICIAN

If someone had told me where I would be and what I would be doing I would have laughed and run!

38-YEAR-OLD PROGRAM DIRECTOR

"Life sucks" . . . "Faded dreams" . . . "I would've run" . . . we heard so much disappointment from so many of our survey respondents. And, from some of them we heard much more than mere disappointment; many respondents spoke of disillusionment and despair. Few were prepared for the politics of organizational life.

THE GOOD OLD BOYS

Boomer women definitely did much to reduce the gender bias in contemporary organizations; but we, their daughters, have certainly not inherited a level playing field. Few of us were prepared for the dark shadows of power and politics that still drain the color from our organizational landscapes. Our survey respondents had a lot to say about this topic. The comments from these seven women are but the tip of the iceberg:

The office politics are something I was not prepared for. I thought I had left those days behind me in high school. It's very hard to be productive and motivated when you're watching your back and wondering who's saying what.

28-YEAR-OLD HUMAN RESOURCES REPRESENTATIVE

There are more politics and people's personal agendas getting in the way of doing the right thing than I thought there would be. . . . Seem to be more double standards than I had expected.

29-YEAR-OLD PROGRAM MANAGER

I didn't expect the viciousness of politics and the power plays. I didn't expect that management as a whole would be self-interested almost to the exclusion of all else. I didn't expect to hate yuppies with all their "self-esteem-building" vapidity as much as I do now. I thought work would be a meritocracy. It isn't. It's junior high school writ large.

30-YEAR-OLD SENIOR SUPPORT TECHNICIAN

I don't think I expected the politics; sometimes it is more who you know and who likes you than what you know. I experienced this in college and high school but thought that people might be more open-minded in the "real world."

34-YEAR-OLD MANAGER

I had believed that if you work hard you will be rewarded but have learned that it is more who you know and how you play the game instead of what are your qualifications and merits.

37-YEAR-OLD NEWS ANCHOR

I expected that if I had a good education and worked hard I'd be successful. However, this is not the case. In the real world it's not what you know. It's a combination of how pretty you are, how charismatic you are, and who you know.

28-YEAR-OLD SENIOR ACCOUNTANT

I expected that if I worked hard and did things well, always got good reviews, I would get ahead. I have found that getting ahead often relates to whom you are friends with or how much you suck up to whomever is in charge.

39-YEAR-OLD PARALEGAL

As Mom and I discussed these survey comments, she reflected on her own corporate journey into the shadowy world of power and politics. This is what she told me:

> > *When I took my first corporate position, I had no idea how to play the political game. I could see that there was more to organizational life than meets the eye, but I didn't even know the rules of the game, much less have the requisite skills to play it. My mentor recommended that I read Betty Harragan's book* Games Mother Never Taught You: Corporate Games- manship for Women, *which was first published in 1977. This book covered topics ranging from how to manage your inner feelings in the presence of men to how to create the right outer image by dressing for success. Harragan dedicated this book to her daughter with these words: "For my daughter, Kathleen, who will enter the workforce in the mid-1980s prepared to accept nothing less than fully vested citizenship in the American economy."*

> *I don't know whether Kathleen found what her mother had hoped for, but I doubt it. Few women have. But for me the important point of reflection is this: Why did I fail to better prepare my daughter for the politics of orga- nizational life? Why did I not teach her the skills that I had struggled so hard to learn? Why did doing so never cross my mind? Why did I think that her workplace experiences would be dramatically different from mine? The answer lies, at least in part, in my propensity for optimism—a propensity that frequently overpowers my own experiences.*

I admire Mom's optimism, but, in this case, it resulted in her pro- viding me with little more knowledge of organizational politics than she had when she entered the workplace. We both wish she had told me more. I realize that she deeply understands the power of negative expectations and didn't want to set me up to unconsciously create a vic- tim experience. But let's face it, organizations do have a dark side. Because Mom and I didn't talk about this side of organizational life, I was surprised to discover just how political organizations are. Based on our survey comments, a lot of Gen Xers were surprised. No one told us about Fred Luthan's research at the University of Nebraska. It's rather shocking!

Luthan investigated how successful managers (defined as those who get promoted most often) spend their time. The specific research question was this: "Do managers who move up most quickly in an organization do the same activities and with the same emphasis as managers who do the best job?" (Robbins 2003, p. 7). The answer was no. "Successful" managers spent almost 50 percent of their time networking (socializing, politicking, and interacting with people outside their department), while "effective" managers spent 44 percent of their time communicating with their departmental staff and only 11 percent of their time networking. I suspect these findings apply to more than just managers. Yet, my friends and I (and most of the 1,200 people we surveyed) entered the workforce believing that skills and knowledge would get us to the top.

Not only are organizations highly political, but they are still very hierarchical. Most of them offer few opportunities for creative or interesting work, and meaningful moments are rare—at least at the bottom rung of the ladder. Contemporary organizations actually aren't very contemporary at all. Even though Gen X expectations about work are different, organizational cultures aren't all that different from what they were fifty years ago. The world of technology has changed how we do jobs, but little has changed in how people do politics. Here are a few more comments:

> I did not expect politics in the workplace to play such a key part in all aspects of my career. I thought if you busted your butt and did more than expected you would be recognized. Instead, I so often see "Golden Boys" who don't know what they are doing become the boss's buddy and get promoted quickly. Also there is still such a problem with the "Men's Club" that it's hard to be promoted in my industry if you are a woman.
>
> 36-YEAR-OLD QUALITY TECHNICIAN

> I never would have imagined that the companies I work for would be so political and unethical. I used to be optimistic that if I worked hard and had the right qualifications I would have a strong chance of moving ahead. I found that to be very untrue. The corporate world is very racist and sexist.
>
> 27-YEAR-OLD BENEFIT AUTHORIZER

Over the past few years of my career I have actually felt the repercussions of sexual discrimination. I grew up during a time that said I could do whatever a boy could do—and sometimes even better! I always felt this way and never noticed any sort of discrimination whatsoever. Over the past few years I have suffered from this. It was not expected and not something I've ever been used to dealing with.

29-YEAR-OLD REVENUE ANALYST

Our Boomer moms know all about the good old boy obstacles, and it must make them incredibly sad to read these quotes. They must be thinking, What happened to fifty years of hard work? What happened to affirmative action legislation? What happened to our attempts to level the playing field for our daughters? It appears that the more things have changed, the more they have stayed the same—at least in the workplace. There's still no way to sashay or sidestep into the good old boy network unless you really are a boy, or a man, as the case may be.

GENDER DIFFERENCES

Daughters are not the only product of the women's liberation movement. Our mothers also raised sons. That means a whole generation of boys grew into manhood under the influence of their working mothers. And while they were growing up, they were surrounded by girls who were getting a new message from their moms, girls who were being told they had every opportunity that boys had. My mother remembers the optimism she and her friends felt as their Gen X sons and daughters left the nest:

> [>>] *Our equal opportunity children went off to universities where they lived in co-ed dorms. Some of our daughters studied medicine and engineering while a few of our sons went to nursing school. It appeared that the brave new world of equal opportunity that we, their mothers, had dreamed about had arrived at last. We envisioned workplaces without stereotypes, where everyone had an opportunity to become all that they were capable of being.*

Our mothers sincerely believed that when those young Gen X men (their sons) entered the workforce, after all that equality stuff had been drummed into them, they'd be more likely to see women as equals, to identify with their career goals, and to understand their experiences. Right? Well . . . not exactly—the gender gap still exists. Gen X men see our plight a lot differently than we do. They are much more likely than Gen X women are to believe that there have been advances for women at work in the past ten years. Catalyst (2001), a leading research organization that focuses on women's workplace issues, found that more than half of Gen X men think advancement opportunities for white women have increased greatly in the past decade; only one-fourth of Gen X women agreed.

Gen X men are also less likely than Gen X women to see the barriers women face. For example, 62 percent of the Gen X men in the Catalyst (2001) study said they believed that men and women are paid the same for similar work. Less than 33 percent of women agreed (on average, women earn 77 cents for every $1 men earn). Almost 50 percent of the Gen X women surveyed said they had to outperform men to get the same pay; only 11 percent of the Gen X men agreed. Sixty-six percent of the Gen X women surveyed said their commitment to personal and family responsibilities was a barrier to their advancement, but only 33 percent of the Gen X men agreed. Women also reported career barriers such as too few mentoring opportunities, lack of women role models, stereotyping, exclusion from informal networks of communication, and lack of awareness of office politics. In each of these areas, significantly fewer men recognized these issues as barriers that might hold a woman back from career advancement.

DRESSING FOR SUCCESS

Recently Mom told me a story about one of her MBA students who came to her frustrated because her manager didn't seem to give her as many opportunities as a female peer with the same credentials (and less relevant job experience). Mom asked this student to identify how this peer was different from her. The student, without a moment's hesitation, said, "Well, the main difference is that she wears makeup and nice clothes." (Mom's student always dressed in a casual, GAP-type style and wore no makeup.)

Mom, with some reservation, suggested that her student conduct an experiment and for one week try to look and dress like the more favored peer. You can probably guess the outcome. There were noticeable changes in the manager's behavior in just a week's time. Obviously, image is still important, even though the books about dressing for success have fallen out of vogue. Interestingly, Mom teaches "Impression Management" to her MBA students, but somehow she never thought it important to teach me. Consequently, I entered the workplace thinking my skills were a lot more important than my looks (and I'm an on-air news reporter). The lessons I didn't learn from Mom I quickly learned from consultants and news directors.

It is apparent that the "wo" woes still exist. Sound like a made-up kid sickness? It's not. Rather, it's the sudden realization that if you could just lose the "wo" in "woman," you'd have a lot more opportunities at work. Successful women don their button-downs and briefcases for a reason. They're playing in a man's world, and they know that the better they are at fitting in and playing the game, the better off they'll be. As Jay Leno once said, "The way to succeed in this world is to look like a man and think like a woman."

We constantly see women shedding their "wo" and acting like men in order to advance their careers. Margaret Heffernan is a good example of a woman who's been there and done that. She ran five companies in a matter of ten years. She's a CEO success story who's writing a book on why there aren't more like her. She believes that one of the major barriers for women is assimilation. In order to succeed, we have to learn to act like guys. "Carly Fiorina's grim stare from the cover of *BusinessWeek*, complete with cropped hair and dull-gray suit, suggests that assimilation works" (Heffernan 2002, p. 62). Carly's grim stare reappeared on the October 13, 2003, cover of *Fortune*. This time she was joined by an equally grim-looking Condoleezza Rice. The seriousness of their expressions mirrors the seriousness of their jobs. Unfortunately, this picture also makes these women look a lot like men, and that makes the price of success seem awfully high.

Here's an over-the-top example of a woman trying to act like a man. It came to me through e-mail forwarding:

> The FBI had narrowed down its search for new agents to three candidates. Those candidates had one final test before they'd become qualified. They took the first candidate to a door and told him, "Behind this closed door your wife is sitting on a chair. Here's a loaded gun. Your final objective tests your ability to follow directions. Take this gun, go in, and kill your wife." The first man sadly shook his head, refused to take the gun, and was sent home. They took the second candidate to the door and told him the same thing. "Behind this closed door your wife is sitting on a chair. To test your ability to follow any instruction, take this gun, go in, and kill your wife." This candidate took the gun, went into the room, and several minutes later came out sobbing. He handed the gun back to the FBI agents and told them he just couldn't do it. They sent him home. The final candidate was a woman. They took her to the door, handed her the gun, and told her she had to go in and kill her husband. She took the gun, walked in, and closed the door. The agents heard several gunshots and then some yelling and banging. Five minutes later the woman came out, sweating and gasping for air. She told them, "That gun you gave me was filled with blanks, so I had to beat him to death with the chair."

OK, it's an extreme example and clearly a joke, but it does illustrate the point. In order to succeed, women sometimes have to put aside their femininity, even their common sense, and not only dress more like a man than a woman but also act more like one. One of Mom's male Gen X students refers to these women as Tiger Ladies. Here are his observations about the problem *and* the cause:

There is no doubt that my company as a whole complies with all federal and state guidelines for equal opportunity employment.

However, when one looks at those in positions of power, it is easy to see that we have a long way to go before a more diverse situation is achieved. As with many tradition-bound companies, the picture of diversity at the management level would not take long to paint. Management is overwhelmingly white and male (with good heads of hair) and many of the women who have managed to work their way into the management ranks tend to carry the stereotypical Tiger Lady mantra with them in all situations. I find this to be very understandable because these women have been forced to work throughout their careers in a much more careful and tough manner than have their male counterparts. A male can try something and fail and be asked what he has learned from it, but a female is not afforded the same luxury. If she makes a mistake she is "blacklisted" and is thought of as being incapable and prone to error.

The situation in this company is not unusual. According to a 2003 survey of 571 women conducted by Hewlett-Packard and the Simmons School of Management (Merrill-Sands, Mattis, and Matus 2003), a majority of women (89 percent) believe that they have to make significant adjustments to their style to succeed in the workplace. Here's a real-life story from someone we'll call Sydney. As she was going through one of the most feminine experiences of life, giving birth to her first child, one of her co-workers turned into a Tiger Lady.

Hostile Takeover

I never thought co-workers would take advantage of my maternity leave. I never thought about it, at least not until it happened. I'd worked in a group practice as a speech therapist for about four years. I offered to take Saturday appointments because I had a couple of parents who could bring their kids only on the weekend. I started out small with three, then grew to nine kids. Eventually we had to add an extra therapist to help handle the Saturday load.

Just before my maternity leave, I began reassuring the parents that as soon as I had the baby, I'd be back. It would be three or four weeks, tops. It ended up being more like eight weeks, because after my baby was born, he ended up in the NICU for ten grueling days. My work was the last thing on my mind. I had to focus on my family. When my baby was well, I called the office to tell them I was ready to see clients again. The scheduler told me she had one new client for me. One new client! What about my old clients? You see, I'd passed them off to another therapist to handle while I was away, figuring she'd return them when I came back. She didn't see it that way. She took the opportunity to step in and take all of the business I'd spent so long building. I feel like I got screwed!

Sydney's female colleague obviously decided to play by men's rules. She executed a hostile takeover, perhaps not even realizing there could be another set of business practices that are more women-friendly. We women need to find ways to work together and support each other rather than perpetuating cutthroat business tactics. In fact, some brain research suggests that women are wired for collaboration. Researchers at Emory University in Atlanta (Angier 2002) found that when women are given the choice to cooperate or compete, they typically choose cooperation— at least in part because it physically feels good. Acts of cooperation activate the reward-seeking part of the female brain—the same part of the brain that responds pleasurably to desserts, pictures of pretty faces, and money. In this experiment, women participated in a laboratory game called the Prisoner's Dilemma. When given the option to choose between greedy behavior and cooperation, most of the women, unlike Sydney's colleague, chose to cooperate.

Though they sometimes don't show it, women inherently want to get along, especially under stress. While the male brain appears to be wired only for fight or flight, according to a research study at UCLA (Taylor et al. 2000), women have a larger response repertoire. This landmark study found that women's brains respond to stress with a cascade of brain chemicals that cause them to move toward others, not away—to tend and befriend, so to speak. Researchers found that when women engage in tending and befriending, the brain releases oxytocin, which counters stress by producing a calming effect. When men are under stress, they produce high levels of testosterone, which does exactly the opposite.

SEX AND POWER

Too bad women can't bottle oxytocin; if we could we might be able to reduce some of the power struggles in contemporary organizations. Perhaps the ultimate power ploy is sexual harassment. I'll let Mom tell you about one of her students who fell victim to sexual harassment in a company that required its managers to attend sexual harassment training every year!

> [>>] *In all my MBA classes I ask my students to keep a learning journal that they submit to me for review on a weekly basis. The journaling process not only helps these students, most of whom are Xers, gain insight into their lives and careers, but I gain a lot of insight as well. A few years ago, Mary, a twenty-something female student, disclosed that she was experiencing a lot of anxiety, the cause of which was sexual harassment and a subsequent job termination. The incident occurred while she was employed with an insurance company.*
>
> *The most disturbing part of Mary's story for me was not the actual harassment by an older male manager (horrendous as that was), but rather the climate of sexuality that the female managers in this company not only accepted but perpetuated. Mary had been at this company about six months when she was asked to give a presentation to some male clients. Before the presentation, Mary's female manager observed how nervous she was and gave her this advice: "Roll up your skirt a couple of inches and show a little knee; then they'll accept our proposal, regardless of what you say." And, she was serious!*
>
> *Mary went on to say that many women in this company used their sexuality to get ahead. Those who had male bosses joked about how the amount of*

cleavage they showed on performance review day correlated with the amount of salary increase they received. After reading these details, I (a former V.P. of human resources) was astounded. I later asked Mary why she had stayed in such an unhealthy environment. She reflected on my question for a while and then concluded that it was due partly to fear and partly to being naive.

Mary mentioned that as a child, she had received somewhat contradictory messages about women, work, and sexuality. While her father had always stressed professional workplace behavior, her mother's role as an elected official exposed Mary to conversations from other female politicians who sometimes discussed using their sexual allure to win votes. During college Mary interned as a legislative assistant in her state's capital. She was on the house floor doing vote calculations on her twenty-first birthday when a gorgeous bouquet was delivered. Though the bouquet was from her parents, few of the male legislators believed her, not because of Mary's morals, but because of their own—almost all of them were having affairs with female legislators or office staff. The flowers triggered an outburst of suggestive comments, and Mary was swamped with dinner offers for the rest of the day.

While Mary's early experiences may have helped desensitize her to sexually charged work environments, her sexual savvy ultimately did not protect her from an abusive male manager whose behavior began with stalking and progressed to physical abuse (he pushed her and bruised her sternum, resulting in a trip to the emergency room, when she refused his advances). Eventually, after filing an EEOC charge and suing the harasser, Mary made this Golden Boy manager and the company pay financially—but the villain was not terminated until four more women came forward with charges.

Recently I met with Mary and asked her what she would do differently if she were given an opportunity to replay this chapter of her life. She said she would report the inappropriate behavior much sooner (though she doesn't think the outcome would change). She also said that she wished she had listened to family, friends, and her own gut instincts. "At the beginning, while my mind was saying he was just trying to be a mentor and coach, my friends, family, and gut were telling me to stay away. If I had it to do over again, I would listen to them, because I believe at the beginning of it all, had I rebuked his attentions a few times, eventually he would have moved on to a new victim, because, as many of his other victims told me later, he smelled out the vulnerable ones and went after them."

It will take Mary years to overcome the professional and emotional damage. Three years (and one MBA degree) later, Mary makes $3,000 a year less than she did at her previous place of employment. This may be due in part to the economic downturn, but it is largely a result of her shifting priorities. Mary commented that at one time she defined herself by her career—she had been taught to do so by parents and grandparents who emphasized educational and professional accomplishments. But now she defines herself primarily as a mother and a wife. She said, "Now I shake my head and wonder how I could have put anything before my family. In some weird way, it was a blessing in disguise." Mary also mentioned that she was trying to be invisible in her new job. Her lingering fear of sexual predators was visually apparent. Even though we met during her workday, she was wearing little makeup and baggy clothes. Her parting words were "I believed what they told me in college. I had good grades and a great resume. I don't know what happened!"

Mary's story is one that is all too familiar to my generation. We well know that sexual harassment didn't go away just because of legislation. Between 1992 and 2000, the number of sexual harassment claims in the United States increased by 50 percent, and my generation was among those most affected (Parkinson 2002). Here's another survey comment that reminds us of just how common this problem is:

> I thought that we as a society were getting past that. But in a predominantly male workforce I find it a day-to-day battle to receive the promotions or even recognition for the work I do. I feel I have to work twice as hard to receive the recognition than, say, a fellow male employee. I left my last job after three and a half years because of what I felt was workplace harassment and discrimination. . . . It was very frustrating and I left in hopes that not all companies stand for that kind of treatment. I never thought things like that would happen to me.
>
> 28-YEAR-OLD GRAPHICS MANAGER

Our public lives as well as our personal lives mirror the problem. In 1991, as teenagers and young adults, we watched Anita Hill graphically accuse Supreme Court nominee Clarence Thomas of sexual harassment during nationally televised congressional hearings. Then, almost a decade later we watched the impeachment hearings of our president, and the nation once again was reminded how readily power can be abused.

THE YOUNG AND THE RESTLESS

In 1983, the average worker in her twenties stayed in one job for 2.2 years. Today, that figure has shrunk by half, to 1.1 years (Eveld 2001). Whether we're more eager or more willing or we simply have to leave (like Mary in Mom's sexual harassment story), we Gen Xers are changing jobs much more often than our parents and their parents did. Job security is something we may never experience. We saw the burst of the dot.com bubble, and we have lived through more organizational restructurings and corporate scandals than we can count. It's not that we're disloyal; we're just wary. We happened to enter the workplace at a time of corporate rightsizing, very aware that when the ax falls, the youngest with the least experience will be the first to go. Baby Boomers are often shielded from cuts by protected class legislation, so it's the Gen Xers who typically get let go. This is reverse ageism, and the statistics support its prevalence. According to an analysis by the National Employment Law Project and Economic Policy Institute (Armour 2003), 45 percent of the long-term unemployed (those who are out of work for more than six months) were ages 25–44 in 2002, compared to 35 percent of workers over 45. Only a few years ago, many Xers were riding high on the technology wave. According to an Ernst & Young survey (Armour 2003), more than 70 percent of college students in 2000 thought they'd someday be millionaires. Now many of them are out of work.

If Xers didn't know before that a promising future isn't a promise, we know it now. We can be very dedicated, but if there's no long-term commitment from management, we're not likely to wait around for a new management team. Whether we are jumping from job to job to dodge layoffs, escape harassment, or land a better opportunity, Xers who don't feel they're getting what they deserve typically move on. Here's how one woman in our survey described the situation:

> **There is hardly any employer loyalty. That's the biggest difference between my dad's career and mine. He stayed with his employer through rough times and good times. In this day you leave during rough times for a higher-paying job somewhere else, and then that job will go through rough times, and the cycle never ends.**
>
> 29-YEAR-OLD SENIOR AUDITOR

There's a widespread belief among Boomers that Xers are not willing to pay their dues. What we've learned from experience is that paying our dues doesn't pay off. We've been laid off or seen it happen to our friends and co-workers. We know how tight the job market is and may even know what it's like to survive on unemployment, as in my case, even with bachelor's and master's degrees. Like many Gen Xers, I have decided that the only source of security I have is me—my ability to do good work, solve problems creatively, and add value to a company. This is something that can't be taken away, and, more important, I can take it from place to place in my ongoing search for that elusive dream job.

CHAPTER 3

The More Things Change

In the United States, girls outnumber boys in student government, debating clubs, and school newspaper and yearbook staffs. There are more girls elected president of student organizations and more girls are members of honor societies. More than 50 percent of high school students in advanced placement classes are female, as are more than 60 percent of college students studying abroad (Sommers 1998). According to the U.S. Department of Education (Conlin 2003), the typical university freshman class is now 55 percent female and 45 percent male. Not only do more women enroll as freshmen, but women also earn the majority of bachelor's and master's degrees—57 and 58 percent, respectively. The 2003 graduating class at the UC Berkeley School of Law was 63 percent female; Harvard's graduating class was 46 percent female, and Columbia's was 51 percent female. Nearly 47 percent of all medical students are female (Belkin 2003). MBA programs, which are only 38 percent female, are one of the few remaining educational enclaves of good old boy graduate programs (Heffernan 2002). Equal opportunity education is certainly something our mothers wanted, and progress has been made; however, equal opportunity in the workplace appears to be taking longer to achieve.

The 1980s and 1990s brought some cosmetic changes to organizations, but deep systemic change hasn't yet occurred. While many more women are graduating with professional degrees, women have not achieved equal representation in the leadership ranks of twenty-first-century organizations. Only 16 percent of law firm partners are women, and even though women and men enter management training programs in equal numbers, only 16 percent of corporate officers are women, and only eight Fortune 500 companies have a woman as CEO (Belkin 2003). Compared to fifty years ago, this is certainly progress, but when it comes time to pass out the paychecks, women are still getting shorted. Their salaries lag far behind men's. Take a look at the statistics in Table 4 from the U.S. Census Bureau (Spraggins 2003) comparing earnings of men and women.

Depending on where you live, the wage gap may be wider or not as pronounced. In a 2002 survey of wages in the United States, the District of Columbia had the smallest gender gap. In D.C., women earned 89.2

TABLE 4	EARNINGS OF MEN AND WOMEN	
	Men	Women
<$25,000	25%	39%
$25,000–34,999	19%	23%
$35,000–49,999	21%	20%
$50,000–74,999	19%	12%
$75,000 & over	16%	6%

cents for each dollar earned by a man; but in Louisiana and Wyoming, the states at the bottom of the list, women earned 64.4 cents for every dollar earned by men. The 2002 national average for women was 77 cents for each dollar earned by a man (Armas 2004). Even when matched for age, education, job experience, and occupation, women made 20 percent less than men.

REALITY CHECK

Despite all the work our feminist moms did to break the glass ceiling, it still exists and it still translates into inequity in the workplace. Many Gen X women like this one notice it every payday:

> **I'm disappointed at the pay I receive. It's about $10,000 less than a male counterpart with the same job title, who doesn't even have an undergraduate degree.**
>
> 29-YEAR-OLD ENGINEERING MANAGER

And this is from our 2003 survey! For women like this engineer, the more things change, the more they stay the same.

Here's a ray of sunshine from the U.S. Department of Labor's Bureau of Labor Statistics (Moore 2002b). The women of Generation X have narrowed the female-male wage gap compared with gender wage gaps of the 1960s, 1970s, and early 1980s. In 2000, women between twenty-five and thirty-five earned, on average, eighty-two cents for each dollar that men of the same age earned. That's not equality, but it's up from the sixty-eight cents on the dollar women earned back in the 1970s (or fifty-nine cents in the 1960s when my mother entered the workforce). It sounds good until you hear some recent findings from the General Accounting Office (GAO), the research arm of Congress. According to a GAO nationwide study, the pay gap widened for women managers in seven of ten industries between 1995 and 2000 (Larson 2002). In each of the following fields, women lost ground in earnings compared to men: communications, business/repair services, entertainment/recreation services, insurance/real estate, retail trade, finance, and professional medical services.

The three industries in which the pay gap narrowed are public administration, educational services, and health care. All three of these industries are either in the public sector or heavily regulated. They are also industries that have traditionally been heavily populated by women. So even though there have been pay gains in pink-collar jobs, the gains are too little, too late. One of our survey respondents, a teacher who tried putting her life into her work and found that her work barely paid for her life, has this to say:

> I expected to enjoy my job. I did not expect that I would have to struggle so hard to keep it from taking over my life, which is very hard to do as a teacher. I also didn't think that salary would matter as much to me as it does now that I realize how little opportunity there is for salary growth; yet paying the bills is a huge struggle. I wonder how long I can make it in this job based on the amount of time I work in relationship to my pay.
>
> 28-YEAR-OLD ELEMENTARY SCHOOL TEACHER

Teaching, like nursing, is a career primarily populated by women. These two careers don't even fall in the top ten most common jobs for men ("Traditional Jobs Provide Most Work for Women" 2003). As kindergarten and preschool teachers, the occupations with the highest proportion of women (98 percent), men earn an average of $22,000, while the average income for women is only $17,000. Among registered nurses, 91 percent are women, but women's average income is $42,000, while men average $45,000 (Armas 2004).

We women may be making moves in the workplace, but many of us aren't making them in the high-paying or fast-growing fields still dominated by men. According to the U.S. Census Bureau (Moore 2002b), men still hold most of the technical jobs, such as systems analyst, software designer, and engineer. Getting a college degree isn't enough to level the playing field. Women need advanced education in science, engineering, and technology. So even though there are a *few* more women in the labor pool these days (in 1983, 44 percent of the workforce was made up of women; by 2000 that number had grown to 46 percent), the gain has not been dramatic, nor has it been well distributed across industries or positions .

There has been some improvement in the number of women in management and professional positions. In 1970 women held only 29 percent of executive, administrative, and managerial jobs. By 1983 this number had increased to 38 percent, and in 2000 the U.S. Department of Labor (Mincer 2003) reported that women held 49 percent of the jobs in this category. But in many cases, women are lower-level managers. You're still *much* more likely to find a man than a woman sitting behind the big desk in the corner office with CEO engraved on the door. In 1995 women held 8.7 percent of the top-ranking executive positions at America's largest companies. By 2000, that number was up to 12.5 percent, and in 2002 it was 15.7 percent. Women are making strides, but it's still an uphill climb.

WOMEN IN MANAGEMENT

The message is clear: Wanna make the big bucks? You gotta be a guy. And if you wanna make the really big bucks (let's say $30 million a year or so), shoot for being the top guy because companies these days are ratcheting up the pay for CEOs. "CEOs of large U.S. corporations earned 42 times as much as the average worker in 1980—but 531 times as much in 2000" (Tobias 2002, p. 9). If that sounds like highway robbery to you, you're probably the average worker, not the top dog. And, by the way, if you average out the total compensation packages of the thirty highest-paid male executives in 2001, they each took home $112.9 million. The top thirty highest-paid female executives' pay averaged $8.7 million

("Bosses' Bonanza" 2002). It is not surprising that 90 percent of the world's billionaires are male.

> Among the super rich, only one woman, Gap Inc. co-founder Doris F. Fisher, made, rather than inherited, her wealth. Men continue to dominate in the highest-paying jobs in such leading-edge industries as engineering, investment banking, and high tech—the sectors that still power the economy and build the biggest fortunes. And women still face sizable obstacles in the pay gap. (Conlin 2003, p. 4)

Gender-based pay differences make little sense in light of research by Catalyst (2004) showing that companies with more women in senior management are more profitable. In fact, the companies with the most women on their senior management team outperformed the businesses with the fewest women by at least 34 percent. Catalyst examined data from a sample of 353 Fortune 500 companies representing five key industry sectors with average revenues of $13.5 billion. Return on Equity (ROE) was 35 percent higher, and Total Return to Stakeholders (TRS) was 34 percent higher, in those companies with a significant number of women in senior management.

The number of women on the senior management team in the strongest-performing (top quartile) companies averaged 20.3 percent; the number of women on the senior management team in the weakest (bottom quartile) performers averaged 1.9 percent. "These findings reaffirm Catalyst's long-standing belief in the business impact of gender diversity. . . . In companies that focus on diversity—developing and leveraging women's talent—the relationship to the bottom line is remarkable" (Catalyst 2004, p. 2). Despite this compelling research, women are vastly underrepresented in senior management positions in most twenty-first-century organizations.

The workplace inequality for women doesn't add up ethically and it just doesn't make good business sense. Here are three more persuasive arguments for companies to implement senior-level gender diversity:

- Employers will be able to attract, recruit, and retain an underutilized segment of the available talent pool; 57.3 and 58.5 percent, respectively, of all U.S. bachelor's and master's degrees are earned by women, as are 44.9 percent of doctoral degrees and 47.3 percent of law degrees.

- Women make or influence most household purchasing decisions; therefore, the company that promotes female talent into strategy-affecting positions will have an edge in the development of products/services that will appeal to female customers.

- Research demonstrates that diverse groups make more innovative business decisions.

If that's not enough to make the men heading companies think about adding more women to their senior-level management ranks, there's also a growing body of research that suggests that women make better managers! A study conducted by the Foundation for Future Leadership (Irwin and Perrault 1996) analyzed a database of assessment results for more than six thousand managers. The data included anonymous performance feedback from each manager's subordinates, supervisors, and peers. According to the findings, women received higher evaluations than men on twenty-eight of the thirty-one behaviors measured—90 percent of all the assessment items.

It seems logical that women would be better at interpersonal skills, but this research suggests women excel in "left-brained" skills as well. Perhaps we have a biological advantage. Though men's brains are about 10 percent larger, women have a larger corpus callosum (the group of nerve cells that connects left and right hemispheres). This makes us faster at transferring data between the verbal, computational left hemisphere and the visual, emotional right hemisphere. And, in today's fast-paced environments, faster integration of verbal and nonverbal information gives women a processing edge.

Men also tend to have a more command-and-control management style, while women tend to be more team focused. In today's lean workplaces, whoever can create the best-functioning team has an edge. Jeffrey Christian, whose executive search firm placed Carly Fiorina at HP, says, "Money is not the primary reason talented people stay on the job or jump! Rather they stay predominantly because of relationships. Women get that" (in Krotz 2004, p. 2). For women, the desire to build relationships is typically stronger than the desire to win at all costs. Here are a few more female leadership strengths (Krotz 2004):

- Women are typically better at empowering others.

- Women encourage open communication.

- Women are more accessible.

- Women leaders respond more quickly to calls for assistance.

- Women are more tolerant of differences.

- Women identify problems more quickly and accurately.

- Women are better at defining expectations and providing feedback.

This list, and a lot of other research, raises an obvious question: If women have a leadership advantage, why don't we see more of them in leadership positions? The answer to the question may be buckled in a car seat in the back of your SUV.

CRITICAL CHOICES

Today, factors other than discrimination are being discussed as reasons for the male domination of senior management jobs. It takes a lot of time and energy to make it to the corporate mountaintop, and some of today's female executives say they're not willing to give, or give up, what it takes to go all the way. Brenda Barnes is a good example. Some have nicknamed her "the woman who walked away." Here's a look at her life: She would get up at 3:30 a.m. to do work before her kids got up, then spend a twelve-hour day at the office, make it home to tuck the kids in, then finish the day with more work. Barnes was the president of the North American arm of PepsiCo. She moved for the company, living for eight years in a different city from her husband. She made huge sacrifices, and, for that, most thought she was next in line when the CEO retired; except Barnes retired first—not from her career, but from the PepsiCo fast track. "When you talk about those big jobs, those CEO jobs, you just have to give them your life," Barnes says (in Tischler 2004, p. 52). "You can't alter them to make them accommodate women any better than men. It's just the way it is." Barnes went on to teach at the Kellogg School of Management and to serve on the boards of six major companies, among other things; but she says she's no longer gunning for the top.

That's something a lot of men wouldn't understand (or ever consider). With all their testosterone and competitive spirit (and low levels of oxytocin), men seem to have what it takes to make it to the top, at least in today's highly competitive (and frequently dysfunctional) organizational cultures. Some claim that women have a different biological destiny. Psychologist Daphne de Marneffe believes that "feminists and American society at large have ignored the basic urge that most mothers feel to spend meaningful time with their children" (in Wallis 2004, p. 55).

"I wish it had been possible to be the kind of parent I want to be and continue with my legal career, but I wore myself out trying to do both jobs well," says Princeton grad Katherine Brokaw (in Belkin 2003, p. 46). This is an intelligent, well-educated woman who took a look at the demands of her profession and decided it wasn't for her. It's not that women can't do it. It's just that many are choosing not to. Jobs that require 100 hours a week don't offer the balance that many women seek. "As a nation, we now clock more time on the job than any other worker on earth, some 500 hours a year more than the Germans, and 250 hours per year more than the British" (in Tischler 2004, p. 58). In a cover story on stay-at-home moms, *Time* reports that, in 1977, dual-career couples with kids under eighteen worked a combined workweek of eighty-one hours. By 2002, that number was up to ninety-one hours (Wallis 2004). While some Boomers may see this as a career-enhancing necessity, many Xers, both women and men, view it as a serious sacrifice that they're not willing to make. In response to Wallis' story, one man wrote back, "The real problem isn't why more women aren't in top jobs; it's why men would want those jobs."

Matt, a psychologist, is a great example of a Gen X guy who doesn't want one of those jobs. Here's what he has to say about his job choice:

Flex Hours

I designed my job for myself. I knew I wanted a flexible schedule and when I saw this opportunity, I took it. I work forty hours a week, but not eight hours in a row. I do psychological evaluations for kids in Houston's juvenile justice system. I typically write reports when I wake up in the morning, then take a shower and go to the office for a few hours. I try to get home fairly early, and, when I need to, I finish up reports late at night after my wife and the baby are asleep. . . . I don't work a sequential eight-hour day, and it works great for me. It not only fits my personality, but it works especially well now that we have a new baby.

Many Gen X men resent the rat race of corporate jobs with e-mails and cell phone calls 24/7. Many of them are just as disappointed about how their jobs don't accommodate their lives and families as Gen X women are; but there are still more Gen X men than women who are willing to accept grueling work schedules. Marta Cabrera, a former JPMorgan Chase executive, believes it has something to do with a mother's nature to nurture. "The sacrifices for women are deeper, and you must weigh them very consciously if you want to continue," she says (in Tischler 2004, p. 54). "I didn't want to be the biggest, best, greatest. I didn't feel compelled to be number one." Neither did Lisa Gartland, previously an insurance claims manager and now the Gen X wife of Myles Gartland, one of Mom's faculty colleagues (and one of the men to whom we dedicated this book). Lisa, the proud mom of four young children, describes her decision to trade career fulfillment for the joys of motherhood. Here's what she has to say:

Giving the Best to the Kids

As far as finding housework intellectually fulfilling, I don't know any woman who does. Although I do know some women who get into cleaning and find it therapeutic, I hate it! It is not therapy for me. You can ask anyone who knows me. I hate it! But I look at it as the yuck part of any job. There's always some part of any job that is just not fun or interesting to do. As far as parenting, I've never been bored with it. I'm always trying to stay one step ahead, trying to figure out what to do and how to guide the troop that I'm leading. It is all too easy to get involved (overinvolved) with activities at school. And if you show an interest, you can lead just about any function you want! For me, this is where the intellectual stimulation is. There are opportunities galore for creativity.

There are certainly bad days, and there are times when I'd love to put on nice clothes and go into an office and have important conversations about important issues. But, I truly feel that the moment I became a parent, I was obligated to give my best to my children. I did not want to give my best to a career and have my kids on the fringes. I know people who work and have a couple of hours with their kids in the evenings. Some don't even get home in time to put their kids to bed. For me, that would be unbearable.

I love that they see me every day at school; that I am able to volunteer whenever; that I have friendly, casual conversations with their teachers (who I am on a first-name basis with); that I know all their classmates and those kids know me. I'm so relieved that I don't ever have to worry that some day-care person is being mean to my kid or ignoring my baby's cry; that I can hurry up to school and pick up my own sick kid; that when my kids are sick I can baby them with soup, TV, and cuddling without worrying about some report or meeting that needs to be taken care of. I love that my kids know that they are my full-time job and that I take the job very seriously. I never felt fulfilled at work like I do as a mother (even before

I had kids). I don't feel like I'm missing a thing by not working. In fact, I would be wondering about all the things I was missing in my kids' lives if I were.

While some would argue that Lisa's mothering needs are biological, others say that biology is a convenient excuse. Whichever way you lean, it's hard to dismiss the fact that some women have a "Get out of jail free" (work = jail) card from day one; that is, some women have the option of leaving to have babies. Some call maternity leave an escape hatch, an option women have that most men don't. It's still not clear, though, whether women make that choice out of an innate sense of responsibility to their family or as an easy way out of a career that's not meeting their needs. What is clear is that it's a choice more women are making. "I don't want to be on the fast track leading to a partnership at a prestigious law firm," says Katherine Brokaw. "Some people define that as success. I don't" (in Belkin 2003, p. 46).

Yes, despite the best efforts of our working Boomer moms, the top jobs are still going to men. But now when you look at the statistics, you may see things a little differently. Mary Lou Quinlan certainly does. In 1998 she stepped down from her CEO job at a big ad agency. She was tired of the rat race. "The reason a lot of women aren't shooting for the corner office is that they've seen it up close and it's not a pretty scene," Quinlan claims. "It's not about talent, dedication, experience, or the ability to take the heat. Women simply say, 'I just don't like that kitchen'" (in Tischler 2004, p. 60).

Lisa Belkin (2003), a work-life writer for the *New York Times*, explains, "Why don't women run the world? Maybe it's because they don't want to" (p. 45). It may be a shocking concept, especially considering the struggle Boomer mothers went through trying to achieve equality. But as those moms begin to look around to see who will take their place when they retire, they're noticing that even their own daughters— the ones they fought so hard for—are sometimes opting out. Shirley Tilghman is the president of Princeton University. She heads a school that did not open its doors to women until 1969. Tilghman, and other successful women like her, can tell many stories about the struggles and sacrifices they made. She personally helped build a legacy for her daughter's generation, but now she says her daughter "is not as ambitious as I was. I think she saw the trade-offs that I made as ones she might not be prepared to make herself. She is looking for more balance in her life" (p. 85).

THE OPT-OUT REVOLUTION

About half of Ivy League grads these days are women. You couldn't say that thirty years ago. The same goes for graduates of law schools and medical schools across the country. Gen X women have broken a lot of educational glass ceilings, thanks to the hard work of their revolutionary mothers. However, when these women enter the workforce, a disparity appears. "Look at Harvard Business School. A survey of women from the classes of 1981, 1985, and 1991 found that only 38 percent were working full time" (Belkin 2003, p. 44). For a group of talented, well-educated Ivy League grads, just over one-third in full-time jobs sounds like a low percentage. However, many of these Harvard-trained lawyers and investment bankers became stay-at-home moms simply because they could afford to do so. They're married to equally talented, highly successful Ivy League husbands.

There has been a plethora of media coverage about this trend and a new jargon is emerging. Xer moms have been called "neotraditional" women because many of them have values closer to those of their Traditionalist grandmothers than those of their Boomer mothers (Peterson 2003). However, their lives are nothing like June Cleaver's. They often have household help and spend their time, not just mothering their children, but also taking care of themselves. They play tennis, go to yoga classes, and attend weekly study groups to stay intellectually stimulated. Rosanna Hertz, professor of sociology and chair of the women's studies department at Wellesley College, believes that these moms approach their "new jobs" with the same kind of zeal that they previously might have given to a corporation. "They even create a little cottage industry out of the people they're employing: someone to clean the house, someone to do the garden, another person to take care of the kids" (in Gaynor 2004, p. 205). These women want the security and comfort of simpler times, but they want it on their own terms.

Cosmopolitan editor-in-chief Kate White, interviewed on CBS's *Early Show* (Smith 2004), stated her views about Generation X. She believes they have a sense of entitlement, "a sense of 'I want to live my best life ever and be passionate.' They may feel, 'I'm not passionate about my job, so why should I be working over the Xerox machine when I could be at home, taking yoga and cooking my husband good gourmet meals that I learned at a great class?' So it's somewhat generational. I also think we've made work seem so incredibly daunting. It lasts all day. It's a 24/7 thing because of the cell phones and fax machines."

USA Today reports that staying home is the new status symbol. "Working used to be high status. Now that same working mom is considered a wage slave" (Peterson 2003, p. 2D). *Cosmopolitan* calls this trend the new wifestyle. In the September 2004 issue Julie Gaynor writes,

> The return of the full-time wife reflects a larger trend of women rethinking their priorities. In the late '70s and early '80s, women age 25 to 44 showed the biggest surge of women pouring into the workplace in history, according to the U.S. Bureau of Labor Statistics, and working mothers with children 1 year old and younger peaked in 1998 at 64 percent. But that number fell to 60.5 percent in 2001, and it's not just new moms who are cashing in their career chips: The total number of women in the labor force declined from 2000 to 2003. (p. 204)

Susan Douglas and Meredith Michaels (2004) refer to this trend as the "new momism," which they believe is a result of fear, fantasy, marketing, and politics. Momism is the latest version of what Betty Friedan labeled the "feminine mystique" in the 1960s. The essence of this trend is as follows:

> that no woman is truly complete or fulfilled unless she has kids, that women remain the best primary caretakers of children, and that to be

a remotely decent mother, a woman has to devote her entire physical, psychological, emotional, and intellectual being, 24/7, to her children. The new momism is a highly romanticized and yet demanding view of motherhood in which the standards for success are impossible to meet. (p. 4)

For those of us with feminist mothers who think like Douglas and Michaels, this generational trend creates a very real dilemma. "I had the sense I was letting down my sex by leaving," Marta Cabrera concluded after taking a close look at her working-mom life and her options (in Tischler 2004, p. 54). Cabrera had worked as a vice president at JPMorgan Chase while maintaining a happy marriage and having two daughters. She seemed like a class-act juggler until one day, when she was watching one of her girls blow out the candles on her birthday cake, she realized that she didn't know her daughters. Making it to the top of JPMorgan Chase to make headway for women in corporate America just didn't seem as important as making a difference in her daughters' lives. That's when Cabrera decided to opt out—not out of the job market, but out of the fast track to the top at JPMorgan Chase. She started her own company, took a huge pay cut, and found that her new arrangement gave her challenging, rewarding work *and* time to spend with her kids.

These neotraditionalist moms are, for the most part, an elite crowd with husbands who make hefty salaries and have good health insurance; however, the opt-out ranks are growing in all economic strata. It's hard to measure the stay-at-home segment of the female population, but the Bureau of Labor Statistics tracks workplace participation by married mothers with a child under age one. In 1997, 59 percent of those moms were working; by 2000 that number had dropped to 53 percent. The drop may sound modest, but a Bureau of Labor Statistics economist says, "That's huge" (Wallis 2004).

There's also an increase in the number of stay-at-home mothers of older children. In 2002, "10.6 million children under 15 in two-parent homes were raised by stay-at-home mothers, up 13 percent in slightly less than a decade" (Wen 2003, p. 1). One of every four mothers age twenty-five to forty-four (the prime career-building years) is out of the labor force (Peterson 2003). Many of our Gen X survey respondents, though employed, have opted for the mommy track.

> I am doing what I want to do professionally, although I am now working only part-time to handle other family responsibilities. I had anticipated continuing full-time employment, but I now have three children and have chosen to make them my focus rather than my career.
>
> 31-YEAR-OLD SERVICE COORDINATOR

> I have taken a step down in status with a recent move after I got married. I will not work when I have children, so to strive to be the VP isn't in my future. My future is to be the CEO of my children and to help raise them to be wonderful people, just like my mom did with me.
>
> 29-YEAR-OLD CREDIT ANALYST

> When I decided to have children I wanted to take a step back from focusing on my career to focusing on my family. So I took an almost 50 percent pay cut . . . I am pregnant with another (our second baby), and after I have this child I am contemplating quitting my job and figuring out what I want to do with my career.
>
> 32-YEAR-OLD DIRECTOR OF PUBLIC RELATIONS

JUGGLE AND STRUGGLE

Many dual-income Gen X parents can't afford to have one parent take a 50 percent pay cut, much less stay home full-time with the kids. So, the opt-out revolution is still a fringe phenomenon, affecting mostly privileged women with high-earning husbands (Tischler 2004). My friend Sheila, a medical coder at a hospital, is an example of someone who'd like to opt out but can't. She has a college degree and went through extensive training after college to make advances at work, but when she had a baby, her interest in advancement got tossed out with the dirty diapers. Sheila suddenly realized that what was most important to her was her son, Ethan. Instead of pushing for the next career move, Sheila went to her boss and asked to cut back on her hours. If she and her husband had been able to afford it, she would have left work altogether. She wanted to stay home with her baby, not put him in day care for nine hours a day, but Sheila never had the option that some of the Ivy League grads we've been talking about did. So, she continues to juggle and struggle. That's how many of our Baby Boomer mothers raised us (even though their super-woman feats were not always apparent to their children). Mom comments about her experiences of attempting to do it all:

>> *I often felt like a master juggler, juggling the needs of those around me—my husband, my children, my employer, my staff, my peers, my friends, my parents, and my civic, church, and social roles. Rarely did I get a good night's sleep. Often I brought paperwork home with me that I didn't begin until everyone else was in bed. The juggling worked until there was a crisis (sick kids, holidays, project deadlines, etc.), then the juggle definitely turned into a major struggle! It was often exhausting. Sometimes when I neared my breaking point, I fantasized about how much I'd enjoy being hospitalized— just so I could do nothing and have someone else take care of me.*

It's obvious that our mothers paid a high price for their careers, and now we, their Gen X daughters, aren't finding the price any lower. Three of our survey respondents comment on their challenges:

What I have actually experienced is this incredibly difficult balancing act between being a mother of three children and the need to maintain a career (I was a single parent for six years). I find that it is very difficult to keep up with both roles at the level that I desire.

37-YEAR-OLD ENERGY ENGINEER

I see the other engineer/mothers who have tried to work part-time and it looks extremely difficult to work out because of the "team" nature of this particular career. I now see the extreme career sacrifices I will be making to have children. I was much more naive when I started.

29-YEAR-OLD ENGINEER

I did not realize how difficult having a child would be when balancing work and life. I was thirty-six when she was born and always very career driven! It's hard to be successful at both!

37-YEAR-OLD MANAGER

Jackie, a friend of mine in New Orleans, longs for a society that supports what she calls "Mommy Jobs." She came up with the idea at college, and at the heart of it is a desire to be in a position in which she can step off the career highway sometime in her late twenties or early thirties and dedicate herself to raising kids. She's a well-educated young woman who spent years after college planning, strategizing, and saving money so she could be in a position to do this. Here's what Jackie has to say:

Mommy Jobs

I met my friend Nicole my first day at university. She and I hit it off immediately. We were roommates, fellow communications majors, and we shared similar dreams for the future. We both aspired to get a degree, land a killer job, and eventually get married. We were both very driven by our future careers. I hoped to work in the news business, and she dreamed of becoming an advertising executive. We were both fairly confident that we would get these great jobs and rise quickly among ranks of young successful people. We had planned our careers up to the day that they would no longer seem important, the day that we had children.

Nicole and I knew that our mothers were the women who fought to show the world that women could work and raise kids at the same time, but we just didn't believe it was possible. We thought if you wanted to work and have kids, one of your interests would suffer. Either you would end up at the bottom of the success ladder at work or your children would turn out to be unsupervised serial killers. Nicole and I promised not to be "has-beens" in our chosen careers, watching everyone else get promoted while we sneaked off to pump breast milk and leave work early for soccer games. We vowed to get "Mommy Jobs."

We came up with the concept of Mommy Jobs during our second semester in college. Mommy Jobs are part-time jobs that make life easy for your family. They allow you to start after 9 a.m. and finish by 3 p.m. so you have plenty of time for the carpool and for piano lessons. The Mommy Job isn't challenging and requires none of your time at home to focus on work. It's a low-maintenance job that allows you to concentrate on your family and not bring home work-related stress.

Our ideal Mommy Jobs had nothing to do with all the communications classes we were taking at the expensive private university our parents were paying for. Our list included working part-time at a women's dress shop during the day, getting a minimum-impact job as a secretary, or starting a small home-run business. All of these ideas allowed us to be available to our children mornings, evenings, and on the weekends. The jobs seemed low-impact enough to allow us to rush off in case of a playground emergency or a forgotten science project. These jobs allowed us to feel like the perfect mom while still letting us make money for shopping trips.

We didn't see these jobs as a necessity; we saw them as something to keep us busy while our kids were in school. In our dreams (boy, would we have a rude awakening), we would marry a man who would carry the family on one salary, and our desire to work would be just that—a desire, not a necessity. We also saw these jobs as something to keep us occupied; we refused to become overly educated women who knew all the names and love trysts of the people on the daytime soap operas.

Many years have passed since my friend and I dreamed up Mommy Jobs. The concept still seems important to me, but my motivation has changed. I would like to switch careers so that I can be there for my children, but I have realized the nature of the job is important to me. I do still want a job in which I can leave the stress in the office and drop everything for my kids, but I want it to be meaningful and fulfilling. I want to be there for my kids and be stimulated at the same time. I think taking a brainless job wouldn't be relaxing; it would be numbing. And alas, dreams don't always come true. I have a fabulous, accomplished husband, but love doesn't pay the bills. When we have children, we may not be able to make it on one full-time and one part-time salary. In today's economy, my Mommy Job may have to carry part of our family budget.

On the other hand, my friend Nicole has developed the ultimate Mommy Job. A single mother of a three-year-old, Nicole got her real estate license. She plans her open houses and shows homes while her son is at school learning to spell his name. In order to spend less time at the office, Nicole has all her calls rerouted to her cell phone. She is very happy with her decision to tailor her career to her son, but she is kind of lonely in the carpool line. She is one of the few mothers there at pick-up time. Nannies or babysitters pick up most of the other kids. I guess we should have told everyone else about Mommy Jobs!

While some Boomer mothers may cringe at the idea of a well-educated Xer daughter abandoning the opportunities they helped create, it's hard to cringe at what Nicole and Jackie are talking about creating. They don't want to check out of the work world and laze away the days by the kiddie pool at the club. They want to be challenged by work but at the same time have flexibility. Jackie and her husband, like a lot of Xers, won't be able to live the lifestyle they want on a single income. But trying to raise kids while they both have full-time jobs isn't an option they like either.

Consequently, many more women (32 percent) than men (21 percent) postpone having children until later in their career. Having children and climbing the corporate ladder just don't seem to mix—for women. "While 60 percent of men in management have children at home, 60 percent of women managers don't" (Larson 2002, p. 2D). In some cases, these women managers may be older and their children may be young adults. But, in many cases, they have delayed raising families to raise their careers instead. That delay sometimes turns into a life decision simply because of the constant ticking of the biological clock.

Two of my close work friends have made that delay decision. Both have told me they would like to have children, but, instead of pursuing the mommy track, both focused on their television careers through their twenties and thirties. As these two women neared forty, they began to talk about the ticking of their clocks. It's a touchy subject for women who wanted children but never took much time for their lives outside of work. Both now say they may have missed their window of opportunity for babies. I don't bring it up much, but I wonder if I wait another decade to make time for a family, will I have waited too long? Is it a choice I will regret for the rest of my life?

And, it's not just baby delays; fewer women than men with MBAs even get married. On Wall Street, 66 percent of men with MBAs have families, while 55 percent of women with MBAs do. "The message here is simple: Men and women have very different views of what is manageable" (Heffernan 2002, p. 62). Allison Pearson, author of the best-selling novel *I Don't Know How She Does It* (2002), went through her own struggle to balance family and an executive job; then she left the corporate world to start her own company. Pearson believes society's definition of success is still based on the traditional male idea of achievement. "Basically, women entering corporations are obliged to say, 'Unsex me here!' like doomed Lady Macbeths. The price of competing equally with men is to remain childless—but men don't have to pay that price," (in Kreamer 2003, p. 64). This woman comments on the price of the trade-off:

> **I am very fortunate to be making the money that I make in the state that I work in. I am also very excited to be in management at such an early age compared to my peers. I have always worked hard and been rewarded for my efforts . . . My parents said if I put my mind to it I could do anything . . . too bad they were not talking about relationships.**
>
> 31-YEAR-OLD RETAIL SALES MANAGER

This woman focused on her career and lost out on relationships. This shouldn't come as a surprise when you stop and think about it, but it comes at a time when more and more of us are wrestling with how to do both. Finding work-life balance is not an easy trick (just ask your mom). In many cases, the career fast track doesn't have a lane for working moms. That's why many Gen X women are remaining childless—and sometimes regretting it. In her book *Creating a Life: Professional Women and the Quest for Children* (2002), Sylvia Ann Hewlett talks about executive women who regret that they never set aside time to have a family. She surveyed 1,647 high-achieving women and found that 49 percent of those who earned over $100,000 were childless. Hewlett believes those women squandered their fertility and their chance for a family to follow men's model of single-minded career focus.

WORK-LIFE BALANCE

Unfortunately, there is a national trend toward increasingly long work hours for both genders (and all generations). About 50 percent of the Gen X men and 42 percent of the Gen X women surveyed by Catalyst (2004) said they were likely to work more than fifty hours per week. In a recent survey of 1,805 American workers of all ages, the biggest worries people had, next to fears of terrorism, involved work and money (Moore 2002a). It's no wonder work is stressing Americans because these days we're being asked to work longer and harder than ever. More than 50 percent of the highly stressed workers in the study said they had to work through their lunch break at least once a week. More than 50 percent said they spent time working at home on job-related assignments. And 45 percent said they'd missed attending their children's school events because of work.

It almost seems like some Americans take a masochistic pride in the long hours they work. There's an assumption that the longer you work, the more important you are and the faster you climb the ladder. "Vacations are the stuff of long weekends and an occasional seven-day stretch. A 35-hour workweek is for the French or some other culture that sips wine at midday. In the U.S., it's all about what you do—not who you are. And those who sleep five hours a night or juggle two seemingly full-time pursuits evoke envy, not sympathy" (Brady 2002, p. 142).

A survey by CareerBuilder.com (Moore 2002c) found that the economic downturn of the early 2000s is forcing companies to try to turn less into more, which means the company has less to work with and you work more. CareerBuilder.com surveyed 1,400 workers and found that more than 33 percent had seen increased workloads in the past six months. Almost 40 percent said they got to work early and stayed late. Another 30 percent said they typically got to work on time and stayed late. The concept of a 9-to-5 workday is history. And gone are the full-hour lunches. Some 50 percent of the workers took 45 minutes or less for lunch and 35 percent took 30 minutes or less. This country's work-life balance is becoming dangerously skewed. No wonder it's so hard to balance being a working woman and being a wife—much less being a mother and having a life!

My friend Lisa is a pediatric resident who works sixty to eighty hours a week and has a baby at home. I asked for a little of her precious free time to talk about one priority that seems to always wind up on the bottom of her to do-list—herself:

Balancing Acts

I'm part of a girl's group. We range in age from twenty-nine to thirty-four and we're all well-educated career women. We used to meet up every other week for dinner or drinks or just hanging out. These days it seems hard to find the time once a month. You see, the group is slowly changing in two significant ways. First, we're starting to have babies, and, second, we're all noticing that personal time is becoming very scarce. It's something that I'm not even sure would have occurred to my mother. She thought her job was her escape. My job is not an escape. It's stressful and time consuming and often rewarding, but it does not fill my need for private time.

Just the other night we put Lily to bed at 8 p.m. and my husband, Steve, turned in about 8:30 p.m. I was tired, but I wasn't about to miss my rare, golden opportunity for some alone time. I had the downstairs to myself! I put the dogs outside, lit some candles, played some music, and for probably the fifth time in the ten months since Lily was born, I sat down and wrote in my journal. These are the things that simply don't factor into the life of a pediatric resident with a husband and a baby. I don't go to yoga class anymore; I don't get to go for a run by myself. Forget reading or even a soak in the tub. When the girls get together, these are some of the things we talk about and we miss. I don't think my mom ever did anything for herself, so she never seemed to miss these things. But I lived by myself for several years when I was in my twenties and got used to having personal time. Then Steve and I lived together, and I still had time for me. Once you get used to that, you don't want to give it up.

Lisa has achieved everything our Boomer mothers could have hoped for. At twenty-nine, she's wrapping up her pediatric residency. She's put in the long, grueling hours and is on her way to a financially rewarding career. But she longs for more balance in her life. Listen to what Lisa has to say about the message she wants to give her little daughter, Lily:

> I definitely felt pressure from my parents to be something. My mom worked full-time while I was growing up, and my parents always expected me to have a career. I lived up to those expectations, now working sixty to a hundred hours a week at the hospital, but there's one thing I've learned: I don't want to put that kind of pressure on Lily. Even though I'm the primary breadwinner for my family and it's my husband, Steve, who stays at home with the baby, I think it's OK for a woman to just be a mom. That's a hard enough job. But if I told my dad I was just going to stay home and be a mom and a wife, he'd have a really hard time with that. He wouldn't understand, and he'd think it was retro. But I feel like I have three jobs now: doctor, mom, and wife. I want my daughter, Lily, to know she doesn't have to do all three. One or two is plenty.

THE BOTTOM LINE

Lisa wants to give Lily a choice—isn't choice what our Boomer mothers fought for? Isn't the feminist agenda about creating a society in which women control their own destinies? Yes, but my mom often reminds me that having the right to choose is not always the same thing as making the right decision. "As Mark Twain said, 'A man who chooses not to read is just as ignorant as a man who cannot read'" (Hirshman 2004, p. 2). There is a societal cost to the opt-out revolution. Linda Hirshman, a lawyer and philosophy professor, speaking of the talented women who are opting out, reminds us of the extent of this cost: "These are the women that would have gone into the jobs that run our world. These were the women who would eventually have become senators, governors. These women would have been in the pipeline to be CEOs of Fortune 500 companies" (p. 2). Hirshman fears a societal regression to male-dominated values, and her angst about the opt-out revolution is shared by many Boomer women.

Mom thinks this is a very complex problem. On the one hand, she believes "right" choices are highly personal and often paradoxical; on the other hand, she is concerned about the future of the workplace (and the world). Here are her thoughts:

>> *As Laura and I have researched the material for this book, I've thought a lot about the paradox of choice. Specifically, how can we Boomer women give Xer women choice about where they work—in a career or at home—without feeling that our struggles have been in vain? I'm beginning to see the issue a bit differently than when we first began writing. I'm starting to take the opt-out revolution much less personally. I now see it not so much as a backlash against us, their parents, as a boycott of a dysfunctional and outdated concept of work. I applaud this generation's needs for a more frugal and less frazzled lifestyle, and I agree with one Gen X woman who told CBS correspondent Leslie Stahl "that a forty-year full-speed-ahead career with no breaks is something that only an all-male world would have dreamed up anyway—and that it's in everyone's interest to make some room for detours along the way" (Hirshman 2004).*

Reframing how I view the opt-out revolution doesn't mean I don't have concerns—concerns about how the values of women and their unique leadership skills can contribute to the myriad problems facing the workplace and the world—concerns about whether Gen X women's high expectations of the workplace will unconsciously be redirected into a quest to become a "perfect" partner and parent. And, I have a lot of concrete questions, such as who will we Boomer feminists pass the torch to? Who is going to lead the diversity and equality charge if all our talented women flee? But . . . in spite of my fears, I have faith—faith that if enough of them leave, change will have to happen. We, their mothers, fought with our fingers, climbing our way up slippery slopes and treacherous pyramids; our daughters are choosing to fight with their feet, and, in so doing, perhaps they'll change the world of work for us all.

The bottom line is this, if organizations are to keep their Gen X women, they must make changes. Family leave policies, job sharing, telecommuting, on-site child care, and flexible work hours are a good first step, but much more is needed—both from organizations and from society at large. Fundamentally, organizations must change who they are and how they do business. Leaders must shift their focus from playing games of power and politics to creating cultures of sanity and satisfaction. In the meantime, leaders will continue to see a brain drain of their best and brightest young moms. This, however, is not all of the story. While Xer moms are exiting corporations in droves, single men and women are in crisis as well. It appears the opt-out revolution has only just begun.

CHAPTER 4

Quarterlife Crises

start with work stress, mix in relationship challenges, money worries, and career disappointments, simmer for a few years, and you've got a recipe for disaster. You've heard of the midlife crisis that comes when everything starts to feel claustrophobic. Well, the feeling Gen Xers have comes on much earlier in life. "Regrets about the past. Yearning for work that is more spiritually fulfilling, not just lucrative. Misgivings about relationships. It turns out that many twenty-somethings are wrestling with the kinds of issues long associated with middle age" (Eveld 2001, p. G1). The whole wide world is before us, but we're feeling overwhelmed by the choices. Robbins and Wilner (2001) call that feeling the *quarterlife crisis.*

The quarterlife crisis is turning into a bona fide social trend. "Oprah dedicated a show to it, bloggers have ranted about it, and punk bands on

both coasts have named themselves after it. It even has its own shelf in
the self-help section of the bookstore" (Thomas 2004, p. 71). *Quarterlife
Crisis* coauthor Abby Wilner recently launched an online forum at
quarterlifecrisis.com that already has more than ten thousand regis-
trants. She's also working to create NARG, the National Association of
Recent Grads. It's sort of like an "AARP for twenty-somethings, offering
quarterlifers the resources and practical advice they need to navigate the
adult worlds of health care, job hunting, finances, and social networking"
(in Thomas 2004, p. 72).

Just as the midlife crisis doesn't hit everyone at the same age, neither
does the quarterlife crisis. Just ask the authors of *Midlife Crisis at 30*, Lia
Macko and Kerry Rubin (2004). Macko, a CNBC producer, says, "What
we found is women (in their 30s) asking themselves where is time going,
versus the questioning of where has time gone that happens in someone's
50s" (in Montoya 2004, p. E8). Macko and Rubin interviewed thirty-
somethings going through this crisis, as well as some well-known women
who'd made it through and succeeded on the other side—women like
political strategist Mary Matalin, who considered dropping out of law
school at age thirty, and former vice presidential candidate Geraldine
Ferraro, who spent years as a stay-at-home mom before entering politics.
The stories of these successful older women help remind Gen Xers that
we can survive a quarterlife crisis, as millions of women before us have.

But, for now, many of us are feeling confused, and some of us feel a
little desperate. "It turns out that being young and educated with good
health and your whole life in front of you isn't all it's cracked up to be"
(Montoya 2004, p. E1). We may not be buying red convertible sports cars,
but hey, let's face it, we might if we could afford one. We certainly can
relate to the feeling of not knowing what we want and questioning where
our lives are going. Gen X Jenny is a good example. Here's her story. Keep
in mind she's only twenty-seven!

Grabbing Life

I must go out there and grab life by the balls. I have this ideal of
what my life is supposed to look like, physically and spiritually. I

can have that. Yes, I can have that, and it is so easy once I accept that if I really want it that badly, I just have to go after it. I am going to go after it! This is my life and I will make the most of it and enjoy every minute of it from here on out. There are so many things I want to do, yet have not done them. I will now. Tomorrow morning is the start of a brand-new day and it is going to be the first day of this metamorphosis. Here comes eternal Happiness. I can't wait to be beautiful on the inside and out. I am going to envy myself!

Jenny wrote this one night a little over a year ago, a month or two after she'd packed up and moved from Omaha to Chicago in search of her dream job. She continues,

I remember I was lying in bed when I wrote it. Now that I think about it, maybe I'd been drinking? I must have had a few because it sounds just like the kind of pep talk I give my girlfriends over a bottle of wine. You know the talks that start with present problems and then kind of amble back in time. Back to when all the work worries began, right after graduation.

Actually, my first job started out great. It was probably good karma or maybe just perfect timing coupled with a heck of a break. I had just graduated from the University of Nebraska–Lincoln (after six years) with a degree in journalism and not a whole lot of experience. I landed a job at a TV station in Omaha producing promotions for the news department. I was proud! My friends and family were proud! I had amazing responsibilities. I learned more in six months than I had in six years of school (I suppose I'm not the first to admit that). But I was also insecure. I kept thinking: God, what if these people see right through me and think to themselves, "She's just a kid, what the hell does she know? What an idiot!"

I was terrified of what some of these people thought of me and the work that I was doing. But I learned and I grew and then along came the BIG ANNOUNCEMENT! Six months into the job, they pulled the plug on four hours of local news, scrapping it all except one nightly newscast. I think about 55 percent of the newsroom employees lost their jobs. I was not one of them. At first I felt a sense of relief. Then the harsh reality hit. Where was I headed? The morale at that place was exceptionally low. Every day people were getting laid off. This sounds so ungrateful, but eventually I was wishing that I had been let go, too. So I started looking for a job. Now, half a dozen job changes later, I'm still chasing a dream and still knowing I have to keep moving to find it.

It's clear that Jenny has a strong drive to succeed. It's something many of our Boomer mothers can relate to. Jenny also had some serious fears about her qualifications as she started her career, but she didn't let those fears slow her down. What sets her apart from her parents' generation is her free-agent mentality. In her first job out of college, she watched a huge company downsizing. At that stage in her career, those layoffs forever shaped her view of the workplace. Less than a year after that, Jenny found herself in the midst of a full-blown quarterlife crisis. Her solution was to pack up and move, leaving her hometown, her new dog and new house, her old boyfriend, her job, and her friends. It's one of the gutsiest things I've seen (though her ex-boyfriend and dog probably didn't see it that way). Luckily, her supportive parents did. I'll let her tell you about it:

I made up my mind to move to Chicago. To continue my career in production, I was going to have to move somewhere else to find the right job. So, I moved . . . without a job . . . just thinking it would only take a short while to land something. ("How could you be so naive?"—the voice in my head says in retrospect). I sent out resumes, applied for jobs, and exhausted what little resources I had in this enormous city. After a few replies and even fewer interviews, I started to have doubts. How could I not? For the most part I really tried to remain calm about the whole thing, but how much longer was this going to go on? I kept worrying: "Will I have to move back to Omaha and everything I left behind?" "Have I really given it my best shot?" Every day I asked myself new questions, slowly becoming more and more unsure about what I had done. Then one day it happened. I went on an interview and three days later I accepted a position as a production assistant for a national talk show. Finally!

I knew going into this job that it was going to be tough. I never imagined it would be unbearable! In any kind of production assisting position, you are gonna have to put up with some pretty ——ty work. However, grin and bear it and you will move up. That's what I did and that's exactly what happened. I was promoted to an associate producer after only three months.

WHAT AM I IN FOR?

(imagine hearing that very slowly and very dramatically)

The rest of my time in this position was unlike anything I ever imagined. I don't mean that in a good way. I can handle a lot. But it didn't take me long to realize I couldn't handle the dirty laundry they were airing on this show, in front of the camera and behind. It was an unhealthy situation, and it was beginning to change me. My family no longer enjoyed talking with me. I lost contact with several of my friends. I was a zombie doing my day-to-day work with less and less emotion.

Enough is enough. This isn't me! Somehow I reached my breaking point and realized that being truly miserable was a good enough reason to leave. I'd been blind to other alternatives—at least until now. I went to a headhunter and had help finding a new job. It's not in broadcast production, but finally I have the freedom to work, continue searching for my next best move, and most important, be happy. It's definitely harder to find that next production job, but I know when I do, it will be worth it. So far it's been a humbling journey. And I'm only twenty-seven years old!

Talk about quarterlife crises! Jenny's been through several. I remember her telling me how she felt trapped in her job and her hometown. To advance in her career, she really needed to make a major move, and she did. But with each decision to step onto the next rung of her chosen ladder, she felt a little like she was stepping off a cliff. Luckily, Jenny packed her own parachute by becoming a skilled and valuable free agent. She never really needed to worry about hitting the ground because she had equipped herself with a rip cord: a good education and the willingness to take risks. Despite that comfort, Jenny will tell you it was a very unnerving couple of years in her life.

BEST YEARS OF MY LIFE?

Though you might see similarities between midlife and quarterlife crises, there are also big differences. For our parents' generation, a midlife crisis is all about bucking the system—escaping a life that feels too routine, too stable. For us, too much insecurity and instability are pushing us over the edge. Robbins and Wilner's (2001) quarterlife theory suggests that for the first twenty-two years (or more, depending on how long you stretch out the college experience), your life is basically planned out. Sure, you may decide where to go to college and which classes to take, but for the most part, those years are structured. Then BAM! You're out of school and suddenly your life is no longer predestined. You are in charge of making life-altering decisions about your future while you adjust to the real world and the responsibilities that go along with it. "Leaving college is a bit like riding a bicycle for the first time—except it's not just that a trusted adult lets go of the bike at a certain time once the twenty-something has learned how to steady himself while moving forward. It's more like the bicycle suddenly disappears" (Robbins and Wilner 2001, p. 104).

Oh yes, we're well aware that this is the time we're supposed to be living it up. You may have heard Boomers discuss with envy the crazy fun we Xers had in college, and according to our parents' generation that fun continues on into our twenties and thirties. They're the best years of our lives. We're young and carefree, right? We're living a real-life beer commercial, in which the sunlight casts a golden glow over everything. We're all hip, funny, and beautiful, and life is good. Hey, put that bottle down and sober up! Many of us may be single, unencumbered with spouses and kids, but it doesn't make our lives easy. We're supposed to take risks to achieve our dreams while we are young and single so that if the risk has a bad outcome, no one else will be affected. Believe it or not, the freedom to take risks can feel like a big burden.

We are faced with huge decisions about relationships and careers, decisions that will influence the REST OF OUR LIVES; and we're making those decisions without the wisdom of years of experience. "The prevalent belief is that twenty-somethings have it relatively easy because they do not have as many responsibilities as older individuals. But it is precisely this reduced responsibility that renders the vast array of decisions more difficult to make" (Robbins and Wilner 2001, p. 9). When we got out of college, degree in hand, we were ready to set the world on fire. But in reality, many of us don't have the experience it takes to do much more than light the match. How can our decisions be anything more than haphazard? We have very little experience on which to base them. Yet, we feel such pressure to make good decisions.

Some of our decisions involve the same basic questions our parents and their parents faced. We have to figure out how we will earn money and how we will spend it, what we will do in our free time, if and whom we will marry, and whether we will have children. But we have a lot more options than our moms (and dads) ever had. We have more choice about marriage, more career options, more ways to spend our money, more chances to travel. Making the right choices feels overwhelming. It feels like the repercussions of the decisions we make today could very likely be felt thirty years from now. We don't want to someday regret that we decided to get out of whatever field we're in to go for something totally different, or regret that we married or didn't, or decided to have children or not.

THE PARADOX OF CHOICE

Barry Schwartz, professor of psychology at Swarthmore College, offers insight into this dilemma in his book *The Paradox of Choice: Why More*

Is Less (2004a). He believes that unattainable expectations, coupled with a tendency to blame ourselves for our failures, makes a lethal combination, which explains why too much choice feels so stressful. He uses a recent cancer research study as an example. In this study, those surveyed were asked whether they would want to be in charge of their treatment decisions if they had cancer. Sixty-five percent said yes—unless they actually had cancer. Then only 12 percent said yes. Those with cancer had an up-close-and-personal experience with the psychological consequences of life-and-death decisions—and they didn't want that responsibility.

Thankfully, most Gen Xers don't have to make such life-and-death decisions, but they do have to make daily decisions that may seem overwhelming. Just buying a pair of jeans is no longer a five-minute event. We have to decide if we want slim fit, easy fit, relaxed, boot cut, flared—the options go on and on. Even on a quick trip to the drugstore we are confronted with myriad choices. We are likely to find more than three hundred types of shampoo and forty types of toothpaste. Such an overabundance of choice tends to trigger feelings of enormous responsibility. We begin to believe that we have to *maximize* all of life's decisions (even the little ones) rather than settle for good enough. Schwartz's (2004b) research suggests that maximizers are less happy, less optimistic, and more depressed. Could an overabundance of choice really be contributing to my generation's angst? Here we are, living at what Schwartz calls the "pinnacle of possibility" and we're wallowing in confusion. "The success of the 21st century life turns out to be bittersweet" (p. 5). Ironically, we Xers wouldn't be happy if we didn't have choices, but we don't seem happy with so many.

STARTER MARRIAGES

Whether we Xers decide to marry, stay single, focus on career, or focus on our families, one thing is true for all of us—relationships matter. In our survey, relationships are at the top of my generation's importance list (more about this in Chapter 5). Another Gen X survey identified "finding and keeping a loving partner" as the greatest obstacle facing Gen X women today, outranking obstacles such as job discrimination and sexual harassment—even money (Whitehead 1998). Why are we as a generation so focused on relationships? The answer is really quite obvious. Many of us grew up as children of divorce, with working moms. Some of us didn't have our intimacy needs met as children; others simply didn't have healthy relationship role models. Consequently, as a generation, we value relationships greatly, even though many of us don't have the skills to sustain lasting ones. This is especially obvious in one of our generation's defining characteristics—"starter marriages" (some authors use the term "training marriages," "practice marriages," or "ice-breaker marriages").

Pamela Paul's (2002) research into this generational marker raises an important question: "Why are today's twenty- and thirty-somethings (the first children-of-divorce generation) so eager to get married and so prone to failure?" Her answer is a complex combination of societal and psychological factors. Some 50 percent of Boomer parents threw in the towel on their marriages, thus failing to model positive conflict resolution skills and creating a societal epidemic of single moms, alimony dads, and latchkey children. However, other societal factors play a role. Contemporary pop culture certainly provides so many role models that the short-term marriage has almost become trendy—at least in Hollywood. Pop icons, ranging from Drew Barrymore and Uma Thurman to Jennifer Lopez and Julia Roberts, have had very public starter marriages. Former *Ally McBeal* star Courtney Thorne-Smith divorced her husband after seven months of marriage—while her picture was still on the cover of *In Style Wedding*. *Entertainment Weekly* (September 2000) included "divorcing in your 20s" on its list of in things to do.

Of course, divorce is never glamorous or trendy. It results in deep wounds and lifelong baggage, regardless of the age at which it occurs. People who enter into starter marriages certainly don't expect them to be temporary. Rather, they walk down the aisle certain that they will "live happily ever after"; but many of these Gen X marriages end before the couple can blow out the candles on their thirtieth birthday cakes. Even though the endings of these marriages are not precipitated by a midlife crisis, they do result in a quarterlife one. Certainly the men and women who've survived starter marriages would never wish one on their friends, but the survivors point out an upside: In most cases, these couples divorce .before having children, so unlike the Boomer divorces that tore families apart, starter marriage divorces leave only two people to suffer the consequences of the quarterlife crisis that follows.

ADULTOLESCENCE

A couple of years after the end of his starter marriage, Gen Xer Chuck found himself in a full-blown quarterlife crisis. He'd tied the knot in his early twenties, but by his late twenties, he was moving back in with his parents. His decision to resign a high-tech job and return to school to finish his degree turned his life (and theirs) upside down. Here's the story of Chuck, a thirty-year-old computer programming student:

Home Again

At twenty-six, I was sitting at the top of my game. My salary was more than double my age (a good sign, I thought). I was traveling the country from coast to coast working as a project manager/trainer for a communications technologies company based in Florida. I had decided to leave college my junior year for what seemed like a once-in-a-lifetime job opportunity, and within a year I had more than doubled my salary and was living the good life in the Sunshine State. I was on the fast track. For almost two years I traveled the country, going from project to project, building a reputation as a real go-getter and someone who could get the job done.

At some point I started to evaluate where I was going and what I was doing with my life. I started to ask myself long-term goal questions. Where did I want to be in five years and what did I want to be doing? Traveling and working in this high-stress corporate environment was fun now, in my twenties. But would I still feel the same way when I had a family? I watched the managers at my company work fifteen-hour days. They were the first in and the last to leave the office. I also watched many employees who were here one day and gone the next. Could or would that be me? What would I do if it did happen? Without a college degree I knew the road would be rough. I wasn't getting any younger and I knew that getting my degree would only get harder as the years added up.

Then, as if someone had been reading my mind, my whole life changed. The rug was yanked out from under me. I was home for the Christmas holidays when I found out that I might be losing my job. I decided to make the first move. So I flew back to Florida, handed in my resignation, and headed back to school. I hadn't saved enough money to cover my tuition and living expenses at a private university, so I applied for college loans and decided that moving back to my parents' home seemed like the best option. One U-Haul later I was back home in the Midwest. Long gone were the warm sunny days of Florida. Long gone were the big paychecks. I was back in the old room that I had left at age eighteen. The room I swore I would never return to was once again mine. Never say never! It was an indescribable culture shock. No more sushi, no more jet-setting across the country at a moment's notice to meet friends on the East or West Coast. No more asking a date back to my place for a night of dinner and a movie. Well, I guess I could, but the picture of my mom, dad, myself, and date all cuddled up on the couch with my bulldog, Maggie, on the floor was more than I could stomach.

Now comes the fun part—facing my family and friends and explaining that I'm back home. Just imagine the awkward silence when I went out to a bar and met someone, then had to explain to them where I used to work and what I was doing now, not to mention where I was living. I never realized how much our career success or lack thereof defines who we are in this country.

> Life with my parents was what it was. I was always very close to my mother, and both my parents were supportive, though maybe a little surprised that their oldest child was moving back in just about the time their youngest was about to move out. Luckily for me, I was not the only person I knew who was making the same transition. When I looked around, I realized that more than a few of my friends were making the same walk of shame back home.

You'll notice a couple of things in this story. After the ending of his starter marriage, Chuck was thinking seriously about his future goals. He spent time evaluating where he was going and what was most important to him; and, like many other Xers, he decided he wanted a job that would enable him to live a more balanced life. Also, after an unexpected job loss, you might guess that this back-in-school-at-age-thirty Xer has some lingering questions about corporate loyalty. Chuck decided to finish his education so that he would be better equipped to survive in a free-agent economy. And how about the "walk of shame" back to his parents' house? People in that situation should realize they're in good company. My brother moved back home to go to graduate school; so did my sister-in-law, and, when she moved back, she brought one of her girlfriends with her to live in her parents' spare room. The U.S. Census Bureau reported in 2000 that almost 4 million Gen Xers (that's about 10 percent) between ages twenty-five and thirty-four live at home with their parents—even after entering the workforce.

In *Newsweek* Peg Tyre and her colleagues (2002) dub these Xers "Adultolescents." They're talking about men and women in their twenties and even thirties who are living with their parents, moving right back into their old bedrooms (with, one hopes, fewer curfew restrictions). The passage from teen to independent adult appears to be growing longer and longer. University of Maryland researcher Jeffrey Arnett calls this rite of passage "emerging adulthood" (in Thomas 2004, p. 71). In a 2003 survey conducted by the University of Chicago's National Opinion Research Center (Thomas 2004), most of the repondents said they didn't believe adulthood actually starts until around age twenty-six. The college-educated sample's "adulthood age" estimate was even higher—twenty-eight to twenty-nine.

In *Quarterlife Crisis* (Robbins and Wilner 2001), Tanya, a 1996 college graduate, says she won't feel entirely like she is an adult until she has children of her own. "This feeling represents a common view among twenty-somethings: that childhood doesn't end until they are responsible for someone else's childhood" (p. 50). And, Gen Xers are having children much later than any previous generation. In 2002, 26.7 million women between ages fifteen and forty-four were childless—up 10 percent from 1990. Those of us who delay marriage and parenting perpetuate adultolescence and avoid some of the stresses and responsibilities of being grown up, but stress still finds us.

GENERATION WRECKED

Nothing can make you feel more grown up than a pile of bills and a heap of debt. According to the General Accounting Office, about half of college graduates leave school with $20,000 in student loans (in "Some Under 30 Are Overextended" 2002). That kind of debt, paired with a weak economy and an iffy job market, has some Gen Xers realizing that flying solo after graduation (or the loss of a job) just isn't feasible. In an online survey conducted by Monster-TRAK.com, a whopping 60 percent of college students said they planned to live at home after graduation; 21 percent of them said they planned to stay there for more than a year (in Tyre, Springen, and Scelfo, 2002). When a college education comes with a six-figure price tag, a recent grad's best option often is to recoup some of that cost by swallowing her pride and moving back in with mom and dad. Doing so does, however, perpetuate our adultolescence. The twenty-somethings of the Boomer generation were fighting in Vietnam, marching for peace, breaking glass ceilings, and having babies. We Gen Xers are still fighting for our identities and striving to find our way in the world (while paying off our student loans and credit card debts).

Fortune (Watson 2002b) labeled us Generation Wrecked. We, who toted Star Wars and Strawberry Shortcake lunch boxes in the 1970s and 1980s, are now toting loads of debt. Even though a thirty-year-old today is 50 percent more likely than her parents to have a bachelor's degree, she's much less likely to own a home. Gen Xers are the most highly edu-cated generation in American history, but we are far from the wealthiest. In fact, young households have a smaller percentage of total U.S. wealth than they did in 1989. While opportunity and abundance grew exponen-tially throughout the twentieth century, economic growth came to a screeching halt just as we entered the workforce. "From 1947 to 1973 it took 27 years for living standards to double. Now it will take 268" (Nelson and Cowan 1994, p. 23). And the job market hasn't seemed to cooperate either. In fact, according to the *Wall Street Journal,* nearly one in three college students who graduate between 1990 and 2005 are expected to take a job that doesn't require a college degree. That's up from one in ten in the 1960s (in Brown 1996). Some are beginning to question whether college is still a good investment:

> Almost 69% of Gen Xers have some college education, and 6.6% have graduate school degrees. The Census Bureau calls their pursuit of higher education the "Big Payoff," since historically a college-educated full-time worker earns 1.8 times more over his lifetime than a high school graduate. When you can't find a job or pay your student loans, though, college can seem like the big Rip-Off. Today, the median student loan debt is at its highest level ever, $17,000, com-pared with $2,000 when the baby-boomers were in their 20s. Ac-cording to educational lender Nellie Mae, graduating students average $20,402 in combined student loans and credit card debt. Those who have borrowed to pay for professional school, especially doctors and lawyers, are increasingly likely to have immense debt that is not reflected in proportionately higher salaries. Twenty-eight per-cent of those surveyed by Nellie Mae had combined undergraduate and graduate student debt of more than $30,000, and for 22%, their loan payments ate up more than one-fifth of their monthly income. (Watson 2002b, p. 2)

So even though lots of Xers are going to college these days, many of them are borrowing money to do so and are racking up quite a debt. Just imagine all the thousands of dollars women owe when they get their diplomas. And, due to salary inequities, the loan bill is harder to pay off on a woman's paycheck than it is on a man's. Let's say your parents, like mine (bless their souls), decided to pay for your college education ("If you don't get it done in four years, don't look to us for more help!"). And let's say they ended up spending somewhere in the range of $100,000 for that four-year experience (by the way, it's going to be in the range of $400,000 by the time Gen Xers' kids make it to college). First, it's not easy to pick a major that's outside the mainstream. I mean, you've got to have very supportive parents if you want to study art history at a private college. (One of my good friends in college did just that, but to secure her financial future, she also majored in business—in Chapter 5 you'll read about what she's doing now. Hint: It has nothing to do with art.) And let's say you have to start at the bottom of the infamous career ladder. At some point you're going to be sitting there in what seems like a dead-end job, answering phones and sending faxes, wondering if college was really worth the investment, feeling pressure to justify your parents' investment, disappointed in your current job, and highly uncertain about your future. In short, you're likely to be a prime candidate for a quarterlife crisis.

Then there are our credit cards! My friends who have zero balances on their Visas, MasterCards, or Banana Republic Luxe cards are few and far between. You get credit card offers in high school, for goodness sake. It seems a lot of us Gen X women are following in the footsteps of fabulous shoe maven Carrie Bradshaw on *Sex in the City*—which has turned eccentric single living into an art form. If Carrie can buy yet another pair of Manolo Blaniks that she can't afford, why can't we? I don't think the show sets a bad example for Gen X women; I think it simply reflects a lifestyle a lot of us are living. Other Gen Xers seem to agree. Here's how one woman described her financial situation:

> **When I was hired I did not believe the guy who told me that no matter how much money I make, I'll spend it. There will never be enough. He was right. I make over 80K a year and can't seem to get out of debt.**
>
> 37-YEAR-OLD SENIOR SYSTEMS ANALYST

A 2001 Sutra Foundation survey of Gen X single women found that 54 percent say they're more likely to acquire thirty pairs of shoes than to save $30,000 in retirement assets. More than 50 percent say they live paycheck to paycheck. About 33 percent would rather talk to her grandmother about her love life than sit down with a financial advisor to talk about investments. So, grab your calculator and let's talk credit card debt. If you're an Xer without a pile of plastic and a bundle of bills, consider yourself smart or lucky. The average credit card carrier under thirty has $10,000 to $12,000 in debt, according to a study by America's Research Group (in "Some Under 30 Are Over-extended" 2002). That's up 50 percent from five years ago. You get the picture. Gen Xers just don't have the same attitude toward debt or even toward filing for bankruptcy as our Boomer parents did. By the way, all you Carrie Bradshaws, men are also doing better than we are at managing debt (again, they also earn more): 47 percent of single Gen X women have credit card debt compared to only 35 percent of single men. Pick up any financial tip sheet and you'll see the number one suggestion is to pay off your credit card, then start stashing your money away, because by the time you're ready to retire, you're gonna need it—especially if you're a woman!

WAKE UP AND SMELL THE COFFEE

The Employee Benefit Research Institute reports that only 23 percent of twenty-somethings contribute anything to a company retirement plan (in Quinn 2003). What this boils down to is that we're the first generation expected to be poorer than our parents. But somehow a lot of us haven't gotten the wake-up call. Maybe we need a cuppa joe to give us a jolt. It should when you consider that the price of a cup of coffee the year I was born (1974) was between 25 and 50 cents. Today my grande, sugar-free, vanilla nonfat latte at Starbucks costs over $3. Nothing's cheap anymore, and that's why we need to start saving. The magic of compounding pays big dividends. "A 30-year-old who eschews double lattes to put $25 a week in an automatic investment plan would have $231,000 by age 65, assuming an 8% annual return" (Gleckman 1997).

We Xers need to save, not only for our retirement, but also to pay for the rapidly escalating health-care costs that will hit us long before we retire. By 2011, Americans are expected to spend about double what they spent in 2000; that's up to $9,216 per person ("Per-Capita Health-Care Outlays" 2002). The cost of prescription drugs and hospital care is going up at the same time life expectancy is stretching out to eighty years and beyond. The U.S. Department of Health and Human Services says part of the reason medical costs are climbing has to do with the demands of Baby Boomers, who increasingly want high-tech tests and treatments, and who fuel the market for the high-priced drugs they see advertised on television (in "Per-Capita Health-Care Outlays" 2002).

Soon these Baby Boomers will be moving into retirement, leaving Generation X and our tax dollars to support the largest number of senior citizens ever. In the foreword to *Revolution X* (Nelson and Cowan 1994, p. xi), Senator Bill Bradley writes, "We once thought it was our American birthright for our children to have a better standard of living than we do, but for the first time in history, that is no longer going to be the case." Our parents are about to pass on to us the biggest debt in the history of America—trillions of dollars of national debt that is exponentially increasing. It is estimated that if there is no change in economic policy, the federal debt will grow by a staggering $5 trillion dollars by 2015 (Broder 2004). Pete Peterson, the former Nixon administration secretary of commerce, made this comment on the PBS *NewsHour with Jim Lehrer*: "The ultimate test of a moral society is the kind of world it leaves to its children. And as I think about the concept that we're slipping our own kids and grandkids a check for our free lunch, I say we're failing the moral test" (in Broder 2004, p. B5).

Morality aside, Traditionalist and Boomer politicians alike seem much more willing to keep piling up IOUs rather than find a way to protect the retirement funds of future generations—like us. A recent survey concluded that more of us Gen Xers believe we will see a UFO than a social security check with our name on it (Seacrest 1996). That may sound a little far-fetched, but you'll start scanning the night sky for saucers after you hear about January 1, 2011. Just another New Year's Day? Not at all! That day marks the beginning of the year when the first of the Baby Boomers become eligible for social security. In the years that follow, "Tens of millions of Baby Boomers will be stepping off the employment treadmill and into their retirement slippers" (Nelson and Cowan 1994, p. 60).

The sheer number of them is mind-boggling. In 1950, seniors made up only 8 percent of the population. By 2030, roughly 20 percent of our nation's population will be senior citizens, who will live longer thanks to advances in health care. Dr. Robert Butler of the International Longevity Center–USA says that in the twentieth century, Americans gained more than thirty years of life. "That's greater than was attained in the previous 5,000 years of human history" ("U.N. Says Population Aging Fast" 2002).

AARP (American Association of Retired Persons) is already one of the most influential voices on Capitol Hill. AARP can mobilize millions of senior citizens to get to the polls, so politicians listen. And, as the Boomers retire, that voice will only get louder. Just imagine millions of Boomers demanding the same extensive health-care and retirement services that today's seniors get. And why shouldn't they? They have been contributing their earnings to this system for their entire careers.

Our parents are accustomed to the good life because they grew up during the wealthiest period in American history. They were raised during a time when America dominated the world economy. In fact, as the Boomers were growing up, personal incomes were going up, rising faster in one year of the 1950s than they did in all ten years of the 1980s combined. With all the personal wealth, the government could afford to hand out benefits to Americans with almost no regard to need (Nelson and Cowan 1994).

The only way to continue to provide Social Security benefits to the large number of retiring Boomers will be with higher taxes on us and the generations that follow. "If today's politics are any indication, Boomers will have more than enough political power to win what they want— whatever the cost to those who come behind them" (Nelson and Cowan 1994, p. 55). Be prepared for an unbearable strain on our economy, our social welfare systems, and our paychecks. A plan that was paying multi-millionaire Marlon Brando $1,856 a month (Newsmakers, 2003) before he died in 2004 will be gone quicker than a B movie from the box office by the time Matt Damon and Ben Affleck retire. Luckily for them, they've made a lot more money than most of us and, we hope, have put plenty of it away for their gray days, because the Social Security system as designed will not exist when Generation X retires. Unless there's some sort of dramatic increase in payroll taxes, the Social Security Administration predicts that the Social Security system will go bankrupt sometime between 2019 and 2036. There are simply too many people who will retire and too few people to pay for it. Here's a great illustration of how quickly the Social Security system is crumbling:

> Ida Mae Fuller of Ludlow, Vermont, the first recipient of Social Security, received $20,000 in benefits from a total initial investment of only $22. But the economic miracle that benefited Ida Mae spells disaster for anyone born after 1960. Throughout the 1970s and '80s, most seniors got back two to five times what they paid in. Today, a retiree can expect to get back roughly double his contribution, while a 25-year-old will receive, at best, only half of what she is expected to pay in during her working career. (Nelson and Cowan 1994, p. 66)

No wonder the women in our survey are so concerned about job benefits (more about this in Chapter 5). They face a long, steep climb to retirement, and no one faces a longer or steeper climb than single women. We may have stopped waiting for a knight in shining armor to take charge of our finances, but we're still not doing enough for ourselves. With a longer life expectancy, lower earnings than men, movement in and out of the workforce, and high debt accumulation, women really must seriously consider saving for the future. We must do more because we're the ones who are going to last longer: In every country except Pakistan and Bangladesh, women outlive men ("U.N. Says Population Aging Fast" 2002). Also, of the 1.6 million people in U.S. nursing homes, 80 percent are women.

While we can't all expect to be millionaires like Regis Philbin, who earned $35 million in one year asking people if that was, indeed, their final answer, we can all work toward improving our financial security. When you're eating Ramen noodles and Budget Gourmet dinners and scrounging just to go out on dollar beer night, when you're weighed down with thousands of dollars in college loans and more in credit card debt, your life choices are seriously limited and you become a prime candidate for a quarterlife crisis. It's a lot easier to live your dream when you're not living paycheck to paycheck.

It's no wonder Gen Xers find themselves stuck in jobs they don't love. Their debt keeps them there. Remember Bianca from Chapter 2? She was one of my good friends from college (the one on the business trip with Mickey Mouse), and she would love to be a preschool teacher. It's her dream. Instead, she's an I.T. consultant making four times what she could as a teacher, and she's finding it hard to give up her paycheck to follow her dream. But she's put a limit on what she can take. After writing "Welcome to Greensboro," she added this: "As an aside, my current plan is to continue working as a consultant for two more years (until Rich and I start our family). I do not plan on ever returning to an office-type work environment."

You see, Bianca wants to trade in her briefcase for some babies but she's putting it on the back burner for a couple of years to focus on her high-paying career. One would think that with all the marriage/parenting delays and the job-hopping, we Gen Xers would have more time to get ourselves figured out, but that doesn't seem to be the case. With all the space we have to find what makes us happy, it seems we're finding the opposite. *Sometimes freedom leaves us feeling more lost than found.*

GROWING PAINS

Despair! Woe is me! Woman, who has gained so much, is still not happy. How can that be? Pick up any magazine or newspaper or flip on the news and you'll likely find a story about women suffering "burnout" and succumbing to an "infertility epidemic." In an article on today's feminism, Susan Faludi (2001) sees bad signs everywhere. "The *New York Times* states: Childless women are 'depressed and confused': and their ranks are swelling. According to *Newsweek:* Unwed women are 'hysterical' and crumbling under a 'profound crisis of confidence.' And from health advice manuals: High-powered career women are stricken with unprecedented outbreaks of 'stress-induced disorders,' hair loss, bad nerves, alcoholism, and even heart attacks" (p. 1).

According to some research, it seems women are less happy today than they were twenty years ago. In 1977 sociologist Norval D. Glenn began tracking reported happiness for young men and women. Since that time, the happiness index for young men has risen slightly, but for young women it's heading down (in Whitehead 1998). When young women were asked what the biggest worries in their lives were, they responded, men and their own bodies. The same problems our mothers and their mothers faced can be added to the career worries of today's young women. And some Gen Xers do more than simply worry about their bodies—they starve themselves or binge and purge. "Even more widespread than eating disorders is disordered eating, the restrictive and obsessive monitoring of food consumption. According to one survey, the number one wish among young women, outranking the desire to end homelessness, poverty, or racism, is to get and stay thin" (Whitehead 1998, p. 1).

For our feminist moms, all this may come as a huge disappointment. After all their struggles, their daughters are still focused on the same old problems—their relationships and their bodies. We Gen X women, as the first full beneficiaries of the achievements of the women's movement, were supposed to have moved on to bigger issues. We grew up with more freedom and choice than our mothers and grandmothers had. But are our values and beliefs keeping pace with the choices? As you read this Gen X mom's story, you may be wondering if it was set in 1965. Nope, this happened in 2004:

Working Mom Guilt

The table was set, the smell of food wafted from the kitchen, and the conversation ebbed and flowed. We were at our first dinner party since our first baby was born. There were three other couples and I really didn't know any of them well. Sitting at the table, I could see it coming. As I was watching the food being passed around the table, I could sense the question headed my way. Our host finally did the honors of asking it: "Why was I going back to work with a baby at home?" Why indeed! The easy answer (and the one I gave the group) was that I HAD to go back to work. We couldn't pay the bills to support our lifestyle without my income. People nodded, sadly it seemed, accepting my answer.

But there was a more complicated answer that I kept to myself. Part of me was looking forward to going back to work, but I'd learned in the eight weeks since the baby was born to be careful whom I told that to. You get a feel, sort of a vibe, from other people when they ask you if you're staying home or going back to work. I feel like I have to explain myself. It's like they're thinking I'm a bad mother because I'm a working mom. Occasionally I get comments like "I think staying home with my kids is the best thing I've ever done." When I hear that, it feels more like an accusation.

Just the other day I was talking to one of my friends and I confessed that I was getting kind of bored at home all day. She was taken aback and asked, "Don't you like staying home with the baby?" Well, we take naps and watch *The Young and the Restless, Oprah,* and Food Network. Maybe if we were rich and I could shop and go out to eat every day, maybe then I'd want to stay home. But I'm sure I'd even get bored with that eventually. At the dinner party that night, I blamed it on bills and left it at that. I wasn't sure they'd understand that I miss adult interaction and the fulfillment of my job. I sure wasn't going to tell them that I'd already gone back to work, doing private practice on Saturdays. If working five days a week didn't seem acceptable to them, I'm sure they would be appalled that I will be working six!

Remember, all the people sitting around the dinner table in this story were Gen Xers—neotraditionalist Xers—all of whom happened to be living the new wifestyle. That's okay—it's their choice. But it's not okay that they judge someone else's choice. We can't trade one set of shackles for another. My generation must learn to create a world in which every woman's choice is valued and supported. Wasn't that what our mothers taught us?

GIRLHOOD PROJECT

The women of Generation X are the beneficiary of what Barbara Dafoe Whitehead (1998) calls the "girlhood project." The idea is that feminist mothers made a systematic, intentional effort to change the culture and prepare girls for lives as liberated, self-determined individuals with successful careers, sexual freedoms, and nearly limitless personal choice. As she raised daughters in the 1970s and 1980s, Whitehead dressed them in jeans and sneakers, fought for their right to play Little League baseball, pushed for more sex education in school, urged them to please themselves rather than to please men, and read them stories like "The Princess Who Could Stand on Her Own Two Feet." No doubt Whitehead raised some bright and talented daughters. But are they happy? Are we Gen X women any happier than our mothers? Here's what a couple of Gen X women in our survey had to say:

> I expected my career to be much more rewarding personally than it actually is. I expected to be a manager, yet (after five years) I have very little decision-making responsibility. I thought I would always be a "career woman," but now I am anxious to stay home and start a family.
>
> 28-YEAR-OLD SENIOR CONSULTANT

> I thought I would find work a lot more fulfilling than I do. . . . I have started shifting the idea of fulfillment more toward my personal life.
>
> 29-YEAR-OLD E-COMMERCE SPECIALIST

Did our Boomer mothers fail? No! There's no doubt that their glass-ceiling-breaking efforts have paid off. The women's liberation movement has helped level the playing field, even the literal playing field. In 1975, only one in twenty-seven high school girls participated in team sports. By 1994, one in three were on the team. And that experience alone can help a young woman prepare for a working world that's still largely shaped by male codes of conduct rooted in competition, combat, and conquest (Whitehead 1998).

So now that we're in the game, shouldn't we be happy? Susan Faludi (2001) writes that women are enslaved by their liberation, unhappy precisely because they are free. "They have grabbed at the gold ring of independence, only to miss the one ring that really matters. They have gained control of their fertility, only to destroy it. They have pursued their own professional dreams—and lost out on the greatest female adventure" (p. 1). Faludi adds her voice to a growing rumble of twenty-first-century women who blame the feminist movement for female Gen Xers' identity crisis.

Faludi's explanation seems much too simplistic. I, for one, am glad I've been presented the opportunities that I have. I don't blame the feminists for where we are today; I credit them with it. And I don't think the surge of well-educated Gen X women who are opting out of the workplace means the women's liberation movement has failed. In fact, as *Cosmopolitan* editor-in-chief Kate White explains, it's actually a sign of success: "I think women's lib was about choice and I like the idea that a mother can say . . . 'If I want to be home with my kids when they're young, I can do it'" (in Smith 2004, pp. 1–2). Or not!

I'm glad I have choices about marriage, children, and work. Even though having choices may sometimes feel like a burden, it's most definitely also the blessing our mothers hoped it would be. Mom didn't give me the wrong impression. She never told me everything I wanted would be handed to me. I knew that I had to work hard for what I wanted and that sometimes there would be disappointments. But I also got the overall impression that in the end, I'd be a success. She'd invested so much love and money in raising me. How could I fail?

Quite easily, it turns out. I found that out when I decided I wanted a new job because I wasn't as happy as I thought I should be and I wasn't making as much money as some of my friends. I applied for job after job and got rejection letter after rejection letter. I still have them all (from the companies that were kind enough to let me know they didn't want me). I have a three-ring binder full of the "thank you for applying, but we've decided to go with someone who better fits our needs" letters. I've certainly faced my share of failure—and it's not that I lacked credentials. At that point I had a master's degree and six years of significant work accomplishments. Mom always told me to see those rejections as a learning experience and "just be patient." She can be very philosophical about those kinds of things, so I try to be, too.

In fact, it was my attempt to better understand my own quarterlife crisis and my generation's dashed dreams that led us to our survey project. So, I'm passing the pen to Mom. In the next four chapters, she'll describe our survey results in more detail (Chapter 5), give you some real-life examples of X-friendly workplaces (Chapter 6), describe four roads to revolution (Chapter 7), and challenge us Gen Xers to learn the Quantum Skills that will enable us to lead a new kind of workplace revolution (Chapter 8). As you read these chapters, you'll see that Mom has a different perspective at fiftysomething than I do at twentysomething. So I turn to her now to explain the survey results and give us some insight into what it all means for the future of the neXt generation.

>> | CHAPTER 5

From Money to Meaning

I grew up in a small midwestern town with two working parents. My mom, a double major in Latin and history, became a school superin- tendent before she turned twenty-five (the male competition were all fighting in WWII). My dad returned from the war to manage the family grocery store that he inherited from his dad and *mom*. My paternal grandmother was ahead of her time. In the 1930s and 1940s she partnered equally in the daily operations of the family grocery: a wife, mother, and businesswoman.

When I was a child, my primary female role models were working women. These women seemed to do it all. They managed jobs and households, while also raising children and actively participating in their churches (and numerous other community organizations). It all looked so easy. They juggled multiple roles without any obvious struggle, perhaps because we lived in a small community where we were surrounded with relatives. My maternal grandparents lived next door, and aunts, uncles, and cousins were always there to lend a helping hand. If my sister, Patti, or I got sick, one of the relatives always came to spend the day with us while Mother and Daddy went to work.

When Patti and I were old enough to go to school, we rode there with our mother, who worked in the same building. When the three of us returned home, my maternal grandma often had dinner ready for us. I grew up in a much simpler world than did my Gen X children, in the midst of an amazing support system. It truly did take a village to raise my sister and me.

I never questioned that I would be a working woman. I was programmed to do so, and I was oblivious to the possibility that there might be obstacles along the way. After all, I had supportive parents, encouraging teachers, and a lot of accomplishments (for example, I was valedictorian, state essay winner, and homecoming queen). The world was my oyster (or so I believed at eighteen). I left for college filled with ambition.

Though I married at twenty-one, my personal history, coupled with an oldest-child drive, led me on to graduate school. Then, when I was twenty-four, our son, Matthew, arrived, followed by Laura when I was twenty-seven. By that time we were living in a city a considerable distance from family. The absence of an extended family support system, coupled with shifting societal values, led me to the feminist movement. I taught assertiveness classes to women at the local YWCA, helped start a shelter for battered women, attended NOW meetings, taught psychology courses at the state university, and parented two children, while my national sales manager husband traveled the country, growing his career.

In spite of the stress, I always loved my work. Our lives were complicated, but my career was such an integral part of who I was that it never entered my mind to stop working. As my children entered adulthood, I naively assumed that their career needs would be similar to mine. I assumed that work would play the same central role in their lives that it had in mine. Well, I was wrong! My children, their friends, and my MBA students (most of whom are Xers) all seem to agree that work is not the purpose of life, but rather a part of life. While members of this generation have high expectations for success, they are not prone to the extreme sacrifices of my generation. It's not simply that they want more balanced lives than we, their parents, modeled; their motivations are much more complex. This generation's needs are, in fact, quite paradoxical. They desire *independence,* but long for *meaningful relationships.* They seek *freedom,* but crave *responsibility.* They want *flexible* work schedules, but are frustrated by a lack of *security.* They are *impatient* and sometimes *impulsive,* but long for *purpose* and *spiritual fulfillment.* They want *balanced lives,* but demand *challenging work.* They want *careers* and *families, prosperity* and *play, advancement* but not *status.* How confusing!

THE SURVEY

In an attempt to better understand these paradoxes (and my children's and students' needs), I did what any good scholar would do—collected some data. More specifically, Laura and I designed a survey that would provide insight into and answers to four key questions that we will discuss in detail throughout this chapter:

1. What factors are most important to Gen Xers at work?

2. How do these factors differ for men and women?

3. How large is the gap between what Xers want and what they have?

4. How did Boomer parents influence the career expectations of their Gen X children?

The survey results provide insights for parents and a road map for Boomer managers. The results also serve as a call to action for Generation X—especially its women, who, with their strong focus on relationships, are the logical leaders of the neXt workplace revolution.

The Survey Process

During a six-month period in 2003, a thirty-four-question survey was administered to more than 1,200 respondents (see the appendix for the survey form). Some of the surveys were collected in MBA classes at Rockhurst University in Kansas City, Missouri, but most of the respondents completed the survey anonymously online. Laura and I distributed the survey form, via an e-mail link, to all of our Gen X contacts. Each recipient was asked (begged) to forward the survey link to all her or his Gen X colleagues and friends. We cast the original e-mail out to Xers from D.C. to San Francisco, from Minneapolis to New Orleans, and from Los Angeles to Chicago. As those Xers forwarded the survey to their contacts across the country, an electronic spiderweb was quickly created, capturing responses from all over the United States.

Profile of Respondents

Our respondents represent a diverse Gen X population with representatives of each birth year from 1964 to 1977. Though the majority of them are Caucasian, each of the other major ethnic categories is represented. As with many surveys, there are more female than male respondents. Slightly more than half are married, but only about one-third of those respondents have children. Overall, the respondents are well educated. The majority hold undergraduate degrees. Their current positions represent a wide spectrum of job and industry types. The typical respondent has between five and ten years of full-time job experience and has worked for her or his current employer for one to two years. Most are in individual contributor/nonmanagement positions. They work in both for-profit and not-for-profit organizations ranging in size from fewer than twenty employees to tens of thousands. A large majority earn between $20,000 and $60,000 annually. Their demographics are summarized in Table 5 (because of rounding off, the categories do not all total 100 percent).

TABLE 5	DEMOGRAPHIC PROFILE OF SURVEY RESPONDENTS	

		Percentage
Gender	Female	65
	Male	35
Race	Caucasian	90
	African American	4
	Hispanic	3
	Asian	1
	Other	2
Age	Born between 1964 and 1970	32
	Born between 1971 and 1977	68
Education	High school	12
	College	59
	Master's degree	23
	Doctoral degree	5
Marital Status	Married	55
	Unmarried	44
Parenthood	Have child/children	35
	No children	64
Years of Work Experience	Less than 5	21
	5 to 10	53
	More than 10	27
Organizational Level	Nonmanagement	59
	Supervisor	12
	Midlevel manager	18
	Senior manager	5
	CEO/owner	5
Size of Organization	Fewer than 20	13
	20 to 99	17
	100 to 499	21
	500 to 999	7
	1,000 to 9,999	23
	More than 10,000	18
Current Salary	Less than 20K	3
	20K to 39.9K	31
	40K to 59.9K	36
	60K to 99.9K	29
	More than 100K	5

ISSUE #1

What factors are most important to Gen Xers at work?

The things that Gen X women and men find important in their work lives are remarkably similar, but we found that women have stronger needs, and their needs are not being met as well as men's. Let me explain the survey data that led us to this conclusion by analyzing the results on question 22 (Table 6). This question consists of a list of fifteen job factors such as *salary* and *job security*. Respondents were asked to rate each factor according to its importance to them (first column) and their current level of satisfaction (second column). The number "1" represents low importance/satisfaction, while the number "5" represents high importance/satisfaction.

In Table 7 you'll see how Gen Xers ranked the importance of the fifteen job factors ("satisfaction" ratings will be discussed later in this chapter). The results are listed in order of priority—most important to least important for females and males. Note that the top four "importance" factors are the same for Gen X women and men, although the rank order is slightly different. It's also important to note that the last three items are identical on both lists and that *status is at the bottom!*

Most Important

Women ranked *positive relationship with supervisor* as number one in importance and *positive relationship with co-workers* as number two. Men ranked these two factors as number two and number four, respectively. Numerous authors have speculated about why relationships are so important to this generation, and most agree that the relationship needs of many Gen Xers were not met when they were children. As latchkey kids of divorced parents, they often spent excessive time alone. Now, as young adults, they find themselves needy of positive relationships in the workplace (yet they're fiercely independent as well). Unfortunately, many twenty-first-century organizations do not have collaborative cultures that align with the relationship values of this generation. Though much

TABLE 6	IMPORTANCE VERSUS SATISFACTION	

	Importance	Satisfaction
Salary	1 2 3 4 5	1 2 3 4 5
Benefits package	1 2 3 4 5	1 2 3 4 5
Job security	1 2 3 4 5	1 2 3 4 5
Interesting work	1 2 3 4 5	1 2 3 4 5
Job status/prestige	1 2 3 4 5	1 2 3 4 5
Performance feedback	1 2 3 4 5	1 2 3 4 5
Recognition	1 2 3 4 5	1 2 3 4 5
Opportunities for advancement	1 2 3 4 5	1 2 3 4 5
Opportunities for learning	1 2 3 4 5	1 2 3 4 5
Opportunities to innovate/be creative	1 2 3 4 5	1 2 3 4 5
Participation in decison making	1 2 3 4 5	1 2 3 4 5
Positive relationship with supervisor	1 2 3 4 5	1 2 3 4 5
Positive relationship with co-workers	1 2 3 4 5	1 2 3 4 5
Casual, relaxed, playful environment	1 2 3 4 5	1 2 3 4 5
Meaningful or spiritually fulfilling work	1 2 3 4 5	1 2 3 4 5

TABLE 7	FEMALE/MALE IMPORTANCE RATINGS

Female	Male
1. Positive relationship with supervisor	1. Interesting work
2. Positive relationship with co-workers	2. Positive relationship with supervisor
3. Interesting work	3. Opportunities for learning
4. Opportunities for learning	4. Positive relationship with co-workers
5. Job security	5. Opportunities for advancement
6. Benefits package	6. Participation in decision making
7. Opportunities for advancement	7. Job security
8. Casual, relaxed, playful environment	8. Opportunities to innovate/be creative
9. Participation in decision making	9. Salary
10. Performance feedback	10. Benefits package
11. Opportunities to innovate/be creative	11. Casual, relaxed, playful environment
12. Salary	12. Performance feedback
13. Meaningful or spiritually fulfilling work	13. Meaningful or spiritually fulfilling work
14. Recognition	14. Recognition
15. Job status/prestige	15. Job status/prestige

lip service is given to team-building activities, most organizations continue to be rigidly bureaucratic, highly political, and brutally competitive entities. One survey respondent describes the cost:

> My career, due to increasing growth in my company, has taken a very depressingly bureaucratic turn. I no longer feel valued as a person but as a number. The bottom dollar is supreme, and no longer is outspoken opposition taken without penalty. Opposition of any kind is characterized as "non-team playing" or a "lack of professionalism," whereas silence and compliance are seen as professional and demonstrative of a "team player." ... I am leaving my current industry in July.
>
> 32-YEAR-OLD QUALITY ASSURANCE TECHNICIAN

Quality relationships don't appear to be valued in this person's workplace; consequently, she's moving on—a typical Xer reaction. The Catalyst study (2001) Laura wrote about in earlier chapters found that Gen Xers are more than willing to box up their cubicles and walk out the door if their relationship needs aren't met.

Interesting work is number one for men (number three for women). Gen Xers grew up entertaining themselves with TV games (like Atari) and later with computer simulations (I remember my children playing "Pac Man" and "Dungeons and Dragons" for hours on end). These electronic games are designed around fast-paced, continuous action. Even when my kids were preschoolers, *Sesame Street* and Saturday morning cartoons provided lots of action and adventure. Consequently, as young employees, Xers tend to have a low threshold of boredom. They need lots of variety. Xers are masters of multitasking. Putting them in a narrowly defined, monotonous role is another sure way to cause them to pack up their cubicles and walk.

Opportunities for learning (ranked number three by men and number four by women) rounds out the top four list. Xers have a lust for learning and a voracious appetite for information. They grew up in a world with instant access to seemingly infinite amounts of information (and they're used to Googling everything). Xers are nonlinear mosaic thinkers. They prefer hands-on action learning to traditional classroom training. This generation's strong learning needs are also driven, in part, by the need for job security. Learning gives Xers an employment edge. It provides new, portable skills they can carry with them in their free-agent search for the perfect job/organization.

Least Important

Job status/prestige is at the very bottom of the Gen X rankings shown in Table 7. Both men and women rated this factor lowest in importance. These survey comments vividly capture the essence of what this means:

> I believe many Gen Xers are looking to do something that counts for humanity when all is said and done. Unlike our parents, we are not interested in country clubs, BMWs, and large homes with circle drives. Money/career to Gen Xers means FREEDOM and nothing more. The vast majority of my peers/friends have taken years off in their life to work in a ski resort or travel through Europe or teach English in foreign countries. Our goals and priorities are very different from those of our parents.
>
> 29-YEAR-OLD DESIGN STUDIO MANAGER

> Many in the "old guard" have different priorities than those my age. Family is absolutely a top priority with those my age who have children. Older attorneys tend to view the job as the number one priority, and family will simply take care of itself. I take greater satisfaction in my role as a husband and father than as an attorney.
>
> 37-YEAR-OLD ASSOCIATE ATTORNEY

> I would rather shovel dirt and be satisfied with a day's work than sit behind a desk and perform monkey-do tasks. Money matters not! Happiness is the most important thing in life.
>
> 29-YEAR-OLD ANALYST

To me, as a Boomer mother and manager, this is most perplexing. Why are Gen Xers so disillusioned about their career progress if the status symbols that accompany success are so unimportant to them? I suspect that only a Boomer would even ask this question. For most of us, status is (or at least was) extremely important. The tangible signs of success were what got us out of bed each morning. Perks such as job titles, corner offices, and reserved parking spaces are extremely important to most folks over forty. And, of course, it is those folks who are leading twenty-first-century organizations. And they have, for the most part, designed their organizations to meet their needs—not the needs of the next generation. Hence, most organizations are designed to use status symbols to motivate performance, and for most Gen Xers, status is simply off their radar screens.

Salary also ranks relatively low in importance for this generation. Table 7 indicates that *salary* ranked twelfth out of fifteen for women and ninth for men. These rankings, coupled with the survey comments, suggest that making lots of money isn't nearly as important to this generation as living a balanced life:

> **I think I expected to be more of a gunner, but I discovered somewhere along the line that there are more important things to life than work. It's a means to support my life, but it's not all that defines me.**
>
> 34-YEAR-OLD RESEARCH MANAGER

> **Before, I felt I had the desire to be a leader one day but as time goes by I am settling to be a high-level support staff for less pay and, I hope, more balance between work and personal time.**
>
> 38-YEAR-OLD PROJECT MANAGER

Many Boomers measure job success in dollars, but Xers appear to measure it in meaning. Both the quantitative data and the comments suggest that the Xer salary frustrations Laura discussed are driven more by external needs than by internal values. For example, adultolescents who move back in with their parents because they can't afford otherwise will, of course, be frustrated about money. However, we Boomers shouldn't infer that money is an important driver for this generation. Apparently the lack of money simply frustrates their basic survival (and independence) needs. It limits their freedom (not to mention their ability to repay their college loans).

Although we found no statistically significant differences in the importance of salary to men and women, significant salary gaps were found, with male respondents earning significantly higher salaries than their female counterparts. While this phenomenon is already well researched (and was discussed at length in Chapter 3), this survey indicates that the gender wage gap appears very early in Gen X careers—before they celebrate their thirtieth birthdays.

ISSUE #2

How do men's and women's importance needs differ?
Without getting you knee-deep in numbers or strangling you with statistics, I should tell you that rank order of importance doesn't tell the whole story (in fact, a statistician would claim it doesn't tell you much at all). To answer our second research question, we had to dig a little deeper and determine whether there are statistical differences in the mean (average) scores of males and females on each of the fifteen importance factors. And, indeed there are! While five of the fifteen factors have mean scores that are similar for men and women, ten of the fifteen factors have average ratings that are statistically different.

For eight of the ten factors with significant gender differences, the women's average scores (importance ratings) are significantly higher than the men's. The following factors were significantly more important to women than to men:

Benefits package
Job security
Recognition

Performance feedback
Opportunities for learning
Positive relationship with supervisor
Positive relationship with co-workers
Casual, relaxed, playful environment

Men identified two factors that were significantly more important to them. Those factors are

Opportunities for advancement
Participation in decision making

Remember, these lists don't tell us anything about the relative importance of these fifteen factors; they just tell us that women chose significantly higher ratings on eight items, while men chose significantly higher ratings on two. The remaining five factors (salary, interesting work, opportunities to innovate/be creative, meaningful or spiritually fulfilling work, and job status/prestige) show no significant gender differences in importance ratings.

It's obvious that women chose significantly higher importance ratings on many more factors than men did. But, before you jump to the conclusion that Gen X women are simply high-maintenance employees, let us offer another possibility: They may want more because they have less. It's a bit like *time;* the more we have, the less we think about it. However, if we have too little, it becomes a highly precious commodity, and we'd likely give it a higher number on an importance scale than would our peers who have time in abundance. (Try replacing "time" in this example with "recognition" or "job security" and it may make more sense.) Of course, our "time" analogy is only one of several possible explanations. The above lists of important factors don't tell us *why;* they just tell us *what.* Regardless of the reasons, the Gen X women in this survey chose significantly higher importance ratings than did the men.

To better understand the male/female importance differences, try imagining the survey as a shopping mall and the factors as fifteen stores.

Like most malls, this metaphorical mall has stores for men, stores for women, and stores that cater to both. The lists show that men like two of the fifteen stores significantly more than women do, whereas women like eight of the fifteen stores significantly more than men do. There is no significant difference in how much men and women like the remaining five stores. If you replace "stores" with factors like *benefits package* and *opportunities for advancement,* you will see that the *amount* of importance each gender puts on a specific factor (store) varies significantly (see the above lists) even though the rank order of priorities is somewhat similar (see Table 7).

Job Factors Women Like

In our survey, eight job factors were significantly more important to women than to men. Two of the eight have to do with *work relationships* (with supervisors and co-workers). Even though both male and female respondents rated these two factors as high in importance, the women chose a significantly higher importance rating than did men. This doesn't mean relationships are unimportant to Gen X men (remember, they rated them as number two and number four in importance); it's just that women place significantly more importance on positive relationships. This may be because women have higher oxytocin and lower testosterone levels (remember the tend-and-befriend research Laura discussed in Chapter 2), or it may simply be a learned value/need.

Performance feedback and *recognition* are also significantly more important to women than to men. Once again, the ratings don't tell us why. Perhaps women place greater importance on these job factors because they are wired to need more feedback and recognition. Or, perhaps they do so because they receive less attention than men do in the workplace. Certainly the salary and promotion discrepancies between the two genders suggest that it could be the latter. Here's what one Gen X woman had to say about the recognition she received from her supervisor (or, more aptly, the lack of it):

I thought that I would receive recognition for hard work and helping others. That has not happened. I expected that working would be a joy, but now it's just a paycheck.

27-YEAR-OLD SCHOOL PSYCHOLOGIST

It is important to remember that even though women selected significantly higher importance ratings for *performance feedback* and *recognition* than did men, these two factors are low in terms of relative priority for both genders. *Performance feedback* is ranked tenth out of fifteen on the women's priority list, and it's twelfth out of fifteen for the men (see Table 7). *Recognition* is ranked fourteenth in importance for both. Neither gender appears to be addicted to feedback or recognition; therefore the higher importance ratings women give these job factors may merely be a reflection of gender inequity issues in their workplaces.

The women in this survey also place significantly more importance on *benefits package* than do their male peers (number five out of fifteen on women's importance lists; ten out of fifteen for men). This may be due to the fact that 45 percent of our female respondents were single and had no spousal insurance coverage, but it's probably a bit more complicated. The comments Gen X women made in this survey suggest that benefits are key to achieving work-life balance. These women have a strong desire for flexible scheduling and generous time-off benefits. Many Gen Xers watched their Boomer parents devote their lives to a single organization—only to be laid off. Others resent the amount of time their parents spent at work and are trying hard not to fall into the same trap. They don't want to be part of another generation of workaholics, so they are placing more importance on personal goals and values than on those related to work:

When I was younger and just out of college my job was my life; but the older I get, my job is just what allows me to have my life outside of work. I am not my job.

34-YEAR-OLD MANAGER

Women's needs for good benefits programs may also be tied to their desire for more *job security,* caused not only by a shaky economy (Sutra Foundation 2001) but also by the likely demise of Social Security. In the Sutra Foundation study Laura discussed in Chapter 4, 40 percent of single Gen X women ranked employee-sponsored retirement plans as number one in importance in a lengthy menu of benefit options. This generation does, however, have a hard time getting excited about a retirement plan that won't kick in until they are sixty-five (no one is sure she'll even be around the next month). More appealing to Xers are portable retirement plans that they can take with them in their ongoing search for security and the perfect job.

Opportunities for learning were also significantly more important to women than to men. Perhaps women place more importance on learning because they believe learning will provide them with the competency edge necessary for overcoming the gender bias many women still encounter. However, this woman's comment suggests that additional skills don't always compensate for gender inequities. Her education and experience have not enabled her to break through her organization's glass ceiling:

> **I didn't know the politics and the "good old boys" system would be as bad as they are. I started here at the same time and in the same role as a male who has no college degree or comparable experience—and he has received two very hefty promotions.**
>
> 34-YEAR-OLD SENIOR PROGRAM REPRESENTATIVE

Unfortunately, she is not an exception. The Gen X women in this survey not only earn significantly less than their male peers, but they are also at significantly lower organizational levels, even when matched for age and education.

A *casual, relaxed, playful environment* rounds out the list of factors that are more important to women than to men. This job factor seems to mean different things to different women. For some it means schedule flexibility, for others it means having fun at work, and for still others it may mean a clothes preference (for example, not having to wear panty hose). The preference list, of course, doesn't clarify how women define this job factor; it just tells us that women place more importance on it than do men.

Job Factors Men Like

The Gen X men in our survey placed higher importance than did the women on *opportunities for advancement.* We can only speculate about why. Perhaps men, with their higher levels of testosterone, have a stronger biological need for achievement, or perhaps they have been programmed by centuries of familial responsibilities to unconsciously believe that it is their duty to strive for advancement. Interestingly, as more and more talented women opt out, men's achievement will become even more important to a family's economic well-being, thus perpetuating these patterns.

Participation in decision making was also more important to men than to women. This job factor seems related to the higher importance that men gave to *opportunities for advancement.* In most traditional organizations, employees must advance up the managerial ladder in order to actively participate in decision-making activities. Thus, in traditional organizations, satisfaction on one job factor could be expected to correlate with the other. However, it doesn't have to be this way. The X-friendly workplaces discussed in the next chapter provide examples of participative decision-making processes managers can use to share power rather than hoard it.

ISSUE #3

How large is the gap between what Xers want and what they have?
In Chapter 2, Laura compared her generation's career reality to its career expectations. She believes (and so do I) that her generation's career frustrations can be explained, at least in part, by an expectation-reality gap.

We explored a similar gap in this survey. We call it the importance-satisfaction gap. Our 1,200 respondents were asked (in question 22) to rate the importance of each of these fifteen factors to them as well as their current level of satisfaction. The results provide a clear picture of what is bugging this generation by identifying the size of the importance versus satisfaction gap for each of the fifteen job factors.

If a particular factor is not important to the respondent, no problem exists, regardless of satisfaction. However, if the importance rating is higher than the satisfaction rating, there's a problem—and the bigger the gap, the bigger the problem. Instead of thinking about salary or benefits, try picturing an importance-satisfaction scale for lima beans. If you love lima beans but you don't get a lot of lima beans for dinner, you might have a problem. If you don't get a lot of lima beans but you don't care for them, there's no problem at all. Two people could end up with the same amount of lima beans, and, based on their tastes, one might be happy, the other disgusted. We designed our survey to stand up to the "lima bean test," so to speak. Therefore, a low satisfaction rating in and of itself may not be a problem. However, when the respondent's importance rating is higher than his or her satisfaction rating, seeds of frustration are usually sprouting. And, as the gap between these two ratings widens, motivation and commitment are likely to decline.

Sadly, we found statistically significant importance-satisfaction gaps on fourteen of the fifteen job factors, and importance ratings were higher than satisfaction ratings on all fourteen factors—for *both* men and women. Using the lima bean example, this means that a lot of Gen Xers want more lima beans than their workplaces are serving up. The size of the gaps does, however, differ by gender. The five largest importance-satisfaction gaps for women are (in descending order)

1. Opportunities for advancement

2. Interesting work

3. Meaningful or spiritually fulfilling work

4. Opportunities for learning

5. Participation in decision making

And the five largest importance-satisfaction gaps for men are (in descending order)

1. Opportunities for advancement

2. Interesting work

3. Participation in decision making

4. Opportunities to innovate/be creative

5. Opportunities for learning

Obviously these two lists have a lot more similarities than differences. Though the rank order of the gaps is a bit different for men and women, four of the five factors appear on both lists, and the first two items on each list are *opportunities for advancement* and *interesting work.* There are also large importance-satisfaction gaps for men and women on *opportunities for learning* and *participation in decision making.* Using our shopping mall example, these factors are like having four stores where both men and women like to shop, but every time they go to one, the store is closed.

Opportunities for Advancement

The largest importance-satisfaction gap for both men and women relates to *opportunities for advancement.* This gap may be caused, at least in part, by this generation's unrealistic career expectations. However, other factors are also at play. Many Gen Xers entered the workforce just when the dot.com bubble burst and the U.S. economy took a major nosedive. Instead of finding opportunities for advancement, Xers found themselves in lean and mean organizations, many of which were undergoing massive rightsizings. During times of cost cutting and belt tightening, few opportunities for advancement exist. The flattening of the organizational pyramid has eliminated a lot of supervisory and midlevel management positions. No wonder there's a significant importance-satisfaction gap.

Interesting Work

The second-largest importance-satisfaction gap for both men and women is *interesting work*. Remember, *interesting work* also appeared on both men's and women's top-four importance lists. As mentioned earlier, Xers grew up entertaining themselves with lots of interesting games and fast-paced technology. All too often, these action-addicted adultolescents find themselves in narrowly defined, boring, entry-level positions like the one described here:

> I expected to be excited and motivated to do a good job and make a difference. I also expected my day-to-day work to have meaning and become ever changing with the direction of the company. I expected to be inspired by my work. I have found that all jobs have some degree of similarity in that the emotional aspect is not really involved. Instead, politics, the work grind (expectations that peers or management may impose on you—such as working 7 a.m. to 7 p.m.), and *menial everyday tasks* exist and tend to grow with job experience. Individual input makes little difference in the big picture.
>
> 31-YEAR-OLD PROGRAM MANAGER (FEMALE)

Opportunities for Learning

Interesting work for Xers typically includes lots of *opportunities for learning* (the fourth-largest importance-satisfaction gap for women and the fifth-largest for men). Learning new skills not only provides a sense of job security, but it prevents "rust-out" (more on this in Chapter 6). Mentoring, coaching, shadowing, and job rotation programs are good ways to expose Gen Xers to new people with diverse skills. Investing in the development of talented young employees pays big dividends in reduced turnover and increased motivation.

Participation in Decision Making

The significant importance-satisfaction gap on *participation in decision making* (the third-largest gap for men and the fifth-largest for women) suggests that Boomer empowerment initiatives are falling short. Even though we've flattened many of our organizations, we have not necessarily done so in a way that engages the hearts and minds of this generation by involving them in critical decision-making processes. Boomer managers (as a result of corporate downsizing) may be delegating more responsibility to their Gen X employees without giving them an equal amount of authority. Managers often talk the empowerment talk, but their power and control needs, too often, keep them from walking it.

Meaningful or Spiritually Fulfilling Work

Even though four of the five largest importance-satisfaction gaps are identical for men and women, two are gender specific: Gen X women experience a significant gap between importance and satisfaction on *meaningful or spiritually fulfilling work*. This finding is not unique to our survey. Robbins and Wilner's (2001) quarterlife crisis research suggests that Xers "have the unshakable belief that this is the time during which they have to nail down the meaning of their lives, which explains why they often experience a nagging feeling that somehow they need to make their lives more fulfilling" (p. 9). Laura explains,

> ⟩⟩ *We're looking for purpose, not just in our lives, but also in our work. And it's not always easy to find in today's organizations. It's not that we don't need money; of course we do. We couldn't survive without a paycheck, but we sure feel better about taking a smaller check home if we're working for a company with a mission—not a cheesy, long-winded mission statement that pops up on your work computer every time you log on, or one that is posted by the front door, but a purpose or mission that energizes us. If most of our time is spent at work, we want that work to be something we can believe in, something that gives more meaning to our lives.*

Allison Pearson's (2002) research confirms that Gen Xers are looking for companies that fill their emotional needs. Unfortunately, her research also suggests that few have found what they're looking for. Certainly our survey comments would support her findings. These comments suggest that many disillusioned Xers aren't willing to stick around and wait for things to change:

> I expected to feel fully satisfied, with a clear vision of my career after all the work that went into my college and advanced degrees. I have yet to find my "true purpose." . . . I continue to look for ways outside of my career to fulfill my passion, which is to add value to the world around me (my current position does not give me the opportunity to truly add value to anyone's life). So I seek extracurricular activities . . . tutoring, coaching youth volleyball teams, teaching journalism classes, and so on. It keeps me busy, but it has not moved me closer to the satisfaction I had once envisioned for myself and my career.
>
> 27-YEAR-OLD SENIOR FINANCIAL ANALYST (FEMALE)

> When I entered the workforce I expected to be at one company for longer periods of time and have more loyalty between myself and the company and the company and myself. Since that time I have been laid off four times and worked in many cutting-edge companies that proved to be exciting learning environments but also proved to burn me (and my co-workers) out at an alarming rate. While I wouldn't change any of it, I find myself searching for more meaningful and creative work that I enjoy. Despite the current economy, it is time to determine what exactly I want to be doing—my life's purpose.
>
> 31-YEAR-OLD MARKETING MANAGER (FEMALE)

While the importance-satisfaction gap for *meaningful and spiritually fulfilling work* is statistically larger for women, you can see from these comments that, for some men, meaning at work *means* something:

I didn't really know what to expect, but I do find myself at times asking myself, Is this all there is? Am I going to be doing this kind of thing for the next thirty years? At times I really wish I had something more spiritually fulfilling. Money heals a lot of your problems, but when I look at my career, I wish I were doing something to benefit the greater good.

31-YEAR-OLD EDITOR (MALE)

I've often been discouraged by the opportunities that exist to truly make a valuable contribution to the world. It seems that most of us become so easily mired in our duties that we stop looking for the chance to make a difference—no matter how large or small. We get comfortable and lazy.

32-YEAR-OLD COUNTY ATTORNEY (MALE)

It is interesting to note that there is no significant difference in the importance ratings that Gen X men and women give to this job factor (thirteenth out of fifteen for both). Even though *meaningful or spiritually fulfilling work* ranks near the bottom in relative importance, there is still a statistically significant gap for our women respondents between what they have and what they'd like to have.

Opportunities to Innovate/Be Creative

Men report a significantly larger importance-satisfaction gap on *opportunities to innovate/be creative* than women respondents do. This suggests that Gen X men are becoming more whole-brained, thus wanting to exercise both *creative* and *analytical thinking*. In fact, many men in our survey sound like workplace *metrosexuals*. Here's what one of them had to say about his workplace creativity expectations:

I expected to be treated like a human being who has *creative* and independent thoughts. However I am continually fighting supervisors who are afraid to think outside the box and am punished for creativity. Additionally, I would like to work in partnership with supervisors, but that has yet to happen, as there is always a power struggle for control; therefore, I have to make the supervisor believe that my good idea is his or hers before I am able to move forward on a project.

28-YEAR-OLD PROGRAMMER

While this man's work situation is certainly disappointing, it is refreshing to hear a male discuss his need to express more creativity at work. It is important to remember that there are no significant differences in the importance ratings that Gen X men and women give to this job factor (eighth out of fifteen for men, eleventh for women); but men's needs are being satisfied less well than women's (i.e., the importance-satisfaction gap is larger). Perhaps women are given more opportunities to express their creativity (or perhaps they choose jobs that better align with their needs for creative expression).

ISSUE #4

How did Boomer parents influence the career expectations of their Gen X children?

Where do generational (and gender) workplace differences originate? Our survey asked Gen Xers to indicate how their Boomer parents had influenced their (sometimes unrealistic) career expectations. Seven of the thirty-four survey questions (questions 23 through 29) explored this issue. In question 23 we asked Gen Xers whether their mother or father had a greater influence on their career expectations. Additional questions asked respondents to identify their parents' educational levels and indicate whether they perceived that their parents had rewarding careers.

It is not surprising, but it was somewhat disappointing for me to learn, that 67 percent of the respondents said their father had more influence on their career decisions than did their mother. Even when sorted by gender, dads still came out as the primary influencers of Gen X careers (78 percent for males, 62 percent for females). Furthermore, these Boomer dads are significantly better educated than the Boomer moms, and Gen X children see their dad as having a much higher level of career satisfaction than their mom. Only half of those surveyed thought their mom had a rewarding career, while three-fourths thought their dad did. There were no significant perceptional differences between the genders.

It is important to point out that 88 percent of the respondents' mothers were employed at some time while their children were growing up (compared to 97 percent of the fathers). Therefore, the mothers' lack of career influence does not appear to stem so much from their lack of employment as from their lack of career satisfaction. One Gen Xer explains it this way:

> **When I was growing up I sensed that my mom did not like her job that much and was basically employed to pay the bills (i.e., mortgage, college for me, family vacations, etc.). I pledged to myself that I would find a career that was fulfilling when I grew up. I wanted to enjoy going to work. It turns out my life is becoming like my mom's—I go to work to pay the bills. I don't look forward to going in to work each day.**
>
> 30-YEAR-OLD FINANCIAL ANALYST

Perhaps our attempts to break the glass ceiling appeared exhausting and unrewarding to our children. Or perhaps those of us without a good education simply had a job, not a career. Or perhaps we working Boomer mothers were so busy juggling and struggling that we failed to talk about our career successes and satisfactions. Regardless of the reason, Boomer women seem to have had a less than optimal influence on their children's—even their daughters'—careers. The survey comments suggest that our efforts to crash glass ceilings may have actually created a boomerang effect. Our Gen X daughters are rejecting the career values we, their mothers, modeled. Here is a good example from the survey:

I had always thought I would be "boss." I've since discovered that I would not enjoy being an attorney. Yet my mother's view of happiness was that of being wealthy. However, I now know otherwise.

32-YEAR-OLD LEGAL SECRETARY

Christy is another excellent example of the boomerang effect. At age twenty-eight she decided to move from the corporation to the classroom—a 180-degree flip-flop of her mom's career. Here's how Christy tells it:

Boomerang Career Choices

When I decided what my major in college would be, I was following my heart—not my sense of what would lead to a job at the end of college. I had a wonderful experience studying art history in college and I felt a sense of balance by having business as a minor (a small part of me knew I had to be somewhat practical).

As I was graduating, I knew that I did not want to enter the art world. Too many politics! I was interning at Southwest Airlines in their marketing department, and they offered me a job around the time I needed one. Thus my career path into marketing and sales was launched. It lasted six years. I came to find out that you can always get a job being a salesperson. And, since I hadn't figured out how to marry my passion for art and my professional life, I was content with the path I was on. I had little hope of ever having one of those "perfect" jobs.

The huge shift that came next was shocking to everyone (including me). I was at the crossroads for a salesperson, when you either have to sell your soul to be the best—or decide to make a change. I liked the person I was and was not interested in having to be the ruthless type. My always-wise mother suggested that I look into being a teacher. She went to college to be a teacher and actually taught high school English for a year. However, she left teaching and became a high-level manager in a well-known telecommunications company. So . . . I was shocked that she would suggest such a thing.

Mom also offered to pay for me to get my credentials to teach. Another factor that made this option attractive was the fact that I was engaged and needed to start thinking about a career that would be conducive to having a family. My desire to have a family and a fulfilling career was more important to me than making lots of money. I was fortunate to have my fiancé to help pick up the slack while I went back to school.

So, almost blindly, I got myself enrolled in a credential program and quit my job. I had only spent a minimal amount of time in a classroom—a handful of hours volunteering for Junior Achievement. But, I just had this gut feeling that this was the right move.

A year later, I am a fully credentialed elementary school teacher. I teach fourth grade in a neighborhood much like I grew up in. I have never been more passionate about a job in my life. I found the perfect job for me. My expensive undergraduate education led to more expensive education, but I wouldn't trade my new job for anything in the world.

Christy's Boomer mother traded in her teaching credentials for a prestigious business career. Gen Xer Christy, with a private-school art/business degree, traded in her business career for teaching credentials. She, like many of her peers, is much more interested in meaningful work and a balanced life than the status, wealth, and power that drove the Boomer generation. Another respondent told us,

> **I never expected I would end up in the education field. I always thought I would want to make as much money as possible, but now I just want a job that means something to me. Teaching has most certainly fulfilled that need.**
>
> 28-YEAR-OLD TEACHER

Having different core values is a true sign of a generation gap, and Xers are not the first to make an about-face on their parents' values. We Boomers rejected the "save, save, save" mentality of our Depression-era parents. Many of us preferred to buy rather than hoard. We lived the good life, at least in a material sense, and our Gen X children seemed to enjoy the things we gave them. Yet, they are increasingly refusing to make the same choices we did . . . a sure sign of shifting generational values. One of our respondents compared her career with those of her parents this way:

I see corporate America as standing for everything that I do not, and unlike my parents I am not willing to spend my best years swallowing my pride unnecessarily.

32-YEAR-OLD QUALITY ASSURANCE TECHNICIAN

Is this woman's desire to live her life differently a condemnation of her parents or a condemnation of the corporation? Could it be that the Boomer feminist revolution empowered this daughter to refuse to settle for dysfunction? If so, then my generation's revolution hasn't failed; it has laid the evolutionary groundwork for the neXt one.

The Rest of the Story

Our research results provide insight into numerous societal trends that are characteristic of this generation. For example, in the United States, young people—especially professional Gen X women—are marrying later than they did a generation ago. However, our data indicate that unmarried women have a significantly lower *life satisfaction* rating (question 31) and also lower *job satisfaction* ratings (question 17) than do married women. This gives a whole new meaning to "happily married." Perhaps single Gen X women are putting all their satisfaction eggs in one basket, thus expecting more and needing more from work than their married peers. Regardless of the cause, traditional organizations are more frustrating for single Gen X women than for married women, who may be less focused on getting all their satisfaction needs met at work.

It is also interesting to note that the larger the organization, the lower the satisfaction ratings (question 22) on *opportunities to innovate/be creative, meaningful or spiritually fulfilling work,* and *casual, relaxed, playful environment.* We believe that as Gen Xers exit traditional corporations, they will either move to smaller, more flexible, workplaces or exercise their creativity to birth their own entrepreneurial ventures. They already are! You'll read more about mom-preneurs in Chapter 7, but here's an advance peek at what the women in our survey had to say about striking out on their own:

> I had full confidence in my ability to show people my potential. But now I feel that in order for me to exercise my skills and talent I will need to strike out on my own and go into business for myself.
>
> 26-YEAR-OLD CUSTOMER SERVICE REPRESENTATIVE

> I have realized that a good salary and benefits package are not enough to convince me to go to someone else's office and make someone else a profit for half of my waking hours. I work for myself and will never have a corporate or cubicle job again. I intend to do whatever I enjoy for the rest of my life regardless of how much money I may or may not make doing it.
>
> 27-YEAR-OLD FREELANCE ARTIST

> By this stage in my career I thought I would hold a higher position in the organization I am currently in and thought I would be making more money. Unfortunately, that did not turn out to be the case. And I believe if I want it to be the case, I will have to start my own company, as corporate America is not meeting my needs.
>
> 31-YEAR-OLD GROUP MARKETING MANAGER

THE NEXT REVOLUTION

These survey comments, along with the other Gen X stories scattered throughout the book, remind me of *Office Space,* a 1990s movie that vividly depicts the workplace value differences of Boomers and Xers. Some managers view this Boomer-Xer gap as simply inevitable. They believe the gap will diminish (or disappear) as Gen Xers mature. Managers who hold this assumption are in denial. They are blind to the seismic sociological shifts that have occurred during the past fifty years. The neXt generation is looking for a dramatically different kind of organization— one that will help them strike a better work-life balance. They want to work in companies that offer the advantages of being a free agent (flexibility in when, where, and how they work; compensation linked to what they contribute; and freedom to move from project to project) *and* they also want the security that comes from belonging to an organization. If organizations are to retain and motivate this generation, especially the women, radical changes must occur.

Unfortunately, the problem is bigger than most people realize. The symptoms appear long before young women enter the workforce. Today few teenage girls see business as an attractive job choice. In a national survey of three thousand middle school and high school girls, conducted by Simmons School of Management in Boston and the Committee of 200, a group of leading businesswomen in Chicago, only 9 percent of the girls listed business as their first career choice (Gerencher 2002). It isn't that these young women plan to be full-time homemakers; 97 percent of them plan to work, and many of them have ambitious career goals in fields like medicine and law—just not in business.

The study's conclusion was that there are two key problems: There are few high-visibility female role models in business; and teenage girls see business as a dry, sterile environment that stifles creativity and forces a loss of personal identity similar to the characters in the Dilbert comic strips. "Another factor that may be turning girls off to business is a perception that business is for money-grubbing, power-hungry people out to enrich only themselves" (Gerencher 2002, p. 4). The societal cost of losing this talent pool of young women is enormous.

Even my Gen X MBA students are fed up with old-style corporations. The stereotypical MBA student is supposed to be single-minded in her desire for material wealth, but this is no longer the case. Many of my students are pursuing their MBAs not for corporate advancement, but for career escape. They want to break their ties with the corporation and escape into more interesting and meaningful work. Their frustration with bureaucratic constraints, whether they be glass ceilings, goading bosses, or grueling schedules, is pushing them out of large corporations into the entrepreneurial and nonprofit arenas in record numbers.

A survey conducted by *BusinessWeek* found that even though 100,000 Xers were enrolling in MBA programs in 2003 (up from about 60,000 a decade ago), few of them are driven by the idea of wealth. Many Xers are looking for an alternative career route that "in many cases, entails a brief loop back into the business world only as preparation for breaking free of Corporate America and doing something brash and new and different on their own" (Stewart 2002, p. 27). A CNN.com article, "Meaning over Money for Business Students" (2004), discusses a new breed of MBA student—one who has been influenced by everything from corporate scandal and the dot.com bust to concerns over the effects of globalization and global warming. This new breed of student wants to use her or his degree to make a difference and wants to have fun along the way.

In order for traditional organizations to retain this new breed of worker, a *cultural revolution* is required. In this revolution women won't need to act (or dress) like men; rather, they will work to help free men to act more congruently with their own quickly emerging metrosexual values. The workplace transformation door unlocked by us Boomer women is now about to be pushed open by our daughters—and sons. "Looked at this way, this is not the failure of a revolution, but the start of a new one. It is about a door opened but a crack by women that could usher in a new environment for us all" (Belkin 2003, p. 86). We encourage Xer men and women to use their workplace frustrations to fuel the neXt revolution; and we invite Boomer managers (and moms) to join their ranks. Together we can create X-friendly organizations.

CHAPTER 6

X-Friendly Workplaces

My Boomer friend Beverly dresses in Saks Fifth Avenue clothes, loves jazz, lunches on yogurt (usually at her desk), and manages an HR department at an innovative, state-of-the-art private hospital. Many of her staff are Xers who dress in GAP clothes and listen to alternative music on headphones as they click away on their computers. They spend their lunch break working out, then take time to eat as well, and think nothing of asking for flexible work schedules. Bev has mixed feelings about their casual and sometimes demanding demeanor. Most Boomers do, especially women managers, who both resent Xers demands for so much flexibility and respect their courage for insisting on that which we didn't have: *work-life balance.*

It is easy for managers like Bev to view Xers as impatient, inattentive, arrogant, skeptical, and demanding. However, these same labels also describe employees who are independent, pragmatic, and good at multi-tasking. As Boomer managers, we get to choose whether we see this generational glass as half-full or half-empty. We can focus on understanding and appreciating the values that characterize the Xer generation, or we can lose the value that this generation brings to twenty-first-century workplaces.

In Chapter 3, Laura discussed how many of her generation's brightest, most talented women are opting out—leaving their dysfunctional workplaces to focus their time and energy on creating functional families; men are leaving, too (in Chapter 7, we'll discuss the Xer exodus into entrepreneurial adventures in more detail). Unfortunately, this talent exodus is occurring at just the time their skills are most needed. The Boomer retirement time bomb is about to explode, and traditional organizations are going to be left with a lot of empty desks. According to the Conference Board, an economic research group, about 76 million Baby Boomers will be retiring in the next fifteen years, but only 45 million Gen Xers are in the pipeline to take their place (in Forster 2003). Executives and economists alike are beginning to ask, Who will sit at the Boomers' desks? Kaihla (2003) explains,

> The cause of the labor squeeze is as simple as it is inexorable: During this decade and the next, the baby boom generation will retire. The largest generation in American history now constitutes about 60 percent of what both employers and economists call the prime-age workforce—that is, workers between the ages of 24 and 54. The cohorts that follow are just too small to take the boomers' place. The shortage will be most acute among two key groups: managers, who tend to be older and closer to retirement, and skilled workers in high-demand, high-tech jobs. (p. 2)

This pending labor shortage has been masked by the economic recession that marked the first few years of the twenty-first century. Two million workers have been downsized or displaced since the recession of 2001, and the national unemployment rate remains high; however, things are about to change dramatically. Very soon the labor shortage will be in full swing, creating a gap of 5 to 7 million skilled workers, and the gap will swell to a canyon of 14 million by 2020 (Kaihla 2003). The first signs appeared in the fall of 2004 when recruiting on college campuses began to resemble the rush of the dot.com days. In a survey by the National Association of Colleges and Employers, college hiring was up 13 percent in 2004 compared to 2003 (in Pope 2004). Forget taking a job just to have a job; new college grads will increasingly be able to pick and choose.

Anthony Carnevale, former chairman of President Clinton's National Commission for Employment Policy, comments, "By comparison, what employers experienced in 1999 and 2000 was a minor irritation. The upcoming labor shortage won't just be about having to cut an extra shift; it will be about not being able to fill the first and second shift too" (in Kaihla 2003, p. 2). The problem is complicated by the fact that Generation X is the first generation that is neither larger nor better educated than the preceding generation. The number of available workers will decrease in the next two decades, and the percentage of the labor force that has been to college will remain at the current ratio of 60 percent. The result will be an unprecedented mismatch between the workforce and the demands of a high-tech economy.

This creates a gap that must be filled primarily by the neXt generation. But there are major obstacles. Not only are there simply not enough Xers, but many of them, especially women, are opting out of the job market. Only 67 percent of women with MBAs are working full-time (compared to 95 percent of the men), and the percentages are even lower among women with prestigious degrees from Ivy League schools. As mentioned in Chapter 3, a recent survey of women from the Harvard Business School classes of 1981, 1985, and 1991 found that only 38 percent were working full-time (Belkin 2003). Most of these women are opting out to be stay-at-home moms or to work part-time. However, our research suggests that the exodus of professional women from the workplace isn't really about motherhood; it's about work—or the lack of meaning and balance therein. In a recent *New York Times Magazine* cover story, one woman used the analogy of a romance gone sour: "Timing one's quitting to coincide with a baby is like timing a breakup to coincide with graduation. It's just a whole lot easier than breaking up in the middle of the senior year" (in Belkin 2003, pp. 85–86). Ambitious women used to aim for a management spot, to get onto the boards of Fortune 500 companies or to make it to the top spot and sit in the CEO seat. "There's a new goal. The aim now is more radical and more ambitious: It is to change the game entirely" (Heffernan 2002, p. 64). And, they're doing it—one resignation at a time!

THE PRICE OF DISSATISFACTION

Though we have focused much of this book on the job frustrations of Gen X women, Gen X men are frustrated as well. Increasingly, younger workers are taking a hard look at two-hour commutes, formal business attire, the glare of fluorescent lights, sixty-plus-hour workweeks, and managers who don't seem to get it, and they're realizing this isn't how they want to spend their lives. In fact, job satisfaction statistics are declining for people of all ages and both genders. There is a rapidly growing gap between what we want and what we get from our organizations. In one survey, a mere 51 percent of workers said they liked their job ("Unhappy at Work?" 2002). That's down from 59 percent in 1995. Job satisfaction increased with salary, but even among those earning more than $50,000 a year, only 67 percent said they liked their job. Another employee survey, conducted by Gallup, found that 71 percent of U.S. workers consider themselves to be "disengaged clock watchers" (in Zuboff 2004, p. 104).

The organizational cost of dissatisfaction and subsequent disengagement is enormous. A 2004 research study conducted by the Future Foundation found that in the United States alone, poor people management costs a shocking $105 billion per year. Another survey of 362,950 employees conducted by International Survey Research (Kulesa 2002) found that levels of employee commitment in the United States are significantly lower than those in half of the world's other major economies. Over three years (1999 to 2001), ISR measured employee commitment levels in forty major global companies and also tracked the financial performance of the companies. Organizations with high levels of employee commitment achieved significant increases in both operating margin and net profit. Organizations with low levels of employee commitment experienced significant declines in both of these performance indicators.

It's time to build workplaces that meet corporate goals *and* feed our souls; and, as the above findings demonstrate, these are not mutually exclusive concepts. Younger women are already helping to reshape the workplace—by refusing to trade meaning for money or balance for prestige. Those who are opting out have punched a growing hole in the labor talent pool. In order to plug this hole, Boomer managers need to deeply understand what Gen X women want, and we, along with Gen X men, need to support this revolution. Why? Because all of us, regardless of gender or generation, are increasingly disillusioned with dysfunctional organizations.

Our recent survey of 1,200 Gen Xers suggests that both women and men are passionate in their desire for a new kind of workplace and crystal clear about what an X-friendly workplace would look like. Members of this generation not only want to live more balanced lives, but they want to work in organizations that nurture positive relationships and provide interesting work with lots of opportunities for learning. An engineer who responded to our survey may be cleaning out his desk soon because these three basic factors are missing in his work. On his survey form he wrote,

> My enthusiasm for my work has been brought down by a poor relationship with my manager and a lack of opportunities for learning. It's boring, mindless work and lacks positive feedback/reinforcement. I am still optimistic though, and I am presently looking for a better job.
>
> 26-YEAR-OLD CIVIL ENGINEER

Positive relationships, interesting work, and *opportunities for learning* were at the top of the "importance" list for our survey respondents (Table 8). They are the key criteria for organizational leaders to use in

TABLE 8	TOP FOUR FEMALE/MALE IMPORTANCE RATINGS
Females	**Males**
1. Positive relationship with supervisor 2. Positive relationship with co-workers 3. Interesting work 4. Opportunities for learning	1. Interesting work 2. Positive relationship with supervisor 3. Opportunities for learning 4. Positive relationship with co-workers

redesigning their organizational cultures in order to make them more satisfying. In this chapter, we'll provide Xers with some concrete examples of X-friendly workplaces (yes, some do already exist), while also providing Boomer managers with some new ideas for supporting this generation's cultural revolution.

POSITIVE RELATIONSHIPS

Many Gen Xers grew up in single-parent or dual-career families in which there was often little time for quality relationships; hence, this generation has entered the workforce with a strong desire to experience a sense of community. Positive workplace relationships are very important to Xers, and a poor supervisory relationship is at the heart of much of their job dissatisfaction. There's a saying that Xers join companies, but they leave supervisors. Our survey results certainly reinforce the importance of the supervisor-employee relationship. The female respondents rated a *positive relationship with my supervisor* as number one on their importance lists and the males rated it as number two. Yet, in most organizations, people are promoted into management positions primarily because of their technical (and political) skills rather than their ability to manage meaningful relationships. This is unacceptable to the neXt generation. They want managers who actually care about people.

One of my Gen X MBA students, Julie, is lucky enough to have such a manager. In one of her weekly learning journal entries she wrote the following description of her five-year working relationship with this highly skilled manager:

Julie's Journal

Over time, as we have worked together on large projects and have been low on resources, we have gotten to know each other well. I am able to anticipate what he needs without having to ask for specific directions and provide it to him in a format he likes. We have lunch several times a month and share stories about our personal lives and children. We have developed a certain "rhythm" and professional connection that has instilled a sense of loyalty in me to him. I have turned down three other job offers (one was a promotion) due to the relationship we have built. Part of this is due to the way he treats people. I could probably write a book on how well he treats others, but suffice it to say that he is very genuine and has a high regard for treating others fairly and respectfully.

While there aren't many managers as skilled at relationship building as Julie's, simply treating employees with caring, fairness, and respect can make a major difference in how any Xer feels about her job, as this survey respondent's comment indicates:

I love my current position and love the people I work with. The VP I work for actually cares about each and every employee. At my previous company some directors wouldn't even speak to you while passing in the hall. There is a lot of respect in my current job, which makes it an awesome work environment.

27-YEAR-OLD TRAINING ASSISTANT

Open communication is a critical ingredient for creating positive work environments, and Xers want to be free to converse with anyone in the organization—president to part-time worker. They also want to be free to offer their opinions, insights, suggestions, and criticisms. Xers don't buy into or tolerate the need-to-know approach to communication, and they aren't likely to respect the more traditional, speak-only-when-spoken-to work environments. Here are some real-life examples of how three senior managers went about developing a climate of open communication in their organizations.

Kinko's CEO Gary Kusin spent his first six months on the front line. He wanted to find out what made Kinko's tick. "I went into every single one of our 24 markets in the United States, visited more than 200 stores, and met with more than 2,500 team members," explained Kusin (Overholt 2002, p. 52).

At Staples Inc., CEO Ron Sargent started out his first day by putting on black pants, black shoes, and the red shirt that his store employees wear. He spent the day in the original Staples store in Brighton, Massachusetts, getting to know his new employees.

These managers recognize the importance of spending time building relationships with those who serve the customers. The time Kusin and Sargent spent developing relationships with frontline employees will pay big dividends.

It is likely that at one time or another, you have eaten at one of Andy Pearson's Tricon Restaurants. You might eat at one every week. Tricon is the largest restaurant chain in the world, consisting of Pizza Hut, Taco Bell, and Kentucky Fried Chicken; and Andy Pearson is the company's CEO. Pearson is a pioneer of what he calls a new form of leadership. After spending years in management giving motivational speeches and not getting results, Pearson realized he was guilty of old-style management. Now, instead of telling employees how to do it, he shows them.

"The benefits of this approach are so obvious, they make you cry," Pearson says of his time-consuming approach (LaBarre 1999, p. 73). He spends half of his time in the field doing more than talking about leadership; he interacts with the restaurant workers, using relationship power to inspire change. Among his strategies are what the KFC folks call "meetings in a bucket." Imagine being a worker at the largest restaurant chain in the world. Let's say you're a cashier or maybe a fry cook. Now imagine that the chief executive of the company stops by your store and shows you how to do something differently, maybe more efficiently. That approach is going to be more effective than posting a new rule on the bulletin board. It meets this generation's need for open and direct communication.

Xers are highly skeptical, and they prefer direct communication; they are much more trusting (and appreciative) of a manager who tells it like it is—and they are likely to do the same. They have little tolerance for politics, brownnosing, and other types of corporate game playing. Openness and honesty are the names of their game. They expect their managers to do what they promise (which all too frequently doesn't happen, as this story from Laura's work demonstrates):

> ⟩⟩ *Every boss is going to have a different idea of how to develop relationships. A manager I worked for launched one of his relationship campaigns as if he were plotting a strategic step in some corporate war. He began by announcing his plan to spend individual time every month with each of his direct reports. When I first heard about it, I was thrilled. An hour of face-to-face time every month with my boss! I started planning what I wanted to say. Then I heard what everyone else was saying: "The plan won't last." And true enough, our boss worked his way through one month of meetings, giving us each an hour, and we never heard of the plan again. Now don't get me wrong; my hour was great. I left his office feeling like I was valued and that my concerns had been heard. To me, one meeting is better than none, and we were all optimistic that sooner or later, he'd launch a new (if slightly short-lived) relationship campaign, but before he had the chance, he left for another job.*

This manager's one-shot attempt at relationship building is unfortunately the norm. Consequently, employees in most organizations have become jaded. They view these campaigns as flavor-of-the-month fads. Xers are particularly skeptical. They don't like gimmicks; they want frequent, ongoing communication. In fact, they want daily communication with their managers—not just once-a-month, once-a-quarter (or, worse yet, once-a-year) performance feedback sessions. All we're talking about is a few minutes a day of conversation between supervisors and employees; but, all too often, bosses don't take the time, as these survey comments reveal:

I (incorrectly) imagined that I'd be likely to end up with a boss who cared about his/her employees and would put an emphasis on feedback and development. In two years I've had exactly six one-on-one conversations with my boss (two of which were performance reviews that included feedback such as "you're doing OK; just keep working hard," and two of which were feedback regarding my objectives for the year).

26-YEAR-OLD BENEFITS ADMINISTRATOR

I expected to be given opportunities and to be judged on how I handled those opportunities. Instead, the path to advancement is some nonquantifiable combination of butt kissing and luck. There is no pattern to what makes a person successful, and a great many people are dismissed as not being "stars." I do not feel that the firm values my abilities or the abilities of any particular person (with very few exceptions) but instead has the attitude that someone else will be happy to do my job if I don't want to keep doing it. I am frustrated that I have to work like a dog to do my job well and nobody seems to notice.

32-YEAR-OLD ATTORNEY

Actually, it takes very little time or energy to meet this generation's feedback needs, and when managers verbally recognize good performance, commitment soars, as this story from Laura's past indicates:

>> *I experienced a painful downsizing just a few months into my second reporter job. It left a bitter taste in my mouth and I decided to look at my next job as just a means to an end—not the "just a paycheck" attitude that some traditionalists have, but rather the idea of "putting in my time" so that*

I could then move on to the next job, where I would find more fulfillment. Commitment never entered my mind. Then my boss changed my mind in a matter of about a week. He found out I was looking for a new job and launched a campaign to keep me. His first bold move came in the quarterly station meeting. The station's general manager (whom we coincidentally referred to as General Jim) made the first tactical assault. I was sitting there looking at overhead projections of quarterly profits when General Jim announced that he would be recognizing someone from each department. I wondered who would be singled out from news as going above and beyond. The General started describing a reporter who really "gets it," someone who embraced the news goals and delivered. I wondered which one of us he was describing . . . all the way up to when he said my name. Believe it or not, those two minutes changed my perception. I realized I was valued, and it changed how much I valued the station.

Xers, like Laura, love feedback (but don't we all?). Xers also love to give feedback, and they don't have much tolerance for managers who aren't willing to *listen*. This generation doesn't automatically respect people just because they are older or wiser. Authority figures must prove themselves by listening to their needs. Boston Philharmonic conductor Benjamin Zander has an innovative way of doing this, one that is especially radical for his profession, which embraces the saying "Every dictator aspires to be a conductor" (LaBarre 1998, p. 110). It wasn't until Zander was forty-five that he realized the conductor doesn't make a sound. It's the orchestra that creates the music. "The conductor's power depends on his ability to make other people powerful," Zander explains. Zander started paying attention to how he was enabling his musicians to be the best performers they could be. To get their feedback, he puts a blank sheet of paper on everyone's music stand before every rehearsal. It's an open invitation for the musicians to tell him if he's accomplishing his goal of helping them become the best performers they can be. Imagine what you'd write if your boss handed you a blank sheet of paper every day.

Zander's X-friendly style fosters a general climate of open communication, and it helps to build the climate of positive relationships that this generation wants and needs—not only with managers, but also with co-workers (number two on women's importance lists, number four on men's). At Dandelion Moving and Storage in northern Colorado, owner Bret Lampres has a workforce composed of Gen Xers. Lampres focuses on building a close-knit group by encouraging employees to learn about one another's backgrounds and form personal, as well as professional, relationships. Lampres surveys new employees, asking about their backgrounds, interests, and goals. This helps him get to know them quickly, but it also helps him pair employees with common interests on job assignments, so they can perhaps discover a new best friend. Interestingly, research by the Gallup organization, based on data from more than 80,000 people in four hundred companies, found that "having a best friend at work" was one of twelve key predictors of both job satisfaction and high performance—regardless of gender or generation (in Buckingham and Coffman 1999).

When a Gen Xer's relationship needs aren't met, she will leave. Business consultant Gregory Smith is trying to help the U.S. Army deal with a severe retention problem. It seems that Gen Xers aren't sticking around there either. Highly skilled Generation X junior officers and enlisted soldiers are bailing out in droves (Smith 2001). They are leaving for higher-paying civilian jobs, though money is only part of the problem. Smith found that the Gen X officers didn't believe their older, more senior officers understood their needs or could manage them properly. Xers just aren't impressed with status symbols like title or position. They want an egalitarian structure (something quite foreign to the military). For an Xer, respect has to be earned; it can't be legislated. This generation is much more impressed with opportunities to learn new skills than with opportunities to earn new titles.

INTERESTING WORK

Xers don't believe in waiting their turn and paying their dues. They want to contribute now—not years from now, and they won't, for any length of time, tolerate routine, menial, or mindless tasks. Interesting work is highly desired by both male and female Xers. It ranked number one on the survey's importance list for men and number three on the women's list. This respondent's complaint captures his generation's frustration:

> I didn't expect to be so bored with my job/company after only four and a half years! I can't believe I have thirty-five to forty years left to go in the workforce! I am satisfied with my salary and have received steady promotions and appreciate the opportunity. However, I dread coming to work on most days. My day-to-day tasks are not fulfilling and don't excite me anymore.
>
> 27-YEAR-OLD FINANCIAL ANALYST

Gen Xers grew up in a fast-paced world and they want fast-moving companies and interesting, action-packed jobs. They're wired that way. We Boomers may think they have short attention spans and lack the ability to focus, but those aren't necessarily problems. Viewed from a different perspective, that rapid-fire consumption of information can be a brilliant coping mechanism in a world that's overloaded with information. Take someone with these kinds of multitasking skills and put her in a job where she has lots of variety, and you'll have the perfect fit, as this comment from our survey demonstrates:

> The company I work for allows me to move around and try different things and make choices. I now feel I have control over my career path and that I can make a difference in the world by the domains I choose to work in.
>
> 29-YEAR-OLD PRODUCT ARCHITECT

Unfortunately, when Xers don't have the ability to do a variety of interesting tasks, they find their own diversions. Here's what one of my MBA students had to say about cyberloafing:

I have spent the past five years in the I.T. industry and have witnessed just as much cyberloafing as I have real work. It occurs for many reasons, but absolute boredom is the main one. There are some days when my tasks are so boring that I find myself checking my personal e-mail or CNN.com just to give myself a "wake-me-up." I believe that if I had more responsibility and were personally accountable for more, then this behavior would change.

27-YEAR-OLD I.T. CONSULTANT

This student's comment suggests that interesting work involves more than task variety; challenge and responsibility are also important ingredients. When George Bauer became the new president of the Daimler-Benz subsidiary Mercedes-Benz Credit Corporation (MBCC), he decided to provide his employees with a very big challenge—reinventing the corporate culture. Bauer saw a future of change and wanted the company to be ready for it. He also wanted every employee to actively participate in the change process. "Let's let the people in the organization find the weaknesses in the organization," Bauer declared (Petzinger 1999, p. 214).

One team of two hundred employees got together to write the mission statement. And they came up with a whopper. It's unlike any mission I've ever read, but it defines their risk-taking goals perfectly. It reads, "We encourage a restless spirit of inquiry. Free-flowing communication is the lifeblood of our organization, an information-rich environment where communications flow freely in all directions . . . we must accept and embrace risk-taking at Mercedes-Benz Credit Corporation" (Petzinger 1999, p. 214).

Bauer created an organizational culture in which redundancy was on the chopping block and waste was in the trash can. He not only encouraged workers to eliminate inefficiencies, but he also rewarded them for doing so, and guaranteed employees that they would have a job no matter what they found. Margaret Brayden is a great example of how Bauer's actions matched his promises. Brayden had spent years as the company's records-retention coordinator. When she came up with new processes that effectively eliminated her job, they moved her to a different department. She eventually eliminated that job, too. The company rewarded Brayden by giving her a position on the company's new change management team.

When Bauer arrived at MBCC, the company's assets were $9 billion. When he left for another division six years later, MBCC's assets were over $23 billion. But equally as impressive as this bottom-line achievement are the massive changes to the company's culture. Employees shed their security blankets and started taking risks. Furthermore, each and every employee was involved in planning and implementing MBCC's cultural revolution. Working together, they created an X-friendly workplace.

Here's another story of *interesting work* from catalog retailer Land's End. Gen Xer Randy Lagman used to spend his days at his desk working out computer kinks. He'd reboot servers and wipe out viruses. Today he's lacing up his boots and dodging viruses in the farthest reaches of the world—a techie turned trekkie! Lagman's career at Land's End took a radical turn in 1997 when the company's head honchos asked him to help with an interesting assignment. A replica of a Viking ship was about to retrace Leif Eriksson's thousand-years-ago voyage to the New World, and Land's End wanted Lagman to take his technology savvy to the field and track the ship's journey on its Web site. "My immediate answer was yes," Lagman chuckles (Halper 1999, p. 52). "Of course, I didn't know how to because I didn't know anything about satellite communications. But with information technology, attitude is more important than immediate knowledge." Today Lagman travels the world packing the digital tools he needs to transmit images and essays back to headquarters. He spends weeks with modern-day explorers. It's a long way from his old desk in Dodgeville, Wisconsin.

The managers at T.G.I. Friday's also offer their Gen X employees opportunities for adventure. The T.G.I.F. "Passport Program" rewards hardworking employees in all positions—cooks and dishwashers to hostesses and managers—with an opportunity to travel and work at any Friday's restaurant in the world. This recognition program is designed so that Xers can indulge their youthful wanderlust, but it also enables Xers to learn firsthand about cross-cultural differences and the challenges of operating a global business. In fact, T.G.I. Friday's "Passport Program" meets at least two of our survey's top four "importance" factors: *interesting work* and *opportunities to learn* (and it gives Xers a chance to build a lot of new relationships!).

Boomer Thomas Kasten spent thirty-three years with Levi Strauss as a vice president and talent advocate learning about what he calls the care and feeding of talent (Layne 2000). Now retired, Kasten has some advice for companies looking to retain their Xers. He suggests that "the two most important factors are the quality of management and employees' ability to work on way-cool things" (p. 1). Kasten showed Levi Strauss workers the balance sheet so they would understand how their work affected it. "When people are educated, they are engaged," Kasten says. "And if they are engaged, they are likely having fun. Who's going to leave a fun, engaging job if it pays well too?" (pp. 1–2). Kasten also created a Levi Strauss "Talent Inventory" database that lists every employee's skills and interests, both professional and personal. The purpose was to move people into jobs they would find interesting and challenging. For restless workers, the company sometimes had to create new positions, but doing so proved to be a good investment. Levi Strauss' strategy helped them retain their talent base.

There's an even simpler way to keep work interesting, Kasten says. Just make it fun! He encouraged after-hours beer bashes, told managers to take their teams out to lunch, and suggested some simple chitchat at meetings before getting down to business. The managers organized field trips to San Francisco fashion shows, to the openings of major movies, and to the wine country. Sometimes team outings were as simple as going en masse to the parking lot when the ice cream truck pulled up. "Spontaneous trips like these communicate a culture of sincerity and fun," Kasten says (Layne 2000, p. 3). This sounds like a culture that would be hard to beat and a place you might look forward to going to instead of dreading your day from the moment the alarm clock buzzes.

Few of us Boomer managers (and moms) know how to whoop it up like Southwest Airline founder Herb Kelleher, who built a company committed to having fun at work, or Wal-Mart's Sam Walton, who danced the hula in a grass skirt on Wall Street. Many of us are, in fact, "fun impaired"; however, fun can turn an Xer's job into a career as this respondent explains,

> I feel I've found a "career" rather than a job. Staying late, coming in on weekends ... they're not a chore because I love what I do. I've learned the value of fun at work, feedback, being able to voice concerns, and being recognized for good work—things that make a less-than-ideal salary bearable.
>
> 27-YEAR-OLD MARKETING COORDINATOR

This Xer agrees,

> I expected less satisfaction from my career—primarily fueled by the previous generation's comments about how boring work is and how money is its own reward. I did not expect to find such a fun job for which I am well paid. I thought if a job was lucrative it would be high-pressure and monotonous. Instead I've found creativity, a relaxed environment, and intellectual challenges that make coming to work enjoyable."
>
> 36-YEAR-OLD SENIOR RESEARCH ASSOCIATE

At the Hyatt Regency Hotel in Lexington, Kentucky, employees have a fun Thanksgiving tradition. They wrap a frozen turkey with electrical tape, then roll it down the loading dock, trying to knock down as many wine bottle "bowling pins" as possible. Winners get a pumpkin pie. Fun, however, doesn't have to be quite so rambunctious. Gen X author and consultant Bruce Tulgan cautions Boomer managers about trying to turn their offices into Romper Room. "This notion of young people bolting for the exits if they're not having a blast at work is probably the most bogus boomeresque misreading of Gen X that is out there," says Tulgan (Caminiti 1998, p. 3).

For Gen Xers, fun is often equated with flexibility. It can be as basic as getting to choose your own work hours or your work attire. Xers find the dress suits and oxford shirts that we wore (wear) to work quite humorous (and uncomfortable). They want to bring their own casual style to corporate America. Catalyst (2001) found that 54 percent of the Gen Xers surveyed want a casual dress code. How much fun are panty hose and high heels (or starched shirts and ties)? Xers grew up with a lot of autonomy, and they resist the restrictions of life in a traditional bureaucracy. They want fun, flexibility, and freedom, and when they find it, their job satisfaction soars, as another respondent's comment indicates:

> I have a lot more freedom to make my own decisions than I was expecting. I work out of my house (sales) in Dallas; my boss is in Chicago; and my company is located in Philadelphia. They are extremely hands-off and allow me to be autonomous. However, the support is there when and if needed. I figured this might just be a stepping-stone when I first entered the workforce, but I love what I do and the company I do it for. I consider myself lucky and try not to take it for granted.
>
> 30-YEAR-OLD ACCOUNT MANAGER

This young woman's job is an Xer's dream come true—freedom *and* flexibility! And, her comments remind us that X-friendly workplaces do exist. Here's another example from an Xer who has been pleasantly surprised:

> I expected the workforce to be very uptight and I was very wrong. I enjoy how laid back my job is and the flexibility of my hours.
>
> 28-YEAR-OLD SALES REP

My Gen X son, Matthew, agrees. His job commitment greatly increased when his employer let him work half-time for two months (with full pay) in order to finish his Ph.D. dissertation. A year later, after the birth of his baby, Matt was given the freedom to spend his mornings writing psychological assessment reports from home. His loyalty soared even higher. It appears that the more freedom we Boomer managers give this generation, the stronger their ties to their employers. Isn't this win-win?

OPPORTUNITIES FOR LEARNING

Gen Xers have a lust for learning! They want a learning curve that would give most Boomers a nosebleed. Money may be one driver, because the more we know, the more we're worth. But money, for this generation, is not the prime motivator for learning. Xers grew up teaching themselves computer skills. They were the first generation to have instant and continuous access to Internet information. No wonder they get bored very quickly with jobs that don't provide opportunities for learning. In fact, an astounding 77 percent of Gen Xers say they'd leave their current job if they could find "increased intellectual stimulation" elsewhere (Catalyst 2001). They fear "rusting out."

"Rust-out" is the lesser-known cousin of "burnout." We're talking about employees who feel uninspired and unchallenged and end up experiencing the same things that a victim of burnout would—depression, apathy, physical ailments, and psychological problems. And these days, it's young employees who are rusting away. University of North Carolina sociology professor Arne Kalleberg explains why: "The explosion of educational achievements has created [a corresponding] burst of underemployment" (Wylie 2004a, p. 40). Even though a labor boom looms, there's still a gap between Xer education/expectation levels and workplace opportunities.

I know you Xers are probably breathing a sigh of relief that someone has come up with a name for that underutilized, bored-to-tears, unchallenged feeling you have at work. You'll breathe even easier when you hear that some managers are taking action. Carolyn and Doug Bell, franchise owners of forty-eight Supercuts hair salons, quickly discovered that one of their Gen X employees' top priorities was to learn new skills. Carolyn now spends a lot of her management time organizing seminars on new hair products and new styling techniques. She even teaches courses in how to manage your own salon. She says, "At first I was a little fearful about bringing that last part up. I didn't want to send the message that we were pushing anyone out the door" (Caminiti 1998, p. 2). Actually, just the opposite has happened. In the first eighteen months of this learning initiative, the turnover in the Bells' salons dropped from 75 percent to 45 percent. Paradoxically, training employees for the next job boosts loyalty to the current one.

Chevron's XYZ program, launched in 2000, is another good example of a corporate program designed for "rust prevention." The "X" is for Gen X employees born between 1965 and 1976. The "Y" is for employees born between 1977 and 2000. And "Z" refers to future Chevron employees born after 2000. Chevron wanted to give younger employees a chance to network, identify mentoring opportunities, and encourage corporate and community involvement (Catalyst 2001). There are more than 250 Chevron employees involved in the XYZ network and about 80 percent of them are Gen X or Gen Y. The other 20 percent are Baby Boomers who recognize these young employees as the future of the company. They got involved as mentors and are trying to pass on their knowledge and expertise. The network is also helping to shape the company's future by lending Xers' unique perspective to the top decision makers. Chevron's strategic planning committee, made up of the CEO and division heads, went to XYZ for input. They used a strategic focus group of young employees to help shape Chevron's long-term business vision and mission. Chevron's XYZ program not only gives younger employees opportunities to network and build relationships throughout the company, but it involves them in key decision-making activities and helps them identify mentors who can assist them in career development.

However, formal mentoring programs are not prerequisite to creating an organization committed to fostering a learning environment. Mentoring should be a key accountability for every manager, but apparently it's not. While 83 percent of Boomers claim they are mentoring others, only 75 percent of Gen Xers report that they have a mentor (Nelson 2000). This is disappointing because mentoring pays big dividends, as this survey respondent's comment indicates:

> **I didn't believe that there could be a position so well suited for my education and experience. My boss is a mentor—something I was not expecting and am now so greatly appreciative of.**
>
> 28-YEAR-OLD PROJECT COORDINATOR

Mentoring involves more than the transfer of skills or knowledge; it includes coaching and career planning. Gen X employees want clearly defined career paths. The Catalyst (2001) research suggests that young professionals want customized career paths, including the opportunity to turn down relocation or to step off the partner track for the chance to handle work-life commitments. Companies that allow employees to plot out their personalized goals and execute them will benefit. Their employees will stick around.

Ernst & Young is a great example. According to a *CBS Evening News* report ("Women Seek Flexible Jobs" 2004), this company's attention to work-family issues is saving it $10 million a year in reduced turnover and improved productivity. Prior to launching reduced schedule and compressed workweek options, this Big Four accounting firm lost women at a much faster rate than men (even though they hired equal percentages of each). Now the statistics have flipped: More women than men stay. Not only have the firm's X-friendly policies led to higher female retention rates, they have also created higher morale *and* higher levels of productivity.

The Ernst & Young initiative is a bit different from simply offering women a mommy track, which typically results in less challenging assignments and a permanent detour from the partnership track. Thanks to the new policies, women are making partner while also making babies. Working reduced schedules or compressed workweeks has not led to career derailment. Accountants at Ernst & Young can have family flexibility without having to sacrifice opportunities to learn and advance. And the company has reduced costs along the way. The decision to offer similar policies should be a no-brainer for any manager—even those who are concerned only about the bottom line!

Smaller accounting firms are taking action as well. Before a mother-to-be at Plante & Moran takes maternity leave, she participates in special strategy meetings. These meetings aren't about how to juggle the demands of work; rather these soon-to-be mothers are paired with one of the firm's experienced parents, who acts as a mentor, helping the soon-to-be mother develop a strategy for handing off clients before her baby is born. The mentor also helps plan a strategy for returning to work, including how to pitch a part-time schedule to the new mother's boss. The parent pair-up is just one of the things Plante & Moran is doing to recruit and retain talented women. The company also offers flexible scheduling, four weeks' paid time off (five after five years), and six months unpaid parental leave for mothers and fathers; and during the busy spring tax season, the firm offers on-site day care. This company's Personal Tightrope Action (PTA) Committee focuses on the difficult balance of family and work, and the firm's handbook is full of tips on how to avoid taking work home and how to "underschedule" yourself (this may be the world's most unusual corporate training manual).

Plante & Moran's X-friendly philosophy can be attributed to one of the firm's cofounders, Frank Moran. Moran ignores the idea of a set work schedule and allows his 1,178 employees to set their own schedules, enabling them to serve their clients while also balancing their lives. Managers promote learning by matching each new employee with a "buddy" (mentor). The organization also offers leadership training designed specifically for women. "The Southfield, Michigan-based firm has the largest percentage of female partners (19%, and those are all equity partners, mind you) of any of the 15 largest accounting firms, including the Big Four" (McGregor 2004, p. 96). And at 14 percent, Plante & Moran also has the lowest turnover rate in the industry. "Bill Bufe, Plante & Moran's Director of Human Resources, estimates that replacing a $75,000 employee costs the firm a year's salary" (p. 97). This company's practices are not just X-friendly; they benefit the bottom line!

WORK-LIFE BALANCE

Xers do not live to work; they work to live. Remember, in our survey, *salary* was ranked twelfth out of fifteen in importance for women and ninth for men, and *job status/prestige* was ranked last by both. For most Xers, making money is not nearly as important as enjoying life, and they're on a quest for organizations that understand their priorities. One such employer is the SAS Institute, a privately owned software company based in Cary, North Carolina. SAS has strong employee loyalty and a turnover rate one-fifth the industry average. The company has fabulous on-site day care that gives parents a chance to eat lunch with their kids and take breaks to go play with them. SAS has a flat organizational structure with few levels of management and lots of employee involvement in decision making. The standard workweek is thirty-five hours and every employee has a private office. SAS is rewarding workers with something better than pay: They're providing an X-friendly work environment (Larson 2002).

Autodesk Corporation, based in northern California, has 3,500 employees around the world. The company provides workers with several X-friendly options, including paid volunteer time, child-care subsidies, and sabbaticals. At Autodesk, there's no such thing as being late. Employees get to design their work around their lives at home. And there is no set number of sick days either. In fact, people don't even track them. Managers simply expect employees to use sick leave responsibly. In a time when young professionals are putting more value on personal and family commitments than they are on work commitments, companies that offer this kind of flexibility will find it easier to recruit the next generation of leaders.

A lot of other companies are jumping on the flexibility bandwagon, allowing employees to have flexible work hours, letting them work from home, or offering part-time options such as job sharing. These options are especially attractive to Gen X moms such as this respondent who wrote,

> My current position is a job share, so I work twenty to twenty-two hours a week. This works well with my balance of life since I have young children. This is very satisfying right now in my career.
>
> 33-YEAR-OLD RECRUITER

Approximately 31 percent of large organizations offer a job share option, but typically this option is not offered to those in management. Verizon is an exception. Two women in the company's Philadelphia office share the title of V.P. of Employee Communications. Charlotte Schutzman works Monday and Tuesday; Sue Manix works Thursday and Friday; and they alternate Wednesdays. "The two women have job shared for ten years, acquiring promotions, numerous bonuses, and a twenty-person staff along the way. With each having children at home, this arrangement allows them the flexibility to better balance their work and family responsibilities" (Robbins 2003, p. 477).

Catalyst (2001) found that 61 percent of women said they would leave their job for one that was more flexible; 52 percent said they'd go elsewhere in order to work fewer hours; and 51 percent said they'd quit if another job offered them the chance to telecommute. According to the U.S. Department of Labor, almost 29 million full-time workers (that's almost 29 percent) are already working in jobs that allow some schedule flexibility ("29 Million Have Flex Schedules" 2003). It is important to note that nearly two-thirds of the companies that allow workers to vary their own schedules report that they don't have official flex-time policies. So, Boomer managers need not wait until there's an official corporate policy—just do it!

OFF/ON RAMPS

X-friendly companies not only need "off ramps" and "slow lanes" for working parents who decide to step off the career track to raise their kids; they also need "on ramps" that ensure a smooth return. In a marketing survey of stay-at-home moms, Reach Advisors found that many Gen X moms plan to return to the working world. Of Boomer moms at home, 34 percent wanted to go back to work, whereas 46 percent of Gen X moms at home plan to resume their careers (Wallis 2004). A week-long *CBS Evening News* series on "Women's Work" in 2004 referred to this as "sequencing." The reporter suggested that women could have it all—just not in the same life season. Getting back on track after a career hiatus is, however, often easier said than done. Here's what one Gen X mother has to say about her decision to return to work after the birth of her baby:

Off Ramps/On Ramps

Part of me would like to leave the working world, if we could afford it, and just be a mom for a while, but I'm pretty sure my career would suffer if I did. Everyone seems to buy into the "use it or lose it" theory. I'd worry about getting back into my profession later on if I completely left work for a while. I know I could do it, but it wouldn't be easy. Staying home for three or four years, then going back to work, would be a hard transition. Things change. I wouldn't lose my knowledge, but I'd question my skills. Going back in for a job interview would be intimidating. If I were up against somebody who was transferring from another job, I would think the employer might want to go with her instead of me because I'd been out of the field for a few years. I think a better option would be to work in a part-time private practice. A co-worker of mine did that. The first year she made $75,000, and the next year she made $30,000. Luckily, they can afford that. For me right now, it's just too risky.

Unfortunately, this Gen Xer's concerns are well founded. Reentry can be difficult. Even though *balance* is the new buzzword, few companies have designated on ramps. Deloitte & Touche is an exception. This organization is confronting the on-ramp challenge head-on. In 2004 it launched a program called "Personal Pursuits" that lets above-average performers take up to five years off. The unpaid leave allows people to leave for personal reasons and then encourages them to come back. In the meantime, the company covers professional licensing fees and pays for week-long annual training sessions. "Such efforts have spawned their own goofy jargon. Professionals who return to their ex-employers are known as boomerangs, and the effort to reel them back in is called alumni relations" (Wallis 2004, p. 56). Programs like these enable women (and men) to fully enjoy all the seasons of their lives, and the managers at Deloitte & Touche have learned that they can support balanced lives and still balance their books.

It is time for all managers to recognize that they can do something to change the workplace. You can do it so your Gen X employees will be more satisfied at work, or you can do it for your bottom line. Satisfied employees not only stick around longer, they are more productive. Even if your Xers don't prove to be lifers, their good feelings will follow them and they will not only recommend your company to their friends, but they may boomerang back to you someday. There aren't many cool places to work, but there are plenty of ways managers can create some.

BECOMING AN EMPLOYER OF CHOICE

It's not that difficult to create a more X-friendly workplace. There are already plenty of existing role models. One only has to pick up a copy of *Fast Company* or *Wired* to see new images of organization. In periodicals like these we read about people like Frank Caccamo, corporate V.P. and CIO of Reynolds & Reynolds. Gen Xers represent 40 percent of his I.T. department, and because of that, Caccamo has altered how his department communicates. He's instituted regular all-hands meetings that allow individual employees to report on their own initiatives and ask probing questions of management. Caccamo has also restructured his two-hundred-employee department by turning tightly structured job roles into broad job families that offer more task variety and, hence, more interesting work. This restructuring was done with the full participation of the employees. This is key! The first step in any culture change initiative is to find ways to get the stakeholders involved. State-of-the-art processes such as Appreciative Inquiry and Future Search are useful tools for involving large groups in the design and implementation of an X-friendly organization.

Don't let budgetary constraints keep you frozen in the status quo. Many X-driven changes will cost nothing at all. For example, Gen Xers look for tangible results on a daily basis. Remember, they grew up in an instant society and they want instant results. Is there a way you can give them more frequent feedback? All employees, but especially Xers, respond positively to feedback that's more frequent than an annual review. Look for more ways in which you can give workers personal credit for the tangible results they achieve.

Remember Xers' lust for learning? A manager may be afraid of giving an employee "too much training" because training increases an employee's marketability, but it also increases employee loyalty. Give an Xer some useful training and you'll find it's like putting a fresh battery in the Energizer bunny. Training inspires most Xers to go out and do their own jobs better, and organizations that provide ongoing development typically have low turnover. Their employees stay around for more opportunities to learn and grow. There is a caveat: Opportunities to learn without opportunities to apply can lead to even greater frustration. The problem in some organizations is not the absence of training opportunities, but rather the absence of appropriate ways to utilize newly acquired skills. In situations of skill mismatch or underutilization, motivation suffers and the organizational investment in learning is lost.

Simply being a prestigious employer means little to this generation. If you want Xers to come to work for you (and stay for more than two years), you will have to create an egalitarian culture, practice open communication, offer frequent feedback, engage them in decision making, make work interesting and fun, provide lots of opportunities for learning, and offer schedule flexibility. In so doing you will become an employer of choice for this generation; not only will your retention rates greatly improve, but you will find it much easier to attract high-talent employees to fill future employment needs. It is well documented that the single best method for recruiting new employees is to do a great job with managing your current ones (Ahlrichs 2000). Create an X-friendly work environment, and then use it to sell your business to new recruits in interviews or at job fairs. Have examples of how your work-life policy is helping individual employees balance home and job responsibilities. It's something prospects won't find at every booth in the room. If you're looking for an edge in recruiting young talent, try offering employee sabbaticals or paid volunteer time off. According to Nancy Ahlrichs, author of *Competing for Talent* (2000), community service buttons on company Web sites get more hits than job openings buttons.

Prudential provides a great example of innovative recruiting practices. The company's recruiters incorporate community service programs into their recruitment efforts, giving prospective employees an idea of what types of volunteer activities and nonprofit organizations the company's employees support. At recruitment fairs, job applicants, while chatting with recruiters, pack backpacks for children who've been removed from their homes and are headed to foster care. Attendance at recruitment functions has quadrupled since Cindy Lowden, Prudential's V.P. of succession planning and accelerated development programs, implemented this Gen X–focused strategy.

The current buyers' job market is about to come to a screeching halt, and, the minute the labor market rebounds, all of your frustrated, overworked, underappreciated employees will leave—in a flash! Companies that haven't taken time to build loyalty will find themselves scraping the bottom of the job-pool barrel, especially for managers and skilled workers. Companies that have built loyalty will find that loyal employees not only stay longer, thus cutting recruitment costs, but refer their friends, thus providing a pool of eager prospects.

Can it really be done? Can we create sane and satisfying workplaces? Sure, but it's not easy and it's not common . . . yet. Out of the 1,200 Gen Xers we surveyed, very few offered up solutions to their disillusionment. This Xer is an exception. She's not willing to passively wait:

I've learned that I have a direct role to play in shaping my career. I've learned that I can create my future and overcome changes imposed on me. I have a choice.

37-YEAR-OLD VICE PRESIDENT

Yes, she does and so do you! We all have a choice. Will you be a follower or a leader in the neXt revolution?

CHAPTER 7

Revolution X

There is much work to be accomplished in order for twenty-first-century organizations to inspire the hearts and souls of their Gen X employees. The values of traditional, bureaucratic organizations are like night to the day of the values of the new workforce, and they increasingly clash with the values of other generations as well. We've seen integrity implosions at Enron, WorldCom, Arthur Anderson, and Fannie Mae (to name only a few), and many of us haven't just read about them in the headlines or heard about them on TV; we've worked for them (or the thousands of other companies that operate in similar ways). We've seen leaders and entire corporations come tumbling down because of a combination of ineptness, big egos, bad judgment, and a lack of integrity. We, their employees, are becoming increasingly disillusioned.

It's very disappointing when we see a large amount of money wasted by top executives daily on frivolous things (landscaping constantly changing with the season or midseason decorating of buildings and offices, done and redone several times because of a whim, even a VERY expensive dog to chase geese from the sidewalk, etc.), yet there are no raises or bonuses and thousands of people are being laid off.

27-YEAR-OLD BUSINESS ANALYST

Management is very lacking.... The owner of my company is in jail, and the VP used one of my computers to look up porn.

26-YEAR-OLD STAFFING SPECIALIST

Employees who work in companies like these react in various ways. They often quit, complain, or commit organizational sabotage (e.g., steal company property or shirk their job responsibilities). Such reactions do not promote positive change and often are more rebellious than revolutionary. So, what are the positive action options? What can a frustrated, disillusioned Gen Xer do to turn her anger (or apathy) into action? She can join the neXt revolution.

Think of this as a feminist revolution with a new twist: one that moves beyond breaking the glass ceiling to breaking the cultural mold of traditional organizations, thus creating saner and more satisfying workplaces for all of us, regardless of gender or generation. While the Boomer feminist revolution focused on job equality, this revolution focuses on job fulfillment. Gen X women (and men) can unite in efforts to eliminate outdated, inflexible organizational policies and unethical business practices. Instead of demanding a key to the executive restroom, you can lobby for new kinds of "rest" rooms: break rooms where people can use play as a vehicle for radical innovation. In so doing, you will help to design workplaces where people are as important as profits, and results are measured instead of face time.

We believe the women of Generation X, with their strong focus on relationships and work-life balance, are in a great position to lead this revolution. Indeed, you must! It is unrealistic to think that those who hold positions of power in traditional organizations will readily change the policies and practices from which they personally profit. They must be shown a new way. This chapter offers a road map that you can use to capture the attention of employers. The time is right to begin: The pending job shortage provides a powerful platform from which you can launch the neXt revolution.

THE ROAD MAP

This chapter lays out four roads to revolution (Figure 2). Even though Gen Xers have shared many defining moments, each person is unique. Each individual's personality and life situation will make some roads look more attractive and viable than others. Therefore, as you take up the mantle of revolution, you have choices about the particular path you may want to follow. As you look at Figure 2, imagine standing in the middle

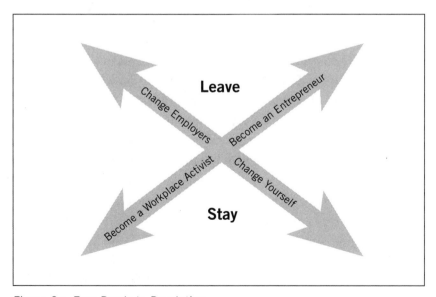

Figure 2 > Four Roads to Revolution

of the "X." The very fact that you are reading this book suggests that you are at a choice point in your life—the proverbial crossroads. Which road are you willing to take? Which best fits your current life situation? Which excites you? Which will enable you to join our revolution? The two roads at the top of the "X" lead to external change. If you choose one of them, you will leave your current employer and either find a more X-friendly workplace or join the millions of Americans who are entrepreneurs. Even though these two options may not appear revolutionary on the surface, if enough people choose them, traditional organizations will be forced to change (remember the pending labor shortage).

The two roads at the bottom of the "X" lead to internal change, either inside your current organization or inside yourself. Taking the road labeled "Become a Workplace Activist" requires learning the behaviors of a positive and proactive workplace revolutionary. The road labeled "Change Yourself" is the most difficult road of all. It requires the willingness to take a quantum leap in personal growth, changing yourself in depth. This road leads to psychological and spiritual revolution. It is premised on the belief that when we change ourselves, everything around us changes as well (including our workplaces).

I don't believe there is one best road to revolution. In fact, I have traveled them all in my thirty-plus years in the workplace. As a child of the sixties, I spent much of my early career as a workplace activist (often an angry and arrogant one). When my activism didn't create the desired results, I left in an ongoing search for an enlightened employer. At midlife I opted out of the corporate rat race and became an entrepreneur. I founded WiseWork, a coaching/consulting organization committed to workplace transformation. Gradually I drifted back inside a traditional organization, perhaps the most traditional of all organizations—a university. I began my reentry quite innocently as an adjunct professor, but over the course of a few years I found myself a full-time employee—immersed in an academic bureaucracy (a Jesuit Catholic one at that). Now, at fiftysomething, I'm focusing much of my revolutionary energy on changing myself, deeply believing that as I "show up" differently at work, the external workplace will reflect my internal changes.

Before we lay out our road map to revolution, we want to make it absolutely clear that we not only believe there is no one best road to revolution, but we also think you can choose to travel multiple roads simultaneously. Many of us were taught either/or decision making, but we advocate that you consider a more pluralistic approach. You may, of course, choose to explore only one road, or you may integrate the skills from the internal roads into your journey down an external road. In systems theory there is a concept called *equifinality*. It means that a system can reach the same final state from differing conditions and a variety of paths. In other words, there is no one right way to get to a targeted destination (Shelton 1999). There are numerous ways to leverage change, and there are at least four roads to workplace revolution.

ROUTE 1: CHANGE EMPLOYERS

We who live in affluent, democratic countries have the freedom to vote with our feet by leaving employers who are abusive and companies that still manage people as if they were machines. If you are in one of these workplaces, we encourage you to actively seek out the kinds of X-friendly organizations discussed in the previous chapter. While they are not yet the norm, they are rapidly increasing in number, and there are many periodicals, books, and organizations you can use to help you with your job search. One of my favorites is the business magazine *Fast Company* (which consistently has the highest percentage of female readers of any business publication). Each issue covers organizations (and leaders) that are daring to do things differently, and the *Fast Company* Web site has a research directory of the world's most interesting and innovative companies.

Other cutting-edge business magazines include *Business 2.0*, *Wired*, and *Business Ethics*. A number of business books also describe X-friendly workplaces. If you read only one such book, read *Maverick: The Success Story Behind the World's Most Unusual Workplace* (Semler 1993). In this book, Ricardo Semler, CEO of Semco, S.A., describes his company's revolutionary journey from rigid hierarchy to an open-book organization with a rotating CEO. My husband, Jim, and I were privileged to visit the Semco headquarters in São Paulo, Brazil, and we found the company to be just as radical (and impressive) as this quote from the book jacket suggests: "*Maverick* is the true and fascinating story of Semco, a company that defies all conventional wisdom and yet is successful in one of the world's most daunting economic climates. A story filled with wisdom and humor, told by those who led and lived through this business revolution, it is must reading for everyone in business, especially those looking for the workplace of their dreams."

Along with these revolutionary books and magazines, there are a growing number of revolutionary business organizations. Most of them sponsor inspiring and enlightening conferences that showcase organizations that are daring to be different, and they leave the attendees with new visions of workplace possibilities. They can give you the fuel you need to make it to your next employment destination. Attending any of the following conferences would be a good way to network with a prospective X-friendly employer:

- *Fast Company*'s Real-Time Conference and Woman-to-Woman Summit

- Great Places to Work Conference

- The International Conference on Business and Consciousness

- Businesses for Social Responsibility Conference

- eWomenNetwork.com International Conference and Business Expo

Bigger Versus Better

As you attend conferences like these and peruse progressive business magazines, you are unlikely to find a lot of large, Fortune 500 companies represented. Their size alone makes them difficult to change, and like dinosaurs of old, they are unlikely to avoid extinction. They are simply too inflexible to survive long-term in a world that is changing at warp speed, and many Xers are starting to realize that bigger doesn't necessarily mean better, as these survey comments indicate:

> I have been granted more opportunity and responsibility than I ever imagined fresh out of college. I have begun my career in a small company with a great deal of potential. I believe this is why I have been given so many opportunities.
>
> 26-YEAR-OLD DIRECTOR OF OPERATIONS

> I started working with smaller companies and I honestly loved it. I thought working at a large company would be even better. I was wrong. We are always stressed about getting laid off. Granted, I make more for doing an easier job, but I liked my first job the best. I felt fulfillment.
>
> 29-YEAR-OLD REVENUE SPECIALIST

The good news is that there are many small businesses—one of which may have just the right culture for you. You may, in fact, be surprised to learn that over 98 percent of businesses in the United States have fewer than a hundred employees (Table 9). This is shocking to most

TABLE 9	NUMBER OF U.S. BUSINESSES BY SIZE OF FIRM
1 to 4 employees	2,697,839
5 to 9 employees	1,019,105
10 to 19 employees	616,064
20 to 99 employees	518,258
100 to 499 employees	85,304
500 to 999 employees	8,572
1,000 to 1,499 employees	2,854
1,500 to 2,499 employees	2,307
2,500 to 4,999 employees	1,706
5,000 to 9,999 employees	871
10,000 employees or more	936

Source: U.S. Census Bureau Web site, www.census.gov

people because we tend to hear about large businesses. However, the really hip companies that I know about are all relatively small organizations. One of my clients, an energy supply/consulting group, is a great example. Boomer founder Dwain Willingham created an organization in which Gen Xers feel at home. Not only do they have access to flex hours and a casual dress code, but they also have the opportunity to create their own job descriptions and set their own salaries (as long as they produce the corresponding results). Open-forum, all-hands meetings are held weekly. There are no sacred cows or executive secrets. This is an open-book organization in which financial information is freely shared. Annually, all employees join together for a strategic thinking/planning retreat. Perhaps the most radical aspect of this unusual culture is the glaring absence of job titles and executive perks (remember, status symbols were at the bottom of the importance list for both male and female survey respondents). All employees share a large open workspace (no cubicles, no offices for the owners). It is an egalitarian work culture that supports communication, learning, and innovation, all of which are very important to the neXt generation.

Our survey results show a statistically significant negative relationship (i.e., bigger company = less happy workers) between the number of employees in a respondent's organization and the ratings on the following job satisfaction/organizational commitment questions:

Q 17: How satisfied are you with your job (the actual tasks you do on a day-to-day basis)?

Q 18: How satisfied are you with your organization as a place to work?

Q 19: How committed are you to your organization—its values, goals, and business practices?

Q 20: How satisfied are you with your organization's leadership?

According to our survey results, employees in smaller organizations are more satisfied with their jobs and more committed to their organizations than are their peers in larger organizations. So you may want to investigate the smaller employers in your preferred employment location. We think you'll find them to be more flexible, and often more enjoyable, places to work. Small businesses operate with a minimum of bureaucracy; there are few rules and little red tape. You're likely to get to dabble in a lot of different projects (rather than work on one narrowly defined task), which means you'll get more opportunities for learning. You're also likely to have more involvement in decision making. And, most small firms tend to operate like a family, offering Xers better opportunities to meet relationship needs. Small businesses don't always pay as much, but your work-life balance needs are much more likely to be met. Of the U.S. firms with fewer than a hundred employees: 62 percent offer flextime; 58 percent offer telecommuting; 41 percent allow employees to bring their children to work in emergencies; and 27 percent offer compressed workweeks (Wall 2003).

Nonprofits

If you decide to explore the road that leads to a smaller organization, you might want to explore small nonprofit organizations. Many of my Gen X MBA students, in their search for more meaningful jobs, have discovered increased job satisfaction in the nonprofit sector. Stacy is one of them:

Show Me the Meaning

Sprint provided my first job out of college. Between my junior and senior years, I worked as an intern within the Sprint Local division. They offered me a full-time position upon graduation. At the time it was a dream come true—working for a prominent corporation close to home. I worked with them for a year on special projects, including revenue recovery and account reconciliation. I then transferred into a finance role supporting the network engineers in the PCS division. I worked on process improvements, developed tools to aid the engineers in their cost-effective decision making, and created executive-level reports. After five years in this role, I started to feel a sort of quarterlife crisis.

What was I doing with my life? I wanted to add value, make a difference in the lives of others. I wanted to spend my forty-plus-hour workweek doing something worthwhile that I felt passionate about and loved. I grew up in a family in which my mom stayed home and my dad was a hardworking blue collar. I saw working as a paycheck. But as I gained experience in the working world, I needed something more fulfilling. I began to grow distant to my job. The values of the company did not even come close to matching what I found valuable. I no longer got satisfaction or motivation from the bottom line.

From my graduate studies, an assignment in Dr. Shelton's Leadership and Motivation class stands out most in my mind. She gave us the task of creating and executing a service project. I learned from this experience that the gift of volunteering returns an incredible amount of fulfillment and enjoyment. So I began to volunteer more and found my passion in working with underprivileged children. I learned the village raises the child. And just one loving, caring adult can change the life of a lost child. I met an individual who works in public relations for an international children's charity. His job was my dream job. He travels to different countries and meets with families who receive great benefits through his organization. He helps to influence and change lives in such a positive way!

So I began researching nonprofit organizations. The more I read, the more I realized that's where my heart is—working for an organization whose mission, goals, and values are to aid humankind. And I found it! Through prayers and research, I was led to an organization that needed someone with my financial systems experience. The organization's mission statement is one I can readily identify with: "We build relationships of mutual respect and support while raising awareness in our own country of the needs and gifts of the poor and the mission outreach of the Church." How fortunate I feel to receive this life-changing opportunity to practice what I cherish most: faith and helping others. You won't find that in the corporate world.

There are many other Gen Xers who are making a move in this direction; and many others, like this survey respondent, are contemplating such a move:

> **Since I am the first person in my family to work in a corporate environment, I had no idea what to expect. I have only worked in large corporations, and over the years I am realizing that I might be more fulfilled working in a small nonprofit environment instead. I'm tired of just being a number and only seeing a very small part of the business.**
>
> 29-YEAR-OLD FINANCIAL ANALYST

Buyer Beware

As you begin to interview for a new position (whether in the for-profit or nonprofit arena), remember the slogan Buyer Beware! Lots of organizations talk the talk, while few of their managers actually walk it. Approach your job search with the optimism of Pollyanna, the diligence of a good auditor, and the sleuth of a CIA operative. Talk to as many stakeholders as possible—not just recruiters and the hiring manager. Ask to visit with folks who would be your peers or co-workers, and, if possible, talk to customers, suppliers, and former employees. Due diligence pays big dividends!

Obtain 360-degree feedback, not only about the organization in general, but about your potential manager in particular. You need to go beyond such standard questions as How much vacation time do I get? and When will I be eligible for a promotion? You need to find out about those job factors that are important to you, whether it's relationships with your boss and peers, interesting work, opportunities for learning, or flexible work policies. Arm yourself with some good questions and go in realizing it's not just the company that's interviewing you; you're interviewing the company! To assist you in making a good decision, we've prepared a baker's dozen questions that you can use to help discern whether a prospective employer deserves an X-friendly stamp of approval.

1. How do you develop positive relationships with your employees?

2. How frequently do you spend time talking to employees about their concerns or ideas?

3. Does the company sponsor periodic team-building activities (e.g., field trips, movie outings, beer nights)?

4. Have you ever had an employee who got bored with her job and wanted something more challenging? If so, what did you do? If not, how would you handle the situation?

5. What training or unique learning opportunities do you offer?

6. If I found a workshop or conference that would improve my job skills, would you help me find a way to go?

7. What's the most fun you've had at work this year?

8. Have you ever "walked in your workers' shoes" by shadowing one of your employees for a day?

9. How frequently do you give your employees feedback on their performance?

10. If I went above and beyond job expectations, how would you recognize my efforts?

11. How do you encourage employees to get better at their jobs?

12. Is there a mentoring or coaching program here?

13. Do you have a flextime or telecommuting policy that will help me balance my work commitments with my life?

As you explore new companies, don't forget to ask how many women are in senior management positions. Remember, the Catalyst research Laura discussed in Chapter 3 shows that companies with at least a 20 percent concentration of women at the senior level not only achieve higher financial performance, but also have more female-friendly people policies as well. Of course, not all Gen Xers will have an opportunity to work in an X-friendly organization. There simply aren't enough of them available—yet. So, even though we encourage you to proactively search for an enlightened employer, there may not be one in your preferred location. If not, you may need to choose a different road to revolution.

ROUTE 2: BECOME AN ENTREPRENEUR

Margaret Heffernan (2002), a successful female entrepreneur who's owned five businesses in the past ten years, believes it's time for women to accept that they work differently from men. She says her generation of glass-ceiling breakers worked hard to fit into a testosterone-driven business world. They were afraid to acknowledge gender differences because they feared that "different from" would be interpreted as "less than" (p. 66). Heffernan refers to Gen X women as "the *Legally Blond* generation." Like Reese Witherspoon's character in the movie, Gen X women are capable of being "girly and smart." Xer women aren't interested in compromise or assimilation. If they're unable to live their values in a traditional organization, they often opt out. "Rather than fight the system, this next generation of women simply *dismisses* the system. Instead, these women seek places to work that value individuals. . . . They seek places that are transparent and collaborative . . . that look more like a network than a pyramid" (p. 66). When Gen X women can't find an X-friendly workplace, they often start one.

Dreams Come True

In 2003 the Center for Women's Business Research counted 10.1 million privately held businesses in the United States in which women owned at least half of the company. That's a lot of women in charge. In fact, if you were to pick eleven women at random from the phone book, one of them would likely be an entrepreneur. Rene Jones, president of the Philadelphia chapter of the National Association of Women Business Owners, explains, "One in 11 women in the U.S. is a business owner. As business owners we are increasingly a dynamic part of the economy in every city in the U.S. But most of all, this information shows that for women, the dream of entrepreneurship can be a viable reality" (Center for Women's Business Research 2003, p. 2).

The number of women-owned businesses has increased 103 percent in the past ten years (Krotz 2004). Women-owned businesses generate 18.2 million jobs and contribute more than $2.3 trillion in sales to the economy (Franklin 2003). Not only are these businesses having a huge effect on the economy, but they also are growing much faster than their men-owned competition. The Center for Women's Business Research estimates that between 1997 and 2002, the number of companies in which women held a majority ownership grew by 11 percent; that's more than 1.5 times the rate of firms overall. During this same period, the employment rate was growing at 8 percent across the country, but at women-owned firms employment increased by 18 percent. Also, whereas sales at firms were up by 24 percent nationwide, at firms where women were in charge sales were up 32 percent (Franklin 2003).

Depending on where you live in the country, you'll find women choosing the road to entrepreneurship at slightly different rates. Women in the South are choosing this option less frequently than their sisters in the North. Mississippi has the lowest percentage of women business owners (4 percent); Alaska has the highest, with 9.4 percent of adult women owning businesses (Center for Women's Business Research 2002). In my city of employment (Kansas City, Missouri), women own 30 percent of all small businesses. Women-owned businesses here have *twice* the growth rate of other small businesses and only *half* the failure rate, according to Lynn Reaser, chief economist and senior market strategist for Bank of America Capital Management.

For the nation as a whole, since 1997, female entrepreneurship has been growing at *twice* the rate of the national average. Plus, the women who are taking the plunge and starting these businesses are more qualified than ever before, and that means they are more likely to succeed. In the past decade, more female entrepreneurs have come from middle management backgrounds or have worked in senior or executive positions. Not only do they have the prerequisite management skills; most are choosing to launch businesses in the same fields in which they've been trained. Only 33 percent of women who started firms twenty or more years ago had worked in a related field before they started their companies; but in the past decade, 51 percent of women launched businesses that were in closely related fields. Harvard Business School professor Myra Hart comments, "This is positive because we know that the more closely related the business is to the owner's previous work experience, the greater the likelihood of success" (Center for Women's Business Research 2001, p. 3).

Historically, women have found it almost impossible to find financial backing to launch their own business ventures, but this seems to be changing. Kathleen Goodwin found the money she needed to start iMakeNews, an electronic marketing company that does work for Shell Oil Company and Oprah. "The environment is far more accepting and far more open," Goodwin said after her company was able to raise $1.7 million in financing in one summer (Rosenberg 2003, p. 1). Women today can turn to national organizations like Springboard, a not-for-profit group that helps connect women-owned businesses with the capital they need to grow. Participants start by going through "boot camp," in which hundreds of women submit business plans. "Only a handful are chosen to participate in a six-week coaching process that includes critique on everything from the business plan to posture, culminating in presentations to a crowd of venture capitalists" (p. 1).

There are plenty of other women who are experimenting with self-employment while still employed. Jeffrey Gruenert (1999) used data collected for the Current Population Survey to analyze this group, which he dubbed the second-job entrepreneurs. Laura and I are good examples. Laura works as a full-time television reporter and wrote this book as a second job, while I work as a professor and consult with businesses as a second job (so this book must make me a third-job entrepreneur). There were about 2 million second-job entrepreneurs in the United States in 1998, but by 2004 that number swelled to 10 million (Fry, Stoner, and Hattwick 2004). Second-job entrepreneuring is a way to take a little test drive down the self-employment road before getting off your employer's full-time paycheck bus.

Gen X-Preneurs

One-fifth of all small business owners in the United States are Gen Xers, and the Gen X start-up rate is three times that of older age groups (Caminiti 1998). "By a two-to-one margin Xers say they'd prefer owning a business to being a top executive in a large company. By a four-to-one margin they choose it over holding an important position in politics or government" (Ericson 1998).

Some Gen X women (and men) become entrepreneurs by default rather than decision. They start their career journey as a passenger on someone else's bus, only to be left stranded by the side of a deserted highway. The recent wave of organizational downsizings, coupled with a weak economy, has put a lot of talented young professionals out on the street:

> **I am an independent consultant and the market is very tough right now. I had always imagined myself to be working in a stable, secure, full-time position somewhere. I couldn't find one that suited my varied interests and my needs for autonomy, so I am determined to make my own path.**
>
> 30-YEAR-OLD CONSULTANT

This woman became a consultant not only because the job market was tight but because she wanted interesting work (the factor ranked number three by the women in our survey) and lots of flexibility. She is certainly not alone. Many of her peers are finding a way to creatively turn their competencies into cash. Rebecca Ryan is a good example. She's a Gen X woman who started a consulting firm after going through five jobs in four years because of the failings of her bosses to connect with Gen Xers (Dresang 2003). Ryan identified an innovative business opportunity: teach Boomer managers how to bridge the Boomer-Xer gap. She launched her own consulting firm and now helps organizations become X-friendly workplaces. The primary product of her five-partner firm is competitive intelligence about the neXt generation of workers. The firm's Hot Jobs–Cool Communities Web site is worth checking out (www.hotjobs-coolcommunities.com). It ranks cities as to their Gen X-friendliness based on such factors as crime rates, commute times, cultural diversity, and night spots. Ryan tells women, "Sometimes the world has a bigger dream for you than you have for yourself." We say, go for it!

Both your current financial situation and your parents' career choices can influence whether you become an entrepreneur (Dunn and Holtz-Eakin 2003). According to data collected from the National Longitudinal Survey, men are more likely to try self-employment if their fathers were self-employed, and women are more likely to become self-employed if their mothers were. But don't let these data keep you from choosing this path! This study also concluded that, for men, financial assets were closely tied to the decision to leave a paid job for self-employment. In contrast, financial assets did not seem to play a significant role in women's self-employment decisions. For a Gen X woman, career frustrations coupled with motherhood are often the driving forces toward entrepreneurship.

Mom-Preneurs

Entrepreneurship is especially attractive to Gen X moms. Many women who feel compelled to parent their children on a full-time basis also want (or need) to earn income. NBC's *Today Show* (Couric 2004) aired a three-part series about this rapidly growing segment of the female population: mom-preneurs. Some of the featured women launched their businesses by accident; others approached their entrepreneurial endeavors more methodically.

Mary Norton, a Charleston, South Carolina, stay-at-home mom, is an example of the accidental approach. Mary started making handbags after the birth of her second daughter in an effort to overcome her postpartum depression and cope with her recent lupus diagnosis. As she engaged in this creative endeavor, her depression went away almost immediately, and the lupus quickly went into remission. Friends loved her designs and convinced her to display three bags at a local salon. All three bags sold quickly. Within six months her business, named MooRoo (her daughters' nicknames), had more than $65,000 in orders. Six years later, these custom handbags have become the rage of celebrities, and a long list of stars (including Halle Berry) have been seen carrying a MooRoo bag down the red carpet on Oscar night. Mary has discovered that she can be a successful businesswoman while also continuing to be a full-time mom. On the *Today Show* she summed up her life with these words: "I'm growing a great business, but more important, I'm growing two great women" (Couric 2004).

Lisa Druxman, another mom-preneur featured on the *Today Show* series, approached her business plan a bit more intentionally. She had worked for seven years in the fitness industry prior to becoming a mother and was searching for a way to build a business that would enable her to use her skills and experience and still be a stay-at-home mom. The result was a fitness class for moms and babies called "Stroller Strides." New mothers sing, stretch, and stride with their babies in tow. What started as a one-person, one-city operation quickly expanded. Within one year, Lisa was receiving calls from women from all over the country. "Stroller Strides" classes are now offered in seventeen states, and more expansion is in the works. Women talk and their businesses grow!

ROUTE 3: BECOME A WORKPLACE ACTIVIST

If you choose not to start your own business or find an X-friendly employer, then perhaps your road to revolution is to stay right where you are and become a workplace activist—an advocator and educator of new ways of doing things within your current organization, continuing the work Boomer women began. As the statistics in Chapter 3 (and the survey results in Chapter 5) indicate, there is still much work to do. The need for workplace reform remains pervasive. Activism is another important road to revolution.

Gen X women are in a position to reinvent the crusade for equality, changing the tone from the anger and distrust of my generation to optimism and trust. Riane Eisler discusses the need to change the face of feminism in her provocative book *The Chalice and the Blade* (1988). For Eisler, the role of women in business is a vital societal issue that goes far beyond breaking the glass ceiling and achieving wage equality. Workplace equality is not merely a question of allowing women to play by the same rules as men. It's about re-creating the game of work. This is the challenge of the neXt revolution.

Eisler's research reveals the limitations of Darwinian thinking (survival of the fittest). She presents biological and archaeological data that indicate cooperation is as important as competition in the evolutionary process. We Boomer feminists certainly worked hard to shift our organizations from domination to partnership. However, like many other social activists before us, we often attempted to eliminate inequities using the tactics of the system we were trying to change. In Chapter 2 I discussed a well-known Boomer corporate guidebook, *Games Mother Never Taught You* (Harragan 1977). This book, and many others like it, encouraged us to use traditional male power tactics to establish our foothold in the "American dream." It didn't work!

If you pick the path of workplace activism, we hope you will learn from our mistakes. You can't create positive change using negative energy. Lots of recent research in both positive psychology and organizational change confirms that the problem-focused or deficit-based approach to change rarely works. It keeps people focused on their problems rather than on imagining creative solutions. Focusing on problems depletes emotional energy and inhibits cognitive functioning, thus reducing one's ability to generate creative ideas for problem resolution.

> Successful solutions are based on the powerful principle that resolution occurs by fostering the positive, not by attacking the negative. Recovery from alcoholism can't be accomplished by fighting intoxication, but, rather, only by choosing sobriety. The "war to end all wars" did no such thing, nor could it possibly have done so. Wars . . . can only be won by choosing peace. (Hawkins 2002, p. 169)

Paradoxically, the easiest (and fastest) way to change organizations (and people) is to find something to appreciate about them—just as they are. Hmmm . . . This may sound nonsensical and naive; yet there is an increasing body of literature that supports the usefulness of this approach to organizational change. The process is called Appreciative Inquiry (AI). AI is premised on the basic assumption that humans construct their experience of reality through their choice of language. What we think and talk about determines what we notice, and what we notice becomes our reality.

Appreciative Inquiry begins with a structured search for stories illustrating an organization's best practices. Once identified, these stories of organizational excellence serve to fuel people's imagination with more positive images of workplace possibility; these positive images in turn refuel organizational energy, replacing stress, burnout, and despair with hope, inspiration, and a commitment to change.

A story about Avon Corporation (a company Boomer moms will certainly recognize) provides insight into the AI process. Avon, an international cosmetics manufacturer and home distributor, wrestled with issues of gender conflict and diversity for several years. Even though Avon's sales force was female, almost all the managers were male. After spending millions of dollars on traditional interventions and finding that the number of lawsuits and complaints just kept increasing (along with negative evaluations from the required sexual harassment training programs), senior management decided to take a dramatically different approach: Appreciative Inquiry. Their first step was to run an ad in the company newsletter, asking employees to volunteer (in pairs) to share their success stories about working effectively with members of the opposite sex. Based on the scope of the problem, management was hoping for a dozen or so internal success stories. Instead, hundreds of people quickly replied.

The next step was to train a hundred employees in the basics of AI interviewing. These volunteer interviewers conducted three hundred interviews with people who had volunteered to share their success stories. At the end of each initial interview, the interviewer asked if the interviewee would be willing to help find more success stories and conduct more interviews. Stories poured in: stories of trust building, shared leadership, innovative conflict resolution, creative diversity management, cross-gender coaching, and minority career advancement (Cooperrider et al. 2000). Using the content of these interviews as examples of internal best practices, management made more than thirty important internal policy changes, including the decision that all committees and project teams would be co-chaired by a woman and a man. Dramatic changes occurred in Avon's management practices, and this cultural revolution rapidly moved beyond the company's U.S. operations. Just a few years later, Avon Mexico (formerly a highly paternalistic organization) received the Catalyst Award as the best place in the country for women to work.

Obviously, the change process at Avon was an organizationwide change initiative sponsored by senior management; however, the theory behind this process works equally well at the micro level in organizations. The truth is this: We can't change others by criticizing what is wrong with them. To do so only generates defensiveness. Defensiveness shuts down one's ability to listen, and when people stop listening to each other, communication comes to a screeching halt. The fallout of such negative encounters typically is some combination of disappointment, hurt, frustration, anger, and blame. Negative emotions rarely lead to positive change.

So, how can one individual—a Gen X workplace activist—use this information to improve job satisfaction and move an organization from domination to partnership? First, commit to shifting your view of the situation from negative (anger, stress, frustration, hopelessness, you fill in the blank) to something more positive—from pessimism to optimism. And, yes, you can learn how to do this! Psychologist Martin Seligman's research strongly suggests that optimism is a learned skill. If you think it's an innate psychological trait, you might want to read Seligman's book *Learned Optimism* (1990).

Optimism (or the lack thereof) is a direct result of what we choose to think (and talk) about. What we think about directs our attention to certain stimuli and causes us to ignore others. Optimists tend to notice what's right in their world. Pessimists, of course, do the opposite. Interestingly, when we choose to see the proverbial glass as half full rather than half empty (or our boss as partially sane rather than mostly insane), our cognitive capacity increases dramatically, and our ability for creative problem solving soars (more about this in Chapter 8). Creative thinking is key to all positive change. It takes a lot of creativity to discover win-win solutions to organizational obstacles; without a win-win option, resistance is sure to occur.

Before we can engage in creative problem solving or win-win conflict resolution (both important milestones on the road to successful activism), we must first master a more basic skill: listening. In fact, refusing to listen to differences is the cornerstone of the dominator dynamic.

> When two people who are supposedly engaged in discussion don't listen to each other, or listen just to see what they can pick apart in the other's argument, you have two people trying to figure out who can come out on top, who can win the argument, right or wrong. This is the dominator dynamic. (Montuori and Conti 1993, p. 266)

Partnership is created by dialogue, and an authentic dialogue requires the willingness to listen. Learning to listen deeply to the "enemy" can paradoxically turn that enemy into an ally. This doesn't mean you tolerate an abusive relationship at work (or anyplace else), but it does mean that in each conflict situation you attempt to see the issue through the eyes of the other person—even if that other is a dictatorial manager or an obnoxious co-worker. Easier said than done! Laura and I both have lots of ongoing opportunities to work on this skill. She's going to tell you about a challenge with one of her co-workers:

>> *OK, I know it's juvenile; it's so immature you'd think I was in fifth grade . . . but when I started my new job, I gave one of my co-workers a nickname. This is a guy I work with a lot. I'm a reporter and he's a photographer; so, on some days, we'd spend six or seven hours together. Some of that time is relaxed, but, more often, in the news business you're racing the clock*

to make deadlines. That can be very stressful. Needless to say, we'd all like to be put in teams with people we get along with well, but as Mom loves to point out, "Where would the learning be if everything were that easy?"

So back to the nickname. This photographer has a penchant for parlance. He has the gift of gab, or maybe it's the curse of conversation. Bottom line, he talks NONSTOP! I started calling him V. V. or Verbal Vomit (behind his back). He drove me insane. I didn't want to work with him. I was miserable every day that I was assigned to work with him. I asked my boss if I could stop working with him. My boss told me I needed to learn how to say two words: "Shut up!" He told me everyone knew V. V. had a lot to say, and when I'd heard enough, I should tell him to "shut up." He promised me it wouldn't hurt V. V.'s feelings; in fact, it was one of the only ways to get him to stop talking.

The idea seemed appalling at first, but I started asking around, and everyone agreed this was the best way to get a few moments of silence from a very non-silent guy. I can remember the first time I tried it. I was tentative, scared of hurting his feelings, but it was either silence him or throw myself off the nearest overpass, so I did it. Well, actually I asked him to "please be quiet so I could think for a minute," but guess what? He shut up. It did wonders for our working relationship (at least from my end). I found that I could tolerate a lot more free-flowing babble knowing deep inside that I could stop it if I needed to.

And then something else happened. We were headed out on a story to interview a congressman and I asked V. V. a question . . . something I'd stopped doing shortly after I met him because it always seemed to open the floodgates to an hour-long response. Well, when I asked V. V. the question, he had the answer. He had more than the answer; he had an explanation of the entire state of politics in Louisiana. I eventually asked him to stop, but I found out that I was riding in the car with a fountain of information. I'd never been able to recognize that before because V. V. was pushing all my buttons (or I was allowing my buttons to be pushed, as Mom would point out). But as I learned to set limits and created a better relationship with him, I finally reached a point where I could appreciate some, even most, of what he had to say. Now, V. V. still talks a lot, but I'm beginning to think of it less as Verbal Vomit and more as Very Valuable.

Listening was key to finding a win-win way to work more peacefully (and productively) with this photographer, but other skills were also needed. Laura had to work to change her pessimism to optimism. She needed to trust that a more functional working relationship was possible, and in order to do this, she needed to catch V. V. doing something right. In other words, she needed to do her own Appreciative Inquiry, searching for something she could appreciate about this very verbal person. Laura also needed assertiveness—another critical skill for the activist's tool kit. Assertiveness is not in-your-face aggression. It is the ability to use "I" messages, the ability to claim your emotions rather than project them onto someone else. For example, Laura might say, "I need a few minutes of quiet to think through how I'm going to write this story," rather than, "You talk way too much. Shut up!" The specific words she chooses will influence V. V.'s response. "I" messages build bridges between people. "You" messages tear them down. And, remember, actions often speak louder than words. Choosing our words carefully, difficult as that can be, is often easier than changing our body language.

The corporate activist also needs patience and perseverance. Patience does not imply passivity; rather, it is the commitment to restate your feelings until they are recognized. I call this "chanting." The challenge is to chant calmly—expressing a need to hear as well as to be heard. Again, this is easier said than done. We'll talk about how to overcome some of the ego's blocks when we discuss the fourth road to revolution (changing yourself). But before we go there, let's discuss how you, as a workplace activist, can use technology to help further Revolution X.

Howard Rheingold, in *Smart Mobs* (2002), gives many examples of how technology enables people to act together in new ways. He discusses how concerned citizens in Manila overthrew the president using cell phone text messaging to organize demonstrations and how the Web site www. upoc.com enables journalists to organize groups of citizen reporters on the fly. Rheingold, reflecting on future societal changes, writes, "Key breakthroughs won't come from established industry leaders but from the fringes, from skunkworks and startups and even associations of amateurs. *Especially* associations of amateurs" (pp. xii–xiii). Informed groups of citizens using high-tech tools can gain a lot of social power.

The British Broadcasting Corporation's (BBC) iCan Web site is a good example of how technology can be used to facilitate change. When Janet Mahoney's beloved dog died a mysterious death after an operation, she was upset and felt alone in her misery—at least until she logged on to iCan and found a whole group of people who'd lost pets because of a vet's mistake. Mahoney used the iCan site to collect the signatures of six thousand like-minded pet owners on a petition to increase oversight and accountability of vets. She then took the petition to the queen. (On the iCan Web site you can research an issue, talk to other concerned people, and find out how to launch a change campaign. You can also learn how to contact everyone from the local government up to members of Parliament.)

"ICan (www.bbc.co.uk/dna/ican) may be the most radical example of 'social software'—the catchall term for Web tools like blogs and wikis (collectively edited sites) that encourage social interaction" (Wylie 2004b, p. 29). A fifteen-person BBC team that's headed up by Martin Vogel runs the site. Vogel believes that iCan "shows people they're not alone and gives them tools to make things happen on a local, national, maybe even global scale. Global campaigns often start locally" (p. 29). Easy access to sophisticated technology helps each of us communicate with many others. Technology can help us create Web-based communities of interest that have the capacity to publicize and promote X-friendly workplaces.

Perhaps Gen Xers could build a global online "appreciation system" similar to the "reputation systems" that already exist on eBay and Amazon, in which the aggregate opinions of the users provide the measure of trust necessary for transactions to flourish. A global, online appreciation system would provide support and reinforcement to those companies and managers who are doing the right things and provide the detailed information necessary to create images of possibility for those who aren't.

Fast Company is already leading the way. They sponsor a "Company of Friends" Web site (www.fastcompany.com/co), where forward-thinking readers can "connect, communicate, and collaborate" with other readers online (as well as in self-organizing face-to-face community groups). Each year *Fast Company* sponsors a "Fast 50" challenge—an annual search for ordinary people who are doing extraordinary things in their organizations. The "Call for Entries" Web page (www.fastcompany.com/fast50_05) states, "The Fast 50 is not just about the bigwigs or bottom line. It's a group of uncompromising leaders, tireless innovators, turnaround artists, truth-tellers, trendsetters—readers who are fueled by courage, integrity, passion and a commitment to results."

Partnership is something we can create with our actions. As Xers begin to live the partnership model and disseminate stories of workplace success, they will raise corporate consciousness. Contrary to popular belief, change doesn't have to happen at the top. In fact, we believe that organizational change can begin anywhere, with anyone. It happens one person at a time.

ROUTE 4: CHANGE YOURSELF

Not all Gen X women (or men) are frustrated with their work experiences. Twenty-seven-year-old Brenna Willingham is one of those who exudes energy and enthusiasm as she describes her four-year journey as a full-time employee. It is, however, important to note that Brenna's journey hasn't always been blissful. After graduating from the University of Colorado with a degree in liberal arts, Brenna went to work in a small technology company as an office manager. Getting things organized took only a few weeks, and Brenna became increasingly bored. Six months later, when her paycheck bounced, she knew it was time to take action. A job placement agency found her a position in a small software company that had just been acquired by a larger technology firm.

Brenna's entry position was not very glamorous: receptionist and assistant to the president of a thirty-person office in Boulder, Colorado. She did her job well but reminded the president of how bored she was, often asking if there was some other project she could tackle. The president eventually took her "cry for more interesting work" to his direct reports, and one of the managers gave Brenna some spreadsheets to work on—still not exciting, but at least it gave her some variety. Brenna's commitment to excellence and her dedication to learning kept earning her more projects. She read everything she could get her hands on about the software industry and this company's products, and she enrolled in a master's degree program in technology management, all the while continuing to seek out new assignments. Brenna commented, "Other than my entry job at BEA Systems, none of my other three positions existed prior to my creating them. I simply looked for managers with a need and found a way to meet that need. Eventually someone would say, 'Let's make this a full-time job.'"

Today Brenna is a software release manager, still working in BEA's Boulder office, which has grown from 30 to 110 employees. Brenna's drive is a key part of her success, as is her courageous risk-taking ability. She also acknowledges the importance of sponsorship at a high level. Brenna's career options grew immediately when the president encouraged his direct reports to use her as an additional resource.

When asked what recommendations she has for frustrated Gen Xers, Brenna replied, "Be sure you choose the right organization and the right boss." BEA has experienced a lot of growth since Brenna was hired, and she is well aware that her career advancement tactics work best in a growth environment. She also acknowledges that sponsorship by a senior manager (in her case, the president) helps a lot. Ambitious Gen Xers need to not only work hard but also identify and meet the needs of key people who will, in turn, open doors of opportunity for them.

When asked what she likes most about BEA, Brenna quickly responded, "The people." She described them as "real people" who like to have fun and don't take themselves or their work too seriously. "They compete with themselves but cooperate with each other." Most of the BEA managers aren't Gen Xers, but they have created an ideal Gen X culture: relaxed, informal, friendly, and fun, with interesting work, lots of opportunities for learning, and a strong focus on relationships. Once a quarter the company has a party day. One quarter it was "ski day." The next quarter everyone went to Boulder Reservoir for a day of sun and fun. During these team outings, employees celebrate past accomplishments and create the relationships that help cement the organization's future success.

Of course, organizations, like people, are not perfect. Until a year ago, Brenna's salary was significantly below market average. Though her role had expanded far beyond her initial receptionist tasks, her pay lagged for three years until a manager went to bat for her and got permission to give her a "huge" salary increase at a time when wage increases were frozen throughout the company. As an aside, Brenna commented that at one time her "starter marriage" husband had worked for the same company, in a lower-grade position but earning considerably more money. So . . . even X-friendly companies may struggle (however unconsciously) with gender equity issues.

On the Gen X survey, Brenna's largest "importance-satisfaction" rating gap was on *performance feedback*. Like many Gen Xers, she is not getting her feedback needs met. (In Chapter 5, we discussed the fact that *performance feedback* and *recognition* are significantly more important to our women respondents than to the men, though neither factor is very high on the women's "importance" list.) Brenna mentioned that even though she has weekly hour-long meetings with her manager, her last performance review was full of surprises. Her recommendation to managers everywhere is "Performance reviews should never contain new information!" Gen Xers want continuous feedback and clear expectations. I think we all do.

Brenna, like most Gen Xers, would like to be more involved in decision making. (We found a significant importance-satisfaction gap on *participation in decision making* for both men and women survey respondents.) Even though Brenna now has a manager title, she doesn't always get invited to the "right" meetings. I asked if she thought this was primarily reflective of her age or her gender. She didn't know the answer but stressed that she'd like to sit in on decision-making meetings, even if only as an observer. (Inviting more junior employees to attend decision-making meetings is a great way to provide no-cost opportunities for learning.)

Brenna, like successful people of all ages, has very clear life goals, both personal and professional. She attributes this to her father, a successful energy entrepreneur who served as her primary career role model during her formative years. (Remember, 62 percent of women respondents said their career was primarily influenced by their dad.) Brenna believes her dad has a rewarding career, and she's extremely optimistic that her career will be rewarding as well. She commented, "There are more things I'd like to do and accomplish in my career, so I won't be resting any time soon." Her drive coupled with her positive attitude will take her far.

The most remarkable thing about Brenna is her high level of emotional intelligence, or EI. Think of emotional intelligence as resilience coupled with self-awareness and social skills. When we have a high level of EI, we are realistically confident in our ability to handle what comes our way. The specific components of emotional intelligence, according to Robbins (2003),

- *Self-awareness:* The ability to be aware of what you're feeling

- *Self-management:* The ability to manage your emotions and impulses

- *Self-motivation:* The ability to persist in the face of setbacks and failures

- *Empathy:* The ability to sense how others are feeling

- *Social skills:* The ability to handle the emotions of others

Brenna's life reflects a high level of resilience; and a high level of emotional intelligence undoubtedly has played a role in her career success. At twenty-seven, she's been through more hours of therapy than most people could imagine (her life has had its share of challenges, including an eating disorder and a starter marriage). However, instead of wallowing in depression or helplessness, Brenna chose to work on changing herself. As a result of her inner journey, she is much more mature than many people twice her age. She realizes she is in charge of her life; she doesn't expect people to fix things for her. She repeatedly uses the terms *hard work* and *dedication.* Brenna thinks many of her Gen X peers have unrealistic expectations. They want to have their organizations hand them success rather than go out and make success happen. Brenna's career demonstrates her ability to be positive and proactive.

Several recent studies document the relationship between emotional intelligence and career success: EI, not IQ, appears to be the key trait of high performers—even in the military. U.S. Air Force officers have found that recruiters with high EI scores are 2.6 times more successful than those with low scores. "By using EI in selection, the Air Force was able to cut turnover among new recruiters in one year by more than 90 percent and save nearly $3 million in hiring and training costs" (Robbins 2003, p. 111). As more and more employers begin to make selection decisions based on emotional intelligence, the EI levels of organizations will leap; positive workplace change is bound to follow.

If you are weak on any of the five EI dimensions, you may want to take corrective action, not just to increase your employability, but also to enhance your effectiveness as a workplace activist. It is difficult, if not impossible, to model the behaviors of a positive revolutionary (for example, optimism, patience, assertiveness, and perseverance) without a high level of EI. Increasing emotional intelligence also leads to increased life satisfaction, regardless of the situations we find ourselves in. As our EI increases we change our perceptions of what is going on around us, and we learn to trust our ability to handle whatever comes our way.

There are several actions one can take to increase EI. For many of us, professional counseling or coaching may be useful. (Brenna thinks therapy is an important factor in her career success.) Why? Because few of us travel through life without emotional baggage, and when that baggage gets heavy, we try to pass it off to others. Psychologists call this projection, and it is a very real obstacle to creating healthy organizations. The relationships within a work group often trigger unfinished emotional business, and we may end up replaying our childhood: new players, but the same game.

For some, coaching, journaling, or therapy will help increase awareness of more positive aspects of the people we work with and the tasks we are given. A spiritual approach to developing EI—yoga, prayer, meditation—can also help break old behavioral habits and teach new ways of being together. Regardless of what path we choose to self-revolution, we have to learn new skills—skills that will help us see life differently and be in the world differently. We call these Quantum Skills because they can enable you to take a quantum leap from life as you have lived it to the life of your dreams. Quantum Skills (discussed in the next chapter) will give you a new power source and enable you to become an authentic change master, changing your workplace and your world—from the inside out.

CHAPTER 8

Leading the Revolution

hanging ourselves is challenging! Old habits die hard, especially when there are so few role models for a new way of being at work (and in the world). Yet, the partnership model will remain but a dream unless we commit ourselves to the work of internal transformation. Organizational structures are mirrors of the values, beliefs, and behaviors of the people who inhabit them. We Boomer managers and mothers must do more than offer Xers encouragement; we must help them learn new skills—Quantum Skills that will enable Gen X women (and men) to lead the neXt revolution, changing themselves and their workplaces from the inside out.

QUANTUM SKILLS

We can't create X-friendly workplaces using traditional management skills. To do so would be like trying to build a quantum computer with 1950s technology. It's simply impossible! An old room-sized IBM was designed using transistors; quantum computers use atomic encoding. It's an entirely new ball game. The same idea applies to re-creating organizations. It is impossible to plan, organize, direct, or control a complex revolution. Old skills are inadequate. New skills are needed—skills that expand our current capacity for leading change. We call these Quantum Skills because they draw heavily from recent research in quantum physics, complexity science, and positive psychology; and using them will enable twenty-first-century revolutionaries to help their organizations take a quantum leap into new ways of being at work. The skills are

- *Quantum Seeing:* The ability to *see* intentionally

- *Quantum Thinking:* The ability to *think* paradoxically

- *Quantum Feeling:* The ability to *feel* vitally alive

- *Quantum Knowing:* The ability to *know* intuitively

- *Quantum Acting:* The ability to *act* responsibly

- *Quantum Trusting:* The ability to *trust* life

- *Quantum Being:* The ability to *be* in relationships

SEEING INTENTIONALLY

Quantum Seeing, the ability to see intentionally, enables us to break free of old perceptual habits and, quite literally, see the world anew. Recent research in both cognitive psychology and quantum physics suggests that the external world is not nearly as objective as we have believed it to be. Rather, the physical world is an infinite mass of perceptual possibilities from which we create an experience of reality based on what we choose to notice. Gary Zukav, writing in *The Dancing Wu Li Masters* (1979), sums this process up well:

> Reality is what we take to be true. What we take to be true is what we believe. What we believe is based upon our perceptions. What we perceive depends upon what we look for. What we look for depends on what we think. What we think depends on what we perceive. What we perceive determines what we believe. What we believe determines what we take to be true. What we take to be true is our reality. (p. 310)

Therefore, if we are to change our external experience of reality, we must first change our internal beliefs. Beliefs drive intentions (expectations), and our intentions determine where we place our attention—what we unconsciously choose to notice. University of Chicago psychology professor Mihaly Csikszentmihalyi (1990) believes that intentions create reality. Our intentions cause us to pay attention to certain things while simultaneously ignoring a plethora of other perceptual possibilities.

As we learn the skill of Quantum Seeing, we become more aware of the subjectivity of human perception, and we become conscious intenders of the lives we desire instead of merely moving through life automatically thinking the same thoughts, doing the same things, and wondering why life keeps showing up the same way it always has. Doing the same thing over and over and expecting a different result is one definition of insanity. The typical person has about sixty thousand thoughts per day. Ninety percent are repeats from yesterday. Is it any wonder that our lives seem to just keep repeating themselves?

If we want our personal lives (or our workplaces) to change, we have to make different choices, as this thought-provoking poem by Portia Nelson (1993) vividly demonstrates:

Autobiography in Five Short Chapters

CHAPTER 1

I walk down the street,
There is a deep hole in the sidewalk.
I fall in.
I am lost . . . I am helpless.
It isn't my fault.
It takes forever to find a way out.

CHAPTER 2

I walk down the same street.
There is a deep hole in the sidewalk.
I pretend I don't see it.
I fall in again.
I can't believe I am in the same place.
But, it isn't my fault.
It still takes me a long time to get out.

CHAPTER 3

I walk down the same street.
There is a deep hole in the sidewalk.
I see it there.
I still fall in . . . it's a habit.
My eyes are open.
I know where I am.
It is my fault.
I get out immediately.

CHAPTER 4

I walk down the same street.
There is a deep hole in the sidewalk.
I walk around it.

CHAPTER 5

I walk down another street.

If we are to walk down a new street, we must set a clear intention to do so; and, we must change our expectations about what we deserve and what we are capable of creating. All change begins with a clear intention. A friend's job search story is a good example.

Mindi, at age thirty-seven, was working in a senior management role in a company whose values were increasingly incompatible with her own. She left that organization and set about clarifying who she was and what was important to her at this stage in her life. As she clarified her interests and values, it became clear that there was one best-fit employer in her local job market. This company was known for its commitment to work-life balance and consistently earned "best place to work" awards. There were, however, potential obstacles. Her educational credentials and industry experience were not directly relevant. Mindi has a Ph.D. degree in pharmaceutical science administration, and all of her previous employment was in health-care related organizations. Her targeted company, a well-known designer and manufacturer of greeting cards, was a long way from health care. Furthermore, this company was in a period of stability, not growth, and thus was not seeking additional executives. In fact, it was about to do some downsizing.

Mindi chose not to focus her attention on these potential obstacles. She set a clear intention to find a position at this company, and she developed a vision of herself as an integral member of the company's management team. She expressed this vision at a social event when she was introduced to a stranger who casually asked her what she did. Mindi explained her situation and shared her desire to work for a specific employer. Unbeknownst to Mindi, this stranger was a retired executive of the targeted company. He was so impressed with the clarity of her intention that he arranged for her to meet the company president. Ninety days later, Mindi began working at this company in a new senior management position that was created just for her. She did not have a detailed game plan for making this career change; rather, she set a clear intention, and the clarity of that intention helped her notice and respond to cues she might otherwise have missed. Without that clear intention, she most likely would have had a very different response to this stranger's question.

Our external lives unfold according to our internal intentions. And, the process of clarifying what is most important to us (our goals) is ongoing. This comment from one of our survey respondents demonstrates the process of continuously redefining what you want.

> **My career has proven to be exactly what I wanted it to be because I feel you have to work to create that. I have been very fortunate in that I am doing what I set out to do. I have always been very goal oriented and knew what I wanted to do for a long time. In the end it turned out that I got to my initial goal quicker than I thought I would. This has proven interesting, as it causes you to redefine what you want from life.**
>
> 30-YEAR-OLD TV NEWS PRODUCER

Unfortunately, the majority of our survey respondents don't seem to have taken the time to fully clarify their intentions. While 76 percent of our 1,200 respondents expect to have a rewarding career (70 percent of the women), only 16 percent have a written vision statement for their lives (see survey questions 30 and 32).

It is difficult to choose a "new road" unless we have a clear picture of the road we want to take. Without a clear vision, we tend to keep re-creating the past, not only our individual histories, but also our family scripts. Many Gen X women didn't have a positive female career role model during their formative years. Only 45 percent of our female survey respondents thought their mothers had rewarding careers. This suggests that 55 percent of these women have negative career scripting to erase. It is imperative that you launch this revolution by developing a positive vision for your life that incorporates both personal and work dimensions. Affirm your commitment to this vision by taking the time daily to review your intentions.

To clarify your intentions, you may need to set aside some time to identify your heart's desires—to decide what kind of life it is that you wish to create. Without intention and desire, no deliberate creation occurs. Instead, we create our lives by default. Many of us have spent our lives suppressing our desires. Some of us were conditioned as children to relinquish wanting in order to protect ourselves from disappointment. We may have thought we were unworthy or have been conditioned to believe that our lives are created by luck or fate. Often, we have simply settled for what is. We have failed to dream of what might be.

To reconnect with our hopes and desires, we may need to awaken our imagination. Imagination is the critical link between life as it currently is and the life of our wildest dreams. What we can't imagine, we can't create. This is why, in the words of Albert Einstein, imagination is more important than knowledge. Once we are able to imagine what we want, we are able to perceive opportunities and resources that will enable us to realize our desires. We are unlikely to see these opportunities until we define our intentions.

Some of us find it easier to imagine than others. If it is difficult for you to create mental images, you may want to use relaxing background music (which opens pathways to the unconscious) or a relaxation/visual imagery audiotape. Ten to twenty minutes of daily visioning can bring dramatic results. As Marcel Proust (1982) wrote, "To go on a voyage of discovery, we don't need new landscapes; we need fresh eyes." The time we devote to reimagining our lives (and our organizations) gives us fresh eyes with which to lead the revolution.

After we have clarified our desires, we begin the moment-by-moment challenge of keeping our intentions at the forefront of our consciousness. Jerry and Esther Hicks in *A New Beginning* (1992) speak of the need to become "selective sifters," gatekeepers at the portals of consciousness, entertaining only those thoughts that match our intentions. Many of us have not learned how to do this. Rather, our minds are like thought salad—a mixture of the useful and the nonuseful. How can we prevent such confusion? How do we let only those thoughts that serve us well come into our awareness?

Affirmations are a good tool. They are simple, short, positive statements of intention, such as "I have the skills and resources I need to be a workplace revolutionary" or, "I deserve a sane and satisfying workplace." It works best if you write them down and read them numerous times a day. I write mine on three-by-five-inch cards and post them where they can serve as frequent visual reminders throughout the day of the things I intend to create. Another useful tool is a dream board—or mind map—a sheet of poster board covered with magazine pictures or drawings that illustrate your intentions. Displaying this in a highly frequented place provides a visual reminder that helps focus your attention on your intentions.

Lily Tomlin, in her starring role as a bag lady in Jane Wagner's thought-provoking Broadway play *The Search for Signs of Intelligent Life in the Universe* (1991), comments, "I knew that when I grew up, I wanted to be somebody. Now I realize I needed to be more specific." The skill of Quantum Seeing enables us to be specific intenders of lives that work and workplaces that satisfy. As we use this skill, we become increasingly conscious of our intentions, and we become increasingly selective in what we choose to notice.

Quantum Seeing presents an interesting paradox. The more aware we become of our ability to intentionally design our reality, the more dependent we find ourselves on others. We live and work in a complex web of interrelationships. Not only am I influenced by my intentions, I'm also influenced by yours. We not only create, we co-create; together we create a shared reality. If we are to transform the workplace, we must create a shared intention of our collective desires. Gen X women, their mothers, and their managers can work together to create a shared vision of a transformed workplace. This vision can be birthed through face-to-face dialogues or in Internet chat rooms. Perhaps Gen X women can even institute a new version of the weekly consciousness-raising groups their mothers may have attended in the sixties or seventies. Whatever the venue, the important dialogue questions are What would be the structure, policies, and practices of a workplace in which positive relationships, trust, respect, equality, continuous learning, empowerment, and open communication are present? How would such an organization hold people accountable? How would it measure results?

If enough of us clarify our vision, we will find a way to create and sustain sane and satisfying workplaces. Are you willing to spend time daily envisioning the kind of workplace you desire? And, are you willing to actively engage others in such a dialogue? If so, you're ready for the revolution!

THINKING PARADOXICALLY

Quantum Thinking is the ability to think paradoxically. Revolutions don't occur according to a logical game plan. They happen when a number of complex variables coalesce at just the right time to move an agenda forward. Serendipity and synchronicity play important roles. Sometimes the smallest events trigger major societal changes. These events can rarely be predicted. In a revolution, slower is sometimes faster, and less is often more.

Quantum Thinking is a critical skill for achieving our goal of a more meaningful workplace. Why? Because logic would suggest it can't be done. After all, "command and control" has long been the modus operandi in organizations. Furthermore, organizations have long been bastions of prejudice and discrimination, places where profits are more important than people and money is more desired than meaning. Within such a value system, equality and empowerment seem highly unlikely. However, miracles may happen when enough people create a shared intention (Quantum Seeing), even if their intention seems highly improbable. Remember how suddenly (and peacefully) the Berlin Wall fell and how quickly capitalism began to replace communism in China? Peaceful revolutions happen! However, they usually make sense only in retrospect. The process rarely can be logically explained in the midst of transformation.

Quantum Thinking is a challenging skill! We in Western countries take great pride in our analytical skills, and our organizations give a lot of lip service to logical thinking and rational decision making (though research suggests that very little "rational" thinking actually occurs in organizations). However, logical analysis will probably predict that this revolution can't occur. So, don't try to calculate the path of this revolution; instead, use your creative energy to imagineer it. Remember, radical change often appears illogical when viewed through the lens of the prevailing paradigm. Logical explanations will eventually follow, but they rarely accompany a quantum leap. Flying an airplane was illogical in the nineteenth century, but the Wright brothers believed it could be done. And they did it . . . even though "common sense" tells us that it should be impossible for a heavy machine to fly through the air.

Garrison Keillor, of *Prairie Home Companion* fame, once commented: "We need to look reality in the eye and deny it." This doesn't mean we should live in a fantasy world; it does suggest that what we're observing is only a part of the possibilities. Quantum Thinking encourages us to think differently—to take a quantum leap into a new way of viewing reality. When we do, we are likely to see brand-new action options. Price Pritchett (1990) reminds us that quantum leaps come when we seek "elegant solutions" (p. 12). These solutions typically aren't as complex or time consuming as we might expect. They are generally less demanding of our energies and emotions. And they probably will not be familiar to us.

Quantum solutions are, in fact, not only unfamiliar but almost always logically impossible. They come to us only when we release our need for a sensible solution. When I was in my early twenties I had a strong desire to complete my Ph.D. degree before I turned thirty. I used the skill of Quantum Seeing to reinforce this intention, and I remained deeply committed to it, even though the external circumstances of my life often made completion look unlikely. There were numerous detours, such as the birth of Matthew when I was twenty-four and Laura when I was twenty-seven, along with several spousal job relocations. These events temporarily refocused my priorities, but my long-term intention remained unchanged.

At twenty-nine I found myself living in LaCrosse, Wisconsin, with a two-year-old, a five-year-old, and a husband whose job caused him to be out of town 90 percent of the time. My Ph.D. target date was fast approaching. My logical options for realizing my intentions were, however, very limited. The closest doctoral program in counseling psychology was 150 miles away at the University of Wisconsin–Madison. I had almost total parenting responsibility for two young children and no relatives within 500 miles. Furthermore, we had no money for such an endeavor. The logical probability of my entering a doctoral program at that time in my life was almost zero.

The rational thing to have done would have been to relinquish my dream, or at least to change the timeline. However, I have always had a propensity for the impossible, so I continued to affirm my intention. I applied for a lucrative scholarship sponsored by a local women's organization, intending to use the money to fly back and forth to class so that I could be home with the children each evening. I didn't get the scholarship, but rather than focus on my disappointment, I continued to visualize walking down the graduation aisle, velvet hood around my shoulders (Quantum Seeing). As I continued affirming and visualizing my intention, new, often illogical, ideas began to emerge (Quantum Thinking).

One idea was to find a free nanny. At first, this seemed highly illogical, but subsequent investigation proved it doable. We lived only a few blocks from the University of Wisconsin–LaCrosse, which has an excellent master's degree program in child development. I found a student who was willing to trade nanny time for internship hours. The child-care problem was solved. Next, I applied for and was granted a student loan. The tuition problem was solved. The only remaining challenge was overnight lodging. I arranged my schedule so that all of my classes were on Monday, Tuesday, and Wednesday, but this still meant that I needed somewhere to sleep two nights a week. An apartment or even a hotel room was not in my budget. The university finally agreed to rent me a by-the-night room in the agriculture dorm, the only dorm that had empty space. I shared a dorm (though not a room) with several hundred male undergrad aggies. Weekly I rode a bus back and forth to Madison, using the commute time to study so that my at-home time could be devoted to my family. This experience was invaluable. It convinced me that if we are willing to hold a vision (Quantum Seeing), and if we are willing to entertain outrageous ideas (Quantum Thinking), solutions to our toughest challenges will emerge. These solutions, though highly illogical, are almost always extremely practical.

The skill of Quantum Thinking is just as applicable to the daily challenges inherent in a traditional workplace as it was to the accomplishment of a major life goal. An e-mail from one of my MBA students employed by a major bank, demonstrates:

> **A senior of mine continues to be friendlier and volunteer more information to a co-worker of mine while the rest of us have to pester that senior for the information we need. And, he has more of a negative attitude with the rest of us. It makes it difficult to stay focused and get work done and not feel rejected. So, how do I best deal with type of situation?**
>
> 29-YEAR-OLD FUNDS ACCOUNTANT

What are the possible solutions? First, she could use Quantum Seeing and begin to resolve this problem by setting a clear intention that she will be noticed and appreciated by this man. Then she could write an affirmation that she will read numerous times throughout the day: "I do good work and I am worthy of being noticed and informed." These are good steps and I recommend them. Next, a Quantum Thinker would identify a seemingly illogical strategy, such as setting an intention to notice this man doing something positive every day and complimenting him on it. In this situation, my student paradoxically is more likely to get what she wants and needs by treating her senior positively than by demanding that he treat her positively. This is hard to do. The ego wants to feel slighted (and my student logically has every right to feel that way). However, being frustrated won't solve the problem. Thinking paradoxically about it may.

Companies like Southwest Airlines, SAS, and Semco remind us that seeing things upside down and backward can create amazing results. It is paradoxical to believe that quality results are primarily a function of the quality of relationships or that putting people first increases profits. These concepts are paradoxical, yet they also are proven! So, as you sign up for this revolution, be willing to frequently engage in creative thought and dialogue (or journaling) about paradoxical questions such as these:

- How can I enrich my life by simplifying it?

- How can I accomplish more by doing less?

- How can I learn to appreciate those whom I most resent?

- How can I live a balanced life and achieve career success?

As you engage these questions (and others like them), be open to the emergence of paradoxical surprises. The skill of Quantum Thinking will enable you to see multiple possibilities and endless creative options for all of life's daily challenges and decisions; and it will provide lots of ideas about how you can help lead the neXt revolution

FEELING VITALLY ALIVE

Quantum Feeling, the ability to feel vitally alive, is another key skill. Revolutions are not easy. They require commitment and focus, sustenance of passion and continuous renewal of their energy. Recent research at the HeartMath Institute provides new insight into how to do this. The physicists and psychologists who work at HeartMath have determined that emotions and energy level are closely related (which should come as no surprise). Negative emotions (for example, frustration, fear, anger, and stress) decrease coherence in the heart's electromagnetic waves and cause us to physically lose energy. Conversely, positive emotions (for example, love, caring, compassion, and appreciation) increase the coherence of these waves, which leads to increased energy and also to improved hormonal and cognitive functioning (IHM Research Update 1995). This research suggests that if we are to be positive agents of change, we must immerse ourselves daily in positive emotions.

This is easier said than done: Stress is a ubiquitous part of life. Stuff happens—daily! However, between every event and each emotion there is a choice point. Unfortunately, making a choice, for most of us, remains an unconscious process. However, we can become more aware of our perceptual choices; we can increase our response-ability, the moment-by-moment ability to monitor and choose our responses. The following exercise is one that I have found useful when I am in a stressful situation:

1. First, I shut my eyes and relax my body by focusing on my breathing.

2. Then, I pinpoint the situation in my life that is causing me discomfort.

3. I imagine a doorway (something like the electronic security checkpoint at an airport).

4. I see myself walking through the doorway, and as I walk through I imagine that all of my negative feelings about this situation are being painlessly removed from my consciousness.

5. I step out the other side of the doorway, free to feel differently.

6. I then identify at least one thing that I can appreciate about this situation.

7. I ask myself, "What do I want to experience? What feeling best supports my vitality?"

8. I open my eyes, fully aware that I have choices about how I respond.

Another useful activity is to take a "walk around" frustrating situations, viewing them from multiple perspectives. Write down a description of whatever (or whoever) is bugging you. Lay the piece of paper on the floor and literally take a walk around it (you may want to do this in private!), challenging yourself to see how many different ways you can view the situation, recognizing that the lens you choose will determine how you subsequently feel.

Here's an example of how this process works. Laura called me one night quite frustrated about work. When I asked her to list all the things that were frustrating her, the first thing she said was, "My boss gives me all the hard assignments." She was obviously viewing this as unfair or punishing. However, I saw it quite differently—as a compliment. I suggested that perhaps he gave her the most complex stories because she was the station's best reporter (I happen to think she's the best there is anywhere). I could sense her emotions shifting immediately. And, I had only identified one new perceptual possibility. If she were to conduct a "walk around," I think she'd discover other possible explanations for her manager's behavior. The point is this: (1) Whatever she sees as his motivations may or may not be accurate, (2) her feelings will be a direct derivative of the way she chooses to perceive the situation, and (3) there is another way of looking at everything that frustrates us.

Frustration is a choice. Regardless of how controlling your manager is, or how incompetent your co-workers appear to be, there is always another way of perceiving them. Regardless of how archaic your departmental policies are, or how inefficient your organizational structure is, you can always find something to appreciate. While this complimentary view may make no logical sense, it makes perfect sense from a psychological perspective. Energetically, we have little probability of changing our negative external realities until we can see them from a positive perspective: As our perceptions shift, so do our feelings. Or, our need to change the external environment may diminish when we cease to focus so much negative energy on it.

It has been a delight for me to watch my children learn to exercise perceptual choice. My son, Matthew, was a new college graduate and three months into his first full-time job when he called home with a wonderful success story. He was working in a group home for dually diagnosed (mentally ill and mentally retarded) men. All three of his patients had "gone off" the same day. One had eaten the TV guide, one had used his feces as modeling clay, and the third had disrobed and thrown his clothing onto the roof, all the while parading naked around the backyard (in a residential neighborhood). Matt, however, didn't sound particularly stressed. When I commented on this, he told me that at first everything had been really "getting to him," but then he realized how useful these experiences would be when he started graduate school in the fall. As he began to see the situation differently, his feelings immediately shifted. He moved from a place of stress to a place where he could appreciate the value of his experiences. He demonstrated response-ability.

As we practice the skill of Quantum Feeling, we learn to see events in ways that enhance our vitality. We choose hope rather than despair, and we choose to find meaning rather than madness in our workplaces. In so doing, we will act as organizational pioneers. We will have a clear vision of a new way of doing work, and we will refuse to be pulled back into the pervasive dysfunction that so often surrounds us. We will remember Eleanor Roosevelt's words: "No one can make you feel inferior without your permission," and we will continuously remind ourselves (and each other) that our ability to feel vitally alive and fully energized at work (and in the world) is primarily a function of how we choose to perceive external reality.

KNOWING INTUITIVELY

Quantum Knowing, the ability to know intuitively, is another important skill for twenty-first-century revolutionaries. The overwhelming amount of information in today's rapidly changing world gives us little choice but to adopt new ways of knowing. Most of our challenges are immediate. For many decisions there is far too much data and far too little time to permit the luxury of engaging in traditional, in-depth problem-solving processes. Fortunately, each of us has a built-in guidance system—our intuition.

Most women recognize the value of intuitive hunches, although many have learned to disregard their inner voice. We have tried so hard to fit into male-dominated workplaces that we have consciously adopted male values and behaviors. We have increasingly come to overrely on sensory data and underutilize the right hemisphere of our brains. I well recall times when I ignored my intuitions. Doing so often led to unfortunate consequences. A few years ago I was faced with a job offer that just didn't feel right. From a logical perspective, it was the perfect job. The salary was great, the culture was compatible with my value system, the work was challenging, the industry offered me new opportunities for growth, and the resources were abundant. It still didn't feel right, but I did take the job. It seemed the only rational thing to do. At the time I was an unemployed single parent with two teenagers, one (Laura) who was about to enter college. So, I disregarded my intuition. This apparently rational decision, however, quickly led me into turmoil.

The company president, whom I so admired, was soon terminated, and the entire senior management team quickly dissipated. The culture changed, almost overnight. I suddenly found myself surrounded by leaders who were hostile to my values and beliefs. Rationality lost credibility in that fiasco, but my confidence in my ability to know intuitively increased dramatically. It was a good lesson for me; because of that experience, I decided to enhance my intuitive skills. I have found the following activities useful:

- Each morning, first thing upon awakening, I record my dreams. If I don't remember any dreams, I write down whatever pops into my awareness. If I'm dealing with a challenging problem or an important decision, I write down my first thoughts on that topic.

- After the journal writing, I generally spend about twenty minutes with my eyes shut, breathing deeply and listening. Some days I save this meditative activity until my daily walk. As I walk, I try to cease my mental chatter and connect with my internal "receiver."

There are many techniques for enhancing intuitive ability (and there are many books that describe them). However, we don't really have to learn how to be intuitive. Research suggests that it's a natural ability that we all possess. Some of us just repress it. Parikh, Neubauer, and Lank (1994) liken intuition to radio waves. Though these waves are continuously "raining down" on us, we either fail to turn on our receivers or we receive the message and fail to heed it.

Certainly there is nothing wrong with using data as a way to make decisions, but sometimes facts are misleading, and sometimes we misinterpret them. Use data, but heed—and trust—your intuition. For example, what would you do if you were working late at night on a huge project (due the next day) and you had computer problems—after all the techies had already gone home? Well, of course, you'd try to reach one (assuming your organization is staffed for after-hours tech support). If you were unable to reach an expert, most likely you would stress out. Anxiety, of course, only decreases your ability to perform effective problem solving. Stress literally reduces blood flow to the brain.

If you were to use the skill of Quantum Knowing in this situation, most likely you would physically walk away from the computer and find the most comfortable, relaxing chair available. Once seated, you would shut your eyes and engage in slow, deep belly breathing, attempting to clear your mind of active thinking (this takes practice). If you became deeply relaxed, you would likely receive a flash of insight—an "aha!" Certainly the probability of success if you do this is much higher than your chance of logically figuring out a solution—all by yourself under extreme stress. Yet, most of us obsessively escalate our direct attempts to solve problems, even when a more indirect approach might work better.

Interestingly, research suggests that many senior managers strongly rely on intuition. Parikh, Neubauer, and Lank (1994) found that 79 percent of the senior managers they surveyed in the United States rated themselves as "above average" on intuitive ability, and internationally, more than 50 percent acknowledged that they used logic/reasoning and intuition almost equally in both their personal and professional lives. Yet, at lower organizational levels, an overreliance on data collection and an underappreciation of other ways of gaining insight linger. Unfortunately, logical analysis typically leads us down a linear path that encourages incremental change rather than transformation.

Ellen Langer, professor of psychology at Harvard University, has developed a theory of *mindful* decision making (in McCarthy 1994). Langer's research suggests that gathering lots of information does not necessarily lead to better decisions. She believes that our culture is focused on an impossible decision-making goal: reducing uncertainty through the gathering of information. Langer sees this as a futile effort because even the amount of information that could be gathered about the simplest of decisions (such as buying a pair of shoes) is endless. Instead of focusing on gathering information, her theory focuses on mindfulness (staying aware). Langer points out that when we are certain, we cease to pay attention. Certainty leads to *mindlessness.* Uncertainty keeps us attentive to both the world outside of us and our internal intuitions. Mindfulness opens pathways to inner knowing.

As we lead this revolution, there won't always be detailed information to guide our path. We will, however, have unlimited access to our intuitions. Our fearful egos may tell us that we need an expert to lead the way and train us in the tactics of a new revolution. But sometimes we just have to "make it up" as we go along. If we take time daily to turn within for guidance, we'll soon discover our own road to revolution.

ACTING RESPONSIBLY

Quantum Acting is the ability to act responsibly. We use this skill to design lives of right action and revolutions that benefit us all. Using the skill of Quantum Acting requires making responsible choices and contemplating the consequences of each action. Zukav (1989) suggests that responsible choice occurs when we take the time to ponder these three questions—before taking action:

1. What is this action likely to produce/accomplish?

2. Do I really want to assume responsibility for creating that?

3. Am I ready to accept all of the consequences of this choice?

As we learn to make more mindful choices, we also become more aware of the feedback that life constantly provides in response to our choices. We then use this feedback to modify actions that are not congruent with our values. I try to reflect each evening on the feedback life provided me in the course of my day, asking myself whether I walked my talk and reflecting on course adjustments I will make in the future. This, of

course, is reactive, but this process, along with my more proactive morning meditation, helps me live each day more consciously, taking steps
toward a life of Quantum Acting—a life in which I model the values that
are most important to me.

I try to frame my day with values by starting each day with prayer and
meditation and ending the day reflecting on my actions and life's feedback. I also practice what Martin Seligman (1990) calls *moral jogging*—
exercising behaviors that benefit the common good. For me, these
activities range from recycling to sharing financial resources in the age-
old practice of tithing. My intention is simply to be a good citizen of the
planet. There are many other ways we can do moral jogging. Seligman
offers numerous ideas, such as giving up some pleasurable activity that
you engage in regularly, such as "eating out once a week, watching a
rented movie on Tuesday night, . . . playing video games when you come
home from work, shopping for new shoes," and instead "spend this time
(the equivalent of an evening a week) in an activity devoted to the well-
being of others or of the community at large." Another of Seligman's suggestions is that we take the time to address heroic or despicable acts by
writing letters. He urges us to "compose the letters every bit as carefully
as you would a crucial report for your company" (p. 289).

The challenge of moral jogging is to learn to express concern while
staying unattached to outcomes. To do so, we must be willing to live
responsibly without being overly concerned with results, giving for the
mere joy of giving without attachment to how the gift is utilized. Moral
jogging does not always have to involve external action; we flex our moral
muscles with each compassionate thought we think and each peaceful
scenario we envision. As we practice moral jogging, we inevitably add
meaning and purpose to our lives—something that is important to most
Gen Xers.

Living responsibly without needing to fix things or change people is
a real paradox (and a very difficult challenge). Just how should a quantum revolutionary respond to moral and ethical violations in the workplace? This is very tricky! Your response, of course, may depend on the
seriousness of the violation. If the act is illegal, the right thing for you to

do is take informed action. If you think your manager is having an affair with a co-worker, taking no action might be in order. Right action is always informed action. And, the right action in one situation is not always the right action in another. This doesn't mean that everything is morally relative. It does mean that our perception is always limited and there may be more to the story than meets the eye.

We design our lives and our workplaces (either intentionally or unconsciously) one choice at a time. When we choose acts of kindness, compassion, honesty, and fidelity, we are, in the words of physicist Danah Zohar (1990), "loading the quantum dice" and increasing the probability that others will choose to act accordingly. As our personal values shift, as we assume more responsibility for who we are, what we do, and what we want to create, the probability increases that others will examine their values as well. Together we can create a collective value system, based on values that will nurture us all.

The skill of Quantum Acting helps us act congruently with our values and make a difference in whatever piece of the workplace (or the world) we inhabit and choose to focus on. "The impact of our leadership will not be defined so much by the scope of the opportunity as by the quality of our response" (Lowney 2003, p. 18). Heider (1985, p. 107) describes how this works:

> If your life works, you influence your family.
>
> If your family works, your family influences the community.
>
> If your community works, your community influences the nation.
>
> If your nation works, your nation influences the world.
>
> If your world works, the ripple effect spreads throughout the cosmos.

As quantum revolutionaries, our actions may be subtle or radical, but they will always be mindful. We may feel guided to spend more time nurturing our workplace relationships, thinking more creatively about the mundane tasks assigned to us, or enrolling in training programs to learn new skills. Or, we may leave our current organizations to find X-friendly employers or become successful entrepreneurs. Regardless of the place or extent of our actions, we will collectively transform the very fabric of the world of work. This is the task of the neXt revolution.

TRUSTING LIFE

Quantum Trusting is the ability to trust life. As we launch a revolution, it is inevitable that we will come face-to-face with our deepest fears. We may doubt our capacity to lead or even participate in this workplace revolution. We may doubt the possibility of transformational change and fear the possibility of dire consequences. Most important, we may realize that to change our workplaces, we have to first change ourselves—our thoughts, perceptions, feelings, and behaviors. This is a daunting task. If we are to summon the courage to act, we must develop our capacity to trust—not only in ourselves, but also in an evolutionary process that we can neither control nor ever fully understand.

We need only look around to see the magnitude of the change that is bombarding our society and the global community to understand that workplace transformation is only part of a systemic change sweeping across the planet. Surely someone or something larger than our individual egos has designed this cosmic drama. Realizing this helps us trust both the larger change process and our role in it. We then begin to appreciate the challenge and trust our ability to add value to the process. We release our fears and accept our role as co-creators with a higher power.

To use the skill of Quantum Trusting, we must first recognize that we live in a friendly universe. Some of us are still unsure. Yet, we continuously display a great deal of faith in the universe's natural processes. We trust in gravity, never questioning that our planet will continue to spin, suspended in space. We trust that our hearts will keep pumping while we sleep. We trust that the bulbs we plant in the fall will bloom in the spring and that an acorn will grow into an oak. Somehow we have failed to transfer this faith in the processes of nature to the unfolding of our own lives. When we do, similar miracles can occur.

I have at times been left breathless by the miracles of my life over the past few years. My experience has been that when I step out in faith, the universe conspires to support me. For me, some of this support has come in a very concrete form: money from unusual and seemingly serendipitous sources. It all began with my recognition that my core values—freedom, creativity, fun, and spiritual fulfillment—were incongruent with the values of my corporate employer. Further reflection on personal mission, vision, and values led me to leave that position and launch out on my own, as an independent consultant.

The decision to act on my values, to build my daily life around them, has provided me with many remarkable experiences. The first year after my exodus from corporate America, my income dropped by two-thirds but my quality of life soared. I was given a no-expense trip to Brazil. I was awarded scholarships to Goddard College's Institute for Socially Responsible Business and the C. S. Lewis Institute on Science and Religion at Cambridge University in England. I received a large, unexpected tax refund. My daughter, Laura, was awarded a full-tuition college scholarship to the private college of her choice. And every day I had time to play and pray, to be creative, to learn and to grow.

Author-philosopher Jean Houston (1982) uses the term "leaky margins" to describe the spiritual process of moving beyond our individual egos and entering into resonance with a larger process, thus becoming co-creators with the whole. In this state of high connectivity we know what to do, when to do it, and how to access the necessary resources. We become miracle makers, and we eventually discover that life is a beautiful "setup" designed to perfectly support our growth and development.

Richard Bach (1977) tells a story that demonstrates just how unnecessary many of our fears are. In this story small creatures are clinging to the bottom of a river in fear, constantly being tugged at by the current, using all their energy to resist the flow, fearing that if they let go they will be dashed against the rocks and killed. Finally, exhausted, one creature releases his tight hold, only to find that what had previously terrorized him in reality effortlessly supported him.

As we learn to use the skill of Quantum Trusting, we discover that we live in a friendly universe where "order is free" (Wheatley and Kellner-Rogers 1996, p. 35). We don't have to plan this revolution. It doesn't have to be difficult or time consuming. We need to "give up our belief that it's a difficult, arduous task to create something or make something manifest" (p. 35). We can learn to trust life and its innate ability to evolve. And, as we learn to do so, we become playful and powerful co-creators of the neXt revolution.

BEING IN RELATIONSHIPS

Quantum Being, the ability to be in relationships, increases our ability to create and sustain positive relationships—at home and at work. This skill enables us to create harmony within a world of differences. The differences do not disappear, but we begin to see them from a new perspective. In so doing, we move from discomfort with those who have different values to a deep appreciation of differences. We begin to realize that differences are vital to our spiritual and psychological growth.

To use the skill of Quantum Being, we must do our own internal work and learn how to reclaim our projections by realizing that what we see in others often says more about us than about them. Here's an example from Laura's distant past. One night while she was still an undergrad, she called me from Dallas. She was quite upset about her job (she was co–photography editor of her university's daily newspaper). Laura felt dumped on. According to her, others were not pulling their weight. People were missing deadlines. Her coeditor was involved in too many other activities and not doing her part of the job. The problems had grown so large that the faculty advisor had scheduled a meeting for the following morning. Laura feared she would be blamed and humiliated in front of the entire staff for problems that were "someone else's fault." As I listened to Laura describe the "faults" of her coeditor—too busy, overcommitted, stressed—it sounded very much like a description of herself. But, at age twenty, she had not yet discovered that the things that bother us are reflections of our own issues. Laura, like most of us, chose to project her frustrations, rather than reflect on their meaning. She wanted someone else to change rather than to explore her own issues. Of course, others rarely comply with our desire to change them. Hence, eventually we are confronted with the need to change ourselves.

Releasing blame and judgment enables us to see others differently. We notice different qualities and behaviors. Others have not necessarily changed; our perceptual focus has simply shifted. When we begin to own our feelings, we also begin to recognize that all of our relationships are extraordinary learning opportunities. And, we begin to suspect that none of them is accidental. We discover that those who have the most to teach us may not be our favorite people, but they may be the most valuable contributors to our psychological and spiritual growth. This realization enables us to practice *forgiveness.*

To forgive is not the same as to pardon. True forgiveness happens when we realize there is nothing to forgive—that every experience is a necessary part of life's curriculum. Forgiveness is a shift in consciousness. It occurs when we realize that resentment does more damage to the vessel in which it is stored than to the object on which it is poured. Forgiveness doesn't mean we allow ourselves to be abused. Rather, it means we learn to sidestep attackers. It's the martial art of consciousness!

As we begin to view our workplace nemeses as teachers, we replace negativity with appreciation, and our workplace relationships are transformed. As Sun Tzu wrote more than 2,500 years ago, "If you know your enemy, you will win most of the time. If you know yourself, there is no enemy" (in Ames 1993). Revolution X is primarily an inside job. It begins with a quantum leap in human consciousness. As Gen Xers commit to their own psychological and spiritual development, they are bound to transform themselves, their workplaces, and the world . . . some already are doing so!

QUANTUM CHANGE

Remember Jenny from the beginning of the book? She went through a quarterlife crisis of sorts and decided to pack her belongings, leave her life in Omaha, and strike out anew in Chicago. Jenny had a vision, a clear intention of what she wanted her life to look like (Quantum Seeing).

Even though it didn't make sense to a lot of people in her life, Jenny believed that she could go to a town where the cost of living was double, without a job, and still land on her feet (Quantum Thinking). In fact, Jenny knew in her heart that she had to make the change because she felt like she was slowly suffocating in her Omaha life. She wanted to feel more passion (Quantum Feeling) about her life in general and about her career in particular. Once she arrived in Chicago, Jenny didn't find the dream job or the ideal life she'd imagined right away. Sometimes discouraged, she kept at it, knowing intuitively (Quantum Knowing) that she had made the right decision and believing she would find her niche eventually (Quantum Trusting). In fact, she worked her way through several jobs that didn't suit her and one that was ethically offensive to her. So, she resigned (Quantum Acting), still trusting in the validity of her intentions. As for Quantum Being, well, today, after all her faith, hope, and hard work, Jenny is being just what she'd envisioned—a producer for the most successful talk show host in the country. She is living her dream!

We challenge you to follow Jenny's example and revolutionize the workplace by revolutionizing your life. Use the skill of Quantum Seeing to envision the workplace of your wildest dreams. Use the skill of Quantum Thinking to think creatively, not only about your future work, but also about how you might enrich and enliven your current work. Use the skill of Quantum Feeling to approach each day with joy and vitality, remembering that you always have choice about where you will focus your attention. Use the skill of Quantum Knowing to intuit your way through challenges and to guide you to right action (Quantum Acting). Along the way, trust your ability to be a constructive change agent in a process that is infinitely larger than any of us can imagine (Quantum Trusting). As you practice these skills, you will create a meaningful life filled with positive relationships (Quantum Being).

When enough of us learn to use these Quantum Skills, we will re-create our workplaces, not so much by redesigning them (though that is sure to happen), but rather by reexperiencing them. We will learn to find joy in that which was previously joyless and hope where there was despair. This is our vision for the neXt revolution. Will you help lead the way?

Gen X Survey Form

CAREER SATISFACTION/EXPECTATIONS

Questionnaire for **Generation X**

Name (optional) _____ **E-mail** (optional) _____

1. What year were you born? _____

2. What is your gender? ____ Female ____ Male

3. What is your race/ethnicity?

   ___ Asian   ___ Hispanic
   ___ African American   ___ Other (_____)
   ___ Caucasian

4. What is the highest degree you have completed?

   ___ High school   ___ Master's degree
   ___ Associate degree/technical training   ___ Doctoral degree
   ___ College (undergraduate degree)

5. Are you married? ___ Yes ___ No

6. Do you have a child/children? ___ Yes ___ No

7. What is your occupational field/profession?

   ___ Accounting   ___ Human Resources
   ___ Advertising   ___ Law
   ___ Administrative Staff   ___ Marketing
   ___ Assembly Line   ___ Public Relations
   ___ Consulting   ___ Purchasing
   ___ Communications   ___ R&D
   ___ Customer Service   ___ Sales
   ___ Education/Training   ___ Social Services
   ___ Engineering   ___ Technology
   ___ Finance   ___ Other (_____)
   ___ Health Care

8. What is your current job title? _____

9. Who is your current employer (optional)? _____

10. How many years have you worked for this employer? _____

CAREER SATISFACTION/EXPECTATIONS

11. How many years of full-time work experience do you have?_____

12. How many other employers have you had since you entered the workforce as a full-time employee?_____

13. What is your current organizational level?

    ___ Nonmanagement
    ___ Supervisor
    ___ Midlevel manager
    ___ Senior executive
    ___ CEO/President/Owner

14. What is is your current annual salary?

    ___ Less than $20,000
    ___ $20,000 to $39,000
    ___ $40,000 to $59,000
    ___ $60,000 to $79,000
    ___ $80,000 to $99,000
    ___ $100,000 or more

15. About how many people work in your organization?

    ___ 1 to 19
    ___ 20 to 99
    ___ 100 to 499
    ___ 500 to 999
    ___ 1,000 to 9,999
    ___ 10,000+

16. How long do you expect to continue working in this organization?

    ___ Less than a year
    ___ 1 to 2 years
    ___ 3 to 6 years
    ___ 7 to 10 years
    ___ More than 10 years

17. How satisfied are you with your job (the actual tasks you do on a day-to-day basis)? (Circle number: 1 = very dissatisfied; 5 = very satisfied.)

    1   2   3   4   5

CAREER SATISFACTION/EXPECTATIONS

18. How satisfied are you with your organization as a place to work?
(Circle number: 1 = very dissatisfied; 5 = very satisfied.)

1   2   3   4   5

19. How committed are you to your organization—its values, goals, and practices? (Circle number: 1 = very uncommitted; 5 = very committed.)

1   2   3   4   5

20. How satisfied are you with your organization's leadership?
(Circle number: 1 = very dissatisfied; 5 = very satisfied.)

1   2   3   4   5

21. How closely did your last performance review (evaluation) match your expectations? (Check one of the following options.)

___ Performance rating lower than I expected
___ Performance rating matched my expectations
___ Performance rating higher than I expected
___ Haven't had a performance evaluation in my current position

22. Rate each of the following factors according to its importance to you; then rate each according to your current level of satisfaction. (Circle number: 1 = low importance/satisfaction; 5 = high importance/satisfaction.)

	Importance	Satisfaction
Salary	1 2 3 4 5	1 2 3 4 5
Benefits package	1 2 3 4 5	1 2 3 4 5
Job security	1 2 3 4 5	1 2 3 4 5
Interesting work	1 2 3 4 5	1 2 3 4 5
Job status/prestige	1 2 3 4 5	1 2 3 4 5
Performance feedback	1 2 3 4 5	1 2 3 4 5
Recognition	1 2 3 4 5	1 2 3 4 5
Opportunities for advancement	1 2 3 4 5	1 2 3 4 5
Opportunities for learning	1 2 3 4 5	1 2 3 4 5
Opportunities to innovate/be creative	1 2 3 4 5	1 2 3 4 5
Participation in decision making	1 2 3 4 5	1 2 3 4 5
Positive relationship with supervisor	1 2 3 4 5	1 2 3 4 5
Positive relationship with co-workers	1 2 3 4 5	1 2 3 4 5
Casual, relaxed, playful environment	1 2 3 4 5	1 2 3 4 5
Meaningful or spiritually fulfilling work	1 2 3 4 5	1 2 3 4 5

23. Who would you say had more influence on your career expectations?
___ Mother ___ Father

CAREER SATISFACTION/EXPECTATIONS

24. What is your mother's educational level?

___ High school
___ Associate degree/technical training
___ College (undergraduate degree)
___ Master's degree
___ Doctoral degree

25. What is your father's educational level?

___ High school
___ Associate degree/technical training
___ College (undergraduate degree)
___ Master's degree
___ Doctoral degree

26. Was your mother employed at any time while you were growing up?

___ Yes ___ No

27. If she was employed, did you perceive that your mother had a rewarding career while you were growing up? ___ Yes ___ No

28. Was your father employed at any time while you were growing up?

___ Yes ___ No

29. If he was employed, did you perceive that your father had a rewarding career while you were growing up? ___ Yes ___ No

30. Do you expect to have a rewarding career? (Circle number: 1 = extremely doubtful; 5 = extremely optimistic.)

1   2   3   4   5

31. How would you rate your current degree of life satisfaction—the quality of your life? (Circle number: 1 = very dissatisfied; 5 = very satisfied.)

1   2   3   4   5

32. Do you have a written vision statement? ___ Yes ___ No

33. Do you have written career goals? ___ Yes ___ No

CAREER SATISFACTION/EXPECTATIONS

34. How has your career thus far proved to be similar to or different from what you expected when you entered the workforce? Please explain briefly.

>> REFERENCES

Ahlrichs, N. 2000. *Competing for Talent: Key Recruitment and Retention Strategies for Becoming an Employer of Choice.* Mountain View, CA: Davies-Black Publishing.

Allen, K. 1998. "Birth of a Third-Wave Feminist." Retrieved June 2003 from http://www.10.com/~wwave/second_third/third_born.html.

Ames, R. 1993. *Sun-Tzu: The Art of War* (Classics of Ancient China). New York: Ballantine Books.

"Analysis Urges Firms to Establish More Family-Friendly Leave Policies." 2002. *Omaha World-Herald,* February 18, p. D1.

Angier, N. 2002. "Why We're So Nice: We're Wired to Cooperate." *New York Times,* July 23, pp. 1–4.

Arellano, K. 2004. "Few Women Hold Top Jobs in Firms." *New Orleans Times-Picayune,* December 23, p. C4.

Armas, G. 2004. "Equal Pay Options Are Few for Women." *Kansas City Star,* June 4, pp. A1, A6.

Armour, S. 2002. "Younger Workers Feel Stuck as Older Ones Don't Retire."
    USA Today, October 10. Retrieved October 2002 from www.usatoday
    .com /money/workplace.
———. 2003. "Young Workers Say Their Age Holds Them Back." *USA Today,*
    October 7. Retrieved June 2005 from http://www.usatoday.com/money/
    workplace/2003-10-07-reversease_x.htm.
Bach, R. 1977. *Illusions: The Adventures of a Reluctant Messiah.* New York: Dell.
Beaudoin, T. 1998. *Virtual Faith: The Irreverent Spiritual Quest of Generation X.*
    San Francisco: Jossey-Bass.
Belkin, L. 2003. "The Opt-Out Revolution." *New York Times Magazine,* October
    26, p. 42–47, 58, 85–86.
"Bosses' Bonanza." 2002. *Utne Reader,* March–April, p. 16.
Brady, D. 2002. "Rethinking the Rat Race." *BusinessWeek,* August 26, pp. 142–143.
Broder, D. 2004. "Burden of Billions." *Kansas City Star,* October 18, p. B5.
Brown, S. 1996. "Generation X: Deficit, Debt, and Entitlements." Retrieved June
    2003 from www.cc.colorado.edu/Dept/EC/generationx96/genx/genx1.htm.
Buckingham, M., and C. Coffman. 1999. *First, Break All the Rules.* New York:
    Simon & Schuster.
Caminiti, S. 1998. "Young and Restless." *Fortune,* February 1. Retrieved June 2003
    from www.fortune.com/sitelets/young and restless/index.html.
Catalyst. 2001. *The Next Generation: Today's Professionals, Tomorrow's Leaders.*
    New York.
———. 2004. *The Bottom Line: Connecting Corporate Performance and Gender
    Diversity.* New York.
Center for Women's Business Research. 2001. "New Generation of Women
    Entrepreneurs Achieving Business Success." Retrieved June 2003 from
    http://www.nfwbo.org/Research/8-21-2001/8-21-2001.htm.
———. 2002. "One in 18 U.S. Women Is Business Owner." Retrieved June 2003
    from http://www.nfwbo.org/Research/7-16-2002/7-16-2002.htm.
———. 2003. "Nearly Half of All Privately Held U.S. Businesses Are Women-
    Owned." Retrieved June 2003 from www.nfwbo.org/Research/5-6-2003.
Ciabattari, J. 2002. "A Day That Opens Doors." *Parade,* March 3, p. 14.
Codrington, G. 1998. "Generation X: Who, What, Why, and Where To?"
    Retrieved June 2003 from http://www.youth.co.za/.
Conlin, M. 2003. "The New Gender Gap." *BusinessWeek,* May 26.
Cooperrider, D., P. Sorensen, D. Whitney, and T. Yager (eds.). 2000. *Appreciative
    Inquiry: Rethinking Human Organization Toward a Positive Theory of
    Change.* Champaign, IL: Stripes.
Corcodilos, N. 2004. "Feedback." *Fast Company,* April, p. 25.
Coupland, D. 1991. *Generation X: Tales for an Accelerated Culture.* Boston: Little,
    Brown.
Couric, K. 2004. "Mom-Preneurs." *Today,* November 2–4.

Csikszentmihalyi, M. 1990. *The Psychology of Optimal Experience.* New York: HarperCollins.

Douglas, S., and Michaels, M. 2004. *The Mommy Myth: The Idealization of Motherhood and How It Has Undermined Women.* New York: Free Press.

Dresang, J. 2003. "Milwaukee Consultant Aims to Bridge Generation Gap Between Firms, Gen X Staff." *Milwaukee Journal Sentinel,* April 6. Retrieved June 2003 from www.galenet.galegroup.com/servlet/BCRC.

Dunn, T., and D. Holtz-Eakin. 2003. "Capital Market Constraints, Parental Wealth, and the Transition to Self-Employment Among Men and Women." NLS Discussion Paper, Report: NLS 96-29. Retrieved June 2003 from http://www.bls.gov/nls/nlsdis29.htm.

Eisler, R. 1988. *The Chalice and the Blade: Our History, Our Future.* San Francisco: HarperSanFrancisco.

Elliott, M. 2004. "Men Want Change Too." *Time,* March 22, p. 59.

Ericson, E. E., Jr. 1998. "Generation X Is OK," part 1. Retrieved from May 2003 from www.theamericanenterprise.org/taejf98i.htm.

Eveld, E. 2001. "Generation Why." *Kansas City Star,* July 15, pp. G1, G8.

Faludi, S. 2001. "Blame It on Feminism," part 1, April 21. Retrieved June 2003 from http://coursesa.matrix.msu.edu/~hst203/documents/faludi.html.

Fields, R., R. Weyler, P. Taylor, and R. Ingrasci. 1985. *Chop Wood, Carry Water: A Guide to Finding Spiritual Fulfillment in Everyday Life.* New York: Tarcher.

Ford, S. 1998. "Generation X Brings More to Job Than Attitude." *Business Journal of Kansas City,* March 20, p. 16.

Forster, J. 2003. "Who Will Replace the Baby Boomers?" *Kansas City Star,* December 4, p. C3.

Franklin, R. 2003. "The Surge in Female Entrepreneurs." *BusinessWeek Online,* May 15. Retrieved May 2003 from www.businessweek.com/smallbiz/content/may2003/.

Fry, F., C. Stoner, and R. Hattwick. 2004. *Business: An Integrative Approach.* Boston: McGraw-Hill.

Gaynor, J. 2004. "An Inside Look at the New Wifestyle." *Cosmopolitan,* September, pp. 204–207.

"Gen X'ers Work for Their Money." 2002. *Omaha World-Herald,* August 26, p. D1.

Gerencher, K. 2002. "The Women Shattering Corporate America's Glass Ceilings May Soon Find There Are Few Other Women Interested in Following Their Lead." *CBS Marketwatch,* October 24. Retrieved June 2003 from www.cbs.marketwatch.com.

Gleckman, H. 1997. "Generation $ Is More Like It." *BusinessWeek,* November 3.

Goldberg, M. 2001. "Where Do Gen-Xers Want to Go Today?" January 23. Retrieved May 2003 from www.thenewrepublic.com/cyberspace/goldberg012401.html.

Gruenert, J. C. 1999. "Second Job Entrepreneurs." *Occupational Outlook Quarterly,* Fall, pp. 18–26.

Hales, D. 2002. "When She Earns More." *Parade,* March 17, p. 6.

Halper, M. 1999. "It's Not a Job, It's an Adventure!" *Fast Company,* January, p. 52.

Harman, E. 2001. "Generational Differences Between Women as Managers and Leaders." Presentation to AIM Women in Management Group, May 29, Sydney, Australia.

Harragan, B. 1977. *Games Mother Never Taught You: Corporate Gamesmanship for Women.* New York: Warner Books.

Hawkins, D. 2002. *Power vs. Force: The Hidden Determinants of Human Behavior.* Carlsbad, CA: Hay House.

Heffernan, M. 2002. "The Female CEO ca. 2002." *Fast Company,* August, pp. 58–66.

Heider, J. 1985. *The Tao of Leadership: Lao Tzu's Tao Te Ching Adapted for a New Age.* Atlanta, GA: Humanics.

Hevrdejs, J. 2003. "Meet the Metrosexual." *Kansas City Star,* August 9, p. F4.

Hewlett, S. A. 2002. *Creating a Life: Professional Women and the Quest for Children.* New York: Hyperion.

Hicks, J., and E. Hicks. 1992. *A New Beginning, I: Handbook for Joyous Survival.* Boerne, TX: Crown Internationale.

Hirshman, L. 2004. "Trading Career for Home." Interview by Leslie Stahl on the CBS *Early Show,* September 2. Retrieved September 2004 from CNSNews .com/stories/2004/08/25/earlyshow/living.

Houston, J. 1982. *The Possible Human.* Los Angeles: J. P. Tarcher.

Hymowitz, C. 2002. "Women Plotting Mix of Work and Family Won't Find Perfect Plan." *Wall Street Journal,* June 11, p. B1.

IHM Research Update. 1995. Boulder Creek, CA: Institute of HeartMath.

Irwin, J., and M. Perrault. 1996. "Gender Differences at Work: Are Men and Women Really That Different?" Foundation for Future Leadership, monograph (serial no. HD6060.6.I78).

Jochim, J. 1997. "Generation X Defies Definition." *Nevada Outpost,* June 1. Retrieved June 2003 from www.jour.unr.edu/outpost/specials/genx/overvw1.html.

Kaihla, P. 2003. "The Coming Job Boom." *Business 2.0,* September. Retrieved September 2003 from www.business2.com/subscribers/articles/mag/print/0,1643,51816,00.

Karp, H., C. Fuller, and D. Sirias. 2002. *Bridging the Boomer-Xer Gap: Creating Authentic Teams for High Performance at Work.* Mountain View, CA: Davies-Black Publishing.

Keller, L. 2000. "Oh, Grow Up! Those Kids in the Conference Room." CNN.com, October 2. Retrieved June 2003 from www.cnn.com/2000/CAREER/trends/09/29/generation.gap/.

Kreamer, A. 2003. "Want to Know How She Does It?" *Fast Company,* February, p. 64.

Krotz, J. L. 2004. "Why Women Make Better Managers." *International Women's Business Exchange,* October 16, pp. 1–3.

Kulesa, P. 2002. "Employee Commitment: U.S. Leader or Follower?" *International Survey Research,* Summer. Retrieved May 2003 from www.isrsurveys.com.

LaBarre, P. 1998. "Leadership—Ben Zander." *Fast Company,* December, p. 110.

———. 1999. "What's New, What's Not." *Fast Company,* January, p. 73.

Lampres, B. 2001. "What Makes Gen Xers Tick?" *BusinessWeek Online,* August 13. Retrieved February 2003 from http://www.businessweek.com/smallbiz/content/aug2001/sb20000813_986.htm.

Lancaster, L., and D. Stillman. 2002. *When Generations Collide: Who They Are, Why They Clash: How to Solve the Generational Puzzle at Work.* New York: HarperCollins.

Larson, V. 2002. "Gender Pay Gap Still Wide." *Omaha World-Herald,* February 18, p. 1D–2D.

Layne, A. 2000. "The Care and Feeding of Talent." *Fast Company,* November. Retrieved from http://www.fastcompany.com/articles/2000/11/ACT_Kasten.html.

Losyk, B. 1997. "Generation X: What They Think and What They Plan to Do." *Public Management,* December, pp. 4–5.

Lowney, C. 2003. *Heroic Leadership: Best Practices from a 450-Year-Old Company That Changed the World.* Chicago: Loyola Press.

Macko, L., and K. Rubin. 2004. *Midlife Crisis at 30: How the Stakes Have Changed for a New Generation—and What to Do About It.* Emmaus, PA: Rodale Books.

Marshall, J. 2004. "Power and Office Politics: Rumor and Reality." *Fusion,* Summer. Retrieved September 2004 from www.naa.org/artpage.cfm.

McCarthy, K. 1994. "Uncertainty Is a Blessing, Not a Bane." *APA Monitor,* September, p. 28.

McGregor, J. 2004. "Balance and Balance Sheets." *Fast Company,* May, pp. 96–97.

"Meaning over Money for Business Students." 2004. CNN.com, April 13. Retrieved April 2004, from www.cnn.com/2004/EDUCATION/2004/13/socially.

Mencimer, S. 2001. "Broken-Fingernail Feminism." *Washington Monthly Online,* November. Retrieved June 2003 from www.washingtonmonthly.com/features/2001/0111.mencimer.html.

Meredith, G. E., C. D. Schewe, and J. Karlovich. 2002. *Defining Markets, Defining Moments.* New York: Hungry Minds.

Merrill-Sands, D., M. Mattis, and N. Matus. 2003. "Women on Work: Is There a Generational Divide?" Retrieved 2003 from http://www.simmons.edu/som/leadership_survey.pdf.

Mincer, J. 2003. "Many Companies Lack Diversity at the Top." *Kansas City Star,* May 13, p. E35.

Montoya, M. 2004. "Generation Vexed." *Times-Picayune,* June 2, pp. E1–E8.

Montuori, A., and I. Conti. 1993. *From Power to Partnership: Creating the Future of Love, Work, and Community.* San Francisco: HarperCollins.

Moore, M. 2002a. "Tensions Rising." Associated Press Newswire, July 9.

———. 2002b. "Work Force Women." Associated Press Newswire, July 9.

———. 2002c. "Working Demands." Associated Press Newswire, September 3.

Neely, H. 2002. "Generation X—More Than a Gap!" February 19. Retrieved June 2003 from www.jobs.com/employerresources/GenX.asp.

Nelson, B. 2000. "The Ins and Outs of Generation X," January 24. Retrieved May 2003 from www.bizjournals.com/extredge/consultants/return_on_people.

Nelson, P. 1993. *There's a Hole in My Sidewalk: The Romance of Self-Discovery.* Hillsboro, OR: Beyond Words.

Nelson, R., and J. Cowan. 1994. *Revolution X: A Survival Guide for Our Generation.* New York: Penguin Books.

"Never Marrieds: Ranks of the Singles Growing Fast." 2002. ABCnews.com, January 9. Retrieved October 2004 from http://ABCLocal.com//kprk//news/010902_4pm_single.html.

"New Report Indicates Faith Is Important in Most Teens' Lives." 2002. *Omaha World-Herald,* March 2, p. E4.

Newsmakers. *Newsweek,* April 7, 2002.

Novicki, C. 1996. "Best Outreach: Homegrown Mindware." *Fast Company,* October–November, p. 28.

Overholt, A. 2002. "New Leaders, New Agenda." *Fast Company,* May, p. 52.

Parikh, J., F. Neubauer, and A. Lank. 1994. *Intuition: The New Frontier of Management.* Oxford: Blackwell Business.

Parkinson, G. 2002. "Women: Don't Expect Corporate Politics to Go Away." Silicon Valley/San Jose Business Journal, October 4. Retrieved from www.bizjournal.com/sanjost/stories/2002/10/7/editorial3.html.

Paul, P. 2002. *The Starter Marriage and the Future of Matrimony.* New York: Villard Books.

Pearson, A. 2002. *I Don't Know How She Does It.* New York: Knopf.

Pekala, N. 2001. "Conquering the Generational Divide." *Journal of Property Management,* November–December, pp. 33–38.

"Per-Capita Health-Care Outlays May Double by '11." 2002. *Omaha World-Herald,* March 12, p. A10.

Peterson, K. 2003. "Gen X Moms Have It Their Way." *USA Today,* May 7, pp. D1–D2.

Petzinger, T., Jr. 1999. "In Search of the New World (of Work)." *Fast Company,* April, p. 214.

Pierce, L. 2003. "Gen X Change the Rules." Retrieved December 2003 from www.nwlegalsearch.com/articles/generation_x.html.

Pope, J. 2004. "It's a Good Time to Be a New College Grad." *New Orleans Times-Picayune,* November 16, pp. C1, C3.

Pritchett, P. 1990. *You2.* Dallas: Pritchett Publishing.

Proust, M. 1982. *Remembrance of Things Past.* New York: Vintage Books.

Quinn, J. B. 2003. "Make Your Money Grow." *Newsweek,* March 24, pp. 58–64.

Quinn, M. 2004. "Family of Choice." *Kansas City Star,* April 26, pp. D1, D7.

Razdan, A. 2002. "Can't You Hear Your Inner Voice?" *Utne Reader,* November–December, pp. 68–69.

Reed, S. 1999. "Stock Options May Be Trendy Benefits, but Other Job Factors Matter More," September 27. Retrieved May 2003 from www.infoworld .com/articles/op.xml/99/09/27/990927opreed.xml.

Reich, R. 1998. "The Company of the Future." *Fast Company,* November, pp. 124–150.

Rheingold, H. 2002. *Smart Mobs: The Next Social Revolution.* Cambridge, MA: Basic Books.

Rhodes, M. 2003. "Can't Beat the Commute: Structure Needed to Work at Home." *Omaha World-Herald,* May 12, pp. D1–2.

Rimm, S. 2000. *See Jane Win.* New York: Three Rivers Press.

———. 2002. *How Jane Won.* New York: Three Rivers Press.

Robbins, A., and A. Wilner. 2001. *Quarterlife Crisis: The Unique Challenges of Life in Your Twenties.* New York: Putnam.

Robbins, S. 2003. *Organizational Behavior,* 10th ed. Upper Saddle River, NJ: Prentice Hall.

Rosenberg, D. 2003. "Something Ventured: Women Entrepreneurs See Opportunity." *Dow Jones Newswires,* November 26. Retrieved November 2003, from www.springboardenterprises. org/press/somethingventured.

Schwartz, B. 2004a. *The Paradox of Choice: Why More Is Less.* New York: Ecco.

———. 2004b. "When It's All Too Much." *Parade,* pp. 4–5.

Seacrest, C. 1996. "Generation X: Facts and Figures." Retrieved May 2002, from www.cc.colorado.edu/Dept/EC/generationx96/genx.

Seligman, M. 1990. *Learned Optimism: How to Change Your Mind and Your Life.* New York: Simon & Schuster.

Semler, R. 1993. *Maverick: The Success Story Behind the World's Most Unusual Workplace.* New York: Warner Books.

Shelton, C. 1999. *Quantum Leaps: 7 Skills for Workplace ReCreation.* Woburn, MA: Butterworth-Heinemann.

Smith, G. P. 2001. "Baby Boomer Versus Generation X: Managing the New Workforce." Retrieved May 2003 from www.businessknowhow.com/manage/ genx.htm.

Smith, T. 2004. "Trading Career for Home." CBSNEWS.com, September 2. Retrieved October 2004 from www.CBSnews.com/stories/2004/08/25/ earlyshow/living/printable638347.shtml.

Smith, W. J., and A. Clurman. 1997. *Rocking the Ages: The Yankelovich Report on Generational Marketing.* New York: HarperBusiness.

"Some Under 30 Are Overextended." 2002. *Omaha World-Herald*, March 11, p. D2.

Sommers, C. H. 1998. "The Girls of Gen X: On the Other Hand." Retrieved May 2003 from www.theamericanenterprise.org/taejf98i.htm.

Spraggins, R. 2003. *Current Population Reports. Women and Men in the United States:* March 2002. Retrieved January 2004 from www.census.gov.

Stewart, C. 2002. "Gen X Rising." *Potentials,* September, pp. 22–29. Retrieved May 2003 from Business and Company Resource Center.

Stone, V. 2001. "Job Satisfaction in TV News." Retrieved May 2003 from www.missouri.edu/~jourvs/tvsaits.html.

Strauch, J. 2002. "Generations at Work: Baby Boomers, Gen-X'ers March to Different Drummers." *Careerbuilder,* February 19. Retrieved June 2003 from www.careerbuilder.com/subcat/wlb/gwlb100108.html.

Strauss, W., and N. Howe. 1997. *The Fourth Turning.* New York: Broadway Books.

Sutra Foundation. 2001. "Financially Speaking, Many Single Young Women Show Signs of 'Carrie Bradshaw' Syndrome," May 1. Retrieved May 2003 from www.sutrafoundation.com/pages/projectsgenxsinglewomen.

Taylor, S. E., L. C. Klein, B. P. Lewis, T. L. Gruenewald, R. A. R. Gurung, and J. A. Updegraff. 2000. "Female Responses to Stress: Tend and Befriend, Not Fight or Flight." *Psychological Review* 107 (3), pp. 421–429.

"Then and Now: Things We Couldn't Do Without," 2004. *People,* April 12, p. 103.

Thomas, E. 2004. "Transcending the Quarterlife Crisis." *Utne Reader,* June 21, pp. 71–72.

Tischler, L. 2004. "Where Are the Women?" *Fast Company,* February, pp. 52–60.

Tobias, A. 2002. "Are They Worth It?" *Parade,* March 3, pp. 8–9.

"Traditional Jobs Provide Most Work for Women." 2003. *Omaha World-Herald,* May 5, p. A3.

Tulgan, B. 1996. *Managing Generation X.* New York: W.W. Norton.

"29 Million Have Flex Schedules." 2003. *Omaha World-Herald,* January 20, p. D1.

Tyre, P., K. Springen, and J. Scelfo. 2002. "Bringing Up Adultolescents." *Newsweek,* March 25, pp. 38–40.

"U.N. Says Population Aging Fast." 2002. *Omaha World-Herald,* March 28, p. A7.

"Unhappy at Work? You're Not Alone." 2002. *Kansas City Star,* August 22, p. C8.

Wagner, J. 1991. *The Search for Signs of Intelligent Life in the Universe.* New York: HarperCollins.

Wall, J. 2003. "Smaller Firms That Can't Pay as Much Use Other Lures." Indianapolis Star/Tribune Business News, January 22. Retrieved June 2003 from www.galenet.galegroup.com/servlet/BCRC.

Wallis, C. 2004. "The Case for Staying Home." *Time,* March 22, pp. 50–59.

Watson, N. 2002a. "Dude, Where's My Job?" *Fortune,* October 14. Retrieved June 2003, from www.fortune.com/fortune/special/special/2002/genwrecked/index.html.

————. 2002b. "Generation X—Generation Wrecked." *Fortune,* October 4. Retrieved June 2005 from http://www.fortune.com/fortune/investing/articles/0,15114,373330,00.html.

Weisbord, M., and S. Janoff. 1995. *Future Search: An Action Guide to Finding Common Ground in Organizations and Communities.* San Francisco: Berrett-Koehler.

Wen, P. 2003. "Stay-at-Home Mothers Finding They're Not Alone." *Boston Globe,* October 12. Retrieved October 2004 from www.boston.com.

Wheatley, M., and M. Kellner-Roger. 1996. *A Simpler Way.* San Francisco: Berrett-Koehler.

Whitehead, B. D. 1998. "The Girls of Gen X: All Is Not Well with the Women of Generation X." Retrieved May 2003 from www.theamericanenterprise.org/taejf98i.htm.

Willimon, W. H., and T. H. Naylor. 1995. *The Abandoned Generation.* Grand Rapids, MI.: Wm. B. Eerdmons–Lightning Source.

"Women Inch up Corporate Ladder." 2002. *Omaha World-Herald,* November 19, p. D1.

"Women Seek Flexible Jobs." 2004. CBSNews.com, November 11. Retrieved August 2005 from www.cbsnews.com/stories/2004/11/10/eveningnews/main654950.shtml.

Wylie, I. 2004a. "Routing Rust-Out." *Fast Company,* February, p. 40.

————. 2004b. "To: The Queen, Subject: My Dog." *Fast Company,* February, p. 29.

Zemke, R., C. Raines, and B. Filipczak. 2000. *Generations at Work: Managing the Clash of Veterans, Boomers, Xers, and Nexters in Your Workplace.* New York: American Management Association.

Zohar, D. 1990. *The Quantum Self: Human and Consciousness Defined by the New Physics.* New York: William Morrow.

Zuboff, S. 2004. "Evolving from Subject to Citizen." *Fast Company,* May, p. 104.

Zukav, G. 1979. *The Dancing Wu Li Masters: An Overview of the New Physics.* New York: Bantam Books.

————. 1989. *The Seat of the Soul.* New York: Simon & Schuster.

>> | INDEX

work, *cont'd*
    spiritually fulfilling, 122–124; stay-
    at-home moms returning to,
    156–157
work attire, 39–40, 149–150
work environment: communication
    in, 139–141, 143–144; description of,
    117–118
work hours: increases in, 71; overtime,
    71; statistics regarding, 70–71
working moms, 97–98
work-life balance, 70–73, 131, 133, 135,
    155–156
workplace: design of, 215; dissatisfac-
    tion in, 2–3, 170–171; equal oppor-
    tunity in, 50; equality in, 181;
    expectations of, 27; flexibility in,
58; gender statistics, 50; opting out
of, 63–64; redesigning of, 220;
restructuring of, 158–159; revolution in. *See* revolution; stress in,
70–71; wage gap, 50–51; X-friendly.
See X-friendly workplaces

Xers. *See* Generation X
X-friendly workplaces: creation of,
158–159; examples of, 151–155; finding of, 167–168; "on-ramps" in,
156–158; overview of, 137–138; positive relationships in, 138–144;
resources, 167–168; restructuring
of, 158–159; role models of, 158–159

Zander, Benjamin, 143